"Not Worth a Straw"

"Not Worth a Straw":

French Colonial Policy and the Early Years of Louisiana

by
Mathé Allain

The Center for Louisiana Studies
University of Southwestern Louisiana
Lafayette, Louisiana

Library of Congress Catalog Card No.: 88-71257
ISBN Number: 0-940984-41-5

Published by The Center for Louisiana Studies
University of Southwestern Louisiana

For my mother

Contents

Foreword

It is, indeed, a pleasant thing to have an idea that just arrived one day seemingly out of nowhere turn up as the thesis of another's book. In a paper delivered before the French Colonial Historical Society in 1984, I suggested that French colonial policy in the early eighteenth century should be studied in the light of the French state ethos. My own research in France, Spain, Austria, Italy, and England concerning the colonial policy of the Regency suggested that colonies were a very low priority indeed in the thinking, or the unthinking, of Philip of Orleans. This indifference explains much about the founding of Louisiana, which could not have been born into anything else except a home-government attitude of neglectful manipulation.

Professor Mathé Allain comes well equipped intellectually to produce this book as her extensive bibliography, both archival sources and published works, indicates. Others have written about the chronological record of how Louisiana came into being and how it fit into the scheme of things devised by Francis I and his descendants, both in the royal family and in the sparkling line of royal ministers. But this short treatise tells us why things occurred as they did, or possibly rolled along as they did! I found that Louisiana became truly intelligible for me, a native Kentuckian, for the first time upon reading this book.

At the outset Professor Allain points out

> Louisiana was the last Ancien Régime colony established in America. Its exploration, establishment, and development fitted into the overall French colonial policy largely determined by European power politics and France's late entry into the imperial race, the delay being itself a consequence of Gallic involvement in European affairs. From Francis I to Louis XIV, from Richelieu and Colbert to Law, Pontchartrain, and Maurepas, colonial expansion was viewed as a facet of foreign affairs, and overseas ambitions were always subordinated to dreams of continental hegemony. (p. 1)

She then enlarges the picture of the colonial system into which Louisiana would be born.

> Francis I did not have true colonization in mind and there is no evidence that he ever foresaw colonization as the 'expansion of the race' or America as a future extension of France. Colonization was a diplomatic ploy which the French king used as long as his dreams of easy wealth and commercial profits endured. (p. 3)

Easy wealth and commercial profits are probably the key to European overseas empires whether they be trading, colonial, or just plain economic penetration.

Professor Allain, however, disagrees, as she thinks that Henry IV might have been more disinterested and that Louis XIII sought more than easy profit from a minimum investment in both men and materials. She is however again quite correct when she writes that "The pursuit of *gloire* on the continent unfortunately interfered with colonial development, as it would repeatedly during the Ancien Régime." (p. 5) I would suggest that *gloire* is "face" and that *gloire* was everything. Even the richest, most powerful potentate or nation in the world must have face (honor, *gloire*) or it has nothing.

That France could not or at least did not capitalize her colonies, specifically Canada and Louisiana, can indeed be explained in part by the French passion for purchasing state offices, institutionalized by the introduction of the *Paulette* during the reign of Henry IV. The head of a rising middle-class family would far rather buy an office with accompanying title of nobility than risk his capital in a colonial venture. Too often heads of these families had learned that a steady 10-15% annual return makes for a far more affluent family than headlong plunges into foreign adventures that occasionally result in windfall profits. It is no wonder that it was the kings themselves, the members of their immediate families, those well within the inner circle of the royal court, and the great crown officers who had to subscribe to the various colonial companies from Henry IV onward. After all, who could better recognize a "Florida land scam" than the head of a wealthy, middle-class merchant/banking family? Not until national governments were willing to commit public revenues, on a forever basis, to guarantee the profits of the upper middle class would merchants and bankers invest in colonial ventures. And that would await a far wider and deeper tax base than the Ancien Régime commanded.

Nor was there much concern with populating the colonies. Few Frenchmen were eager to go to the New World. Richelieu was conscious enough of the problem to provide that vagabonds, beggars, and petty criminals would be taken into the employ of the company. Forced immigration would provide a cheaper, hence more attractive, alternative to a commercial company." (p. 9) But this policy would have required that the crown plan from not just one year to the next but from one generation to the next and give colonies a high priority. Given the continental aspirations of Louis XIV it is not surprising that the French populations in Canada and Louisiana remained tiny, especially when compared to the burgeoning English seaboard colonies.

And to give Richelieu full credit, he did recognize the need for colonies and "laid down the principles of social policy that Colbert would adopt," but he could not convince either the financiers to invest nor the church to send missionaries. The discrepancy between the minister's policy and its implementation is most revealing of a political system no longer attuned to the economic realities of the nation." (p. 12)

Despite anything that Colbert may have wanted to do, Louis XIV supervised all aspects of French policies," but some aspects were closer to his heart than others. Colonial ventures were not the dearest. Louis displayed, according to the reports of the Venetian ambassador, "a natural disinclination toward far-flung adventures. His natural bent lay in the direction of European domination, and he disliked entrusting his prestige to an element as unpredictable as the sea." (p. 13) But whenever colonies existed they were to be ruled directly from Paris just like any other portion of the Bourbon monarchy for, ". . . at all times commercial colonies and settlement colonies were judged by a single criterion, the interest of France and the French monarchy. Colonies existed by and for the mother country. Colonies were not held as important under the ancien régime. No solid upper-middle-class French family would invest in something unimportant—let alone live there!

Colbert could dream of fabulously wealthy, heavily populated colonies, but it remained a dream, for the crown was never keenly interested. The French attitude toward their own overseas possessions was that they were "Not Worth A Straw." And if you look at net revenues versus net outgo, just in terms of defense expenditures, it is debatable that even Canada at beaver's heyday, was worth the trouble, let alone tiny Louisiana. Colbert acknowledged this state of affairs when he ". . . laid down the law for North America." The French Empire was to be kept compact instead of spreading over vast areas which could never be "inhabited or possessed by the French." (p. 31)

Unfortunately for the future of French North America, Colbert's policy was soon frustrated by human greed and the fact that the fur trade, which was the economic lifeblood of French North America, required expanding the reach of the fur trappers. La Salle and other expansionists would not have their way until there was a Bourbon on the throne of Spain and the English could be considered a threat in the Gulf of Mexico. Biloxi and New Orleans would remain dependent military colonies into the eighteenth century.

It mattered little whether the minister of Marine was totally-negative or nearly-positive, whether the crown blew cold or hot, whether adventurers like Cadillac and John Law dreamed up economic bubbles and land scams. The colony would remain small and weak. When Iberville began the fort at Biloxi in 1699, he had but a handful of soldiers and there would never be more than a handful in all of Louisiana throughout the French period. To found a colony required a steady supply of people to fell trees and break the land, acre by acre. New France and Louisiana were not that lucky. Not only did the French crown, even after it committed itself to territorial expansion in the New World, not provide sufficient soldiers, it did not pursue a vigorous population policy. "As far as the [state] was concerned, keeping the English out was sufficient. Establishing a powerful striving colony would be entirely excessive." (p. 50) As Professor Allain points out, "Louisiana's importance, however, remained purely strategic, and crown support remained niggardly." (p. 50)

Chapter V, *In Search of a Policy, 1701-1731,* unfolds the French crown's policy toward the infant colony of Louisiana.

> The colony at the mouth of the Mississippi had thus become strategically indispensable. After Utrecht, there were no more suggestions that Louisiana be abandoned, though in 1712 Louis XIV was still trying to negotiate the exchange of the Mississippi colony for the Spanish half of Hispañola. [This would have been a very good deal. C.S.] But the recognition of its strategic importance did not bring large-scale crown investment. On the contrary, with their treasury bankrupt [and they remained bankrupt until after 1789 and all that! C.S.], Louis XIV and Pontchartrain looked to private initiative to take the colony off their hands. (p. 65)

Schemes came and went, but they made little difference. A string of Ohio and Mississippi Valley forts would be built, some few reinforcements would be sent but never enough to halt the onrush of English settlement: ". . . as always, the French crown committed itself parsimoniously so that the colonies were not given the means to hold at bay their antagonistic neighbors." (p. 65) Law's scheme did bring in badly needed settlers, but by 1721 there were still far fewer than 3,000 family units in Louisiana.

Chapter VI will probably generate discussion. Relationships between the races, the true meaning of the famous *Black Code,* the problem of eligible white females and the use/misuse of Indian women are treated in this intriguing chapter. It stresses the continuity between the Old World attitudes and the ethos developing in the New World. As it points out, "the colonists were not coming to create a brave new classless society, but to re-create their old world, with themselves as the privileged." (p. 72) Thus, for example, the settlers were as concerned as the Versailles courtiers with *préséances:* "On the Louisiana frontier, in the wretched hut which served as a church, the same quarrels [of *préséances*] were repeated when the hapless Capuchin curate auctioned off his pews to the highest bidder thus dispossessing some ladies of their front seat in favor of base-born rivals." (p. 72)

As the chapter concludes:

> The most enduring legacy of the New France idea has been the persistence of the feudal ethos which suffused Ancien Régime society. Wealth did not purchase social position, as it does in a class society, but instead, prestige and rank were expected to bring one fortune. This attitude, totally inimical to the spirit of capitalism, would persist into the nineteenth century and doom the French Creoles to disappearance as a political and economic elite. (p. 88)

The three pages of conclusions succinctly summarize this excellent, well-researched book.

Claude C. Sturgill
University of Florida
April 15, 1988

Preface

This book grew out of years of discussions in the Center for Louisiana Studies at the University of Southwestern Louisiana. Trying to figure out personalities and puzzle out the whys and wherefores of Louisiana's colonial past, I gradually reached the conclusion that the answers lay partially back in France, the French attitudes toward social mobility, in the French passion for state employ (still evident today in the elephantine *fonction publique* of Chirac's France), in the French feudal ethos, but also in the French monarchy's fruitless attempt to articulate colonial policies which it had neither the bureaucratic infrastructure to enforce nor the financial resources to underwrite. The niggardliness of the crown, on the one hand, and, on the other, the ineffectualness of its legislating—which colonial officials usually managed to evade, obfuscate, or bend—explain the sense of aimlessness and uncertainty one experiences when trying to pin down French colonial policy in North America. It is not that the crown lacked a policy, but that it could not impose its will on distant lands, adventurous traders, and ambitious empire-builders. In the New World, greed and distance frustrated the very relative absolutism of the Sun King and his descendants.

During these years of reading and discussing I incurred great debts of gratitude, most of all to Glenn R. Conrad, Director of the Center, who combines a meticulous attention to documents with a passion for integrating the most minute detail into a broad picture. Carl A. Brasseaux, Assistant Director, knows the French colonial documents housed in the Center the way Massachussetts Puritans knew their Bible. His help is always available and ever invaluable.

I also greatly benefitted from suggestions from members of my dissertation committee: Richard C. Cusimano, Robert. J. Gentry, and Allen E. Begneaud, and owe much to the readers whose comments kept me from committing a number of egregious errors. William J. Eccles directed me to Canadian sources I had overlooked just as Claude C. Sturgill indicated studies of French bureaucracy and bureaucrats which should be incorporated. Cornelius J. Jaenen pointed out a need for focusing which, I hope, has been addressed.

The library at the University of Southwestern Louisiana revealed surprising resources, aside from the million-odd pages of microfilmed documents. But it also had unfortunate *lacunae* which were filled with the help of interlibrary loan librarians Fay Backie and Anna Jane Marks. Their relentless pursuit of ephemeral publications and long (and often rightly) forgotten monographs enabled me to allay at least part of the fear experienced by almost anyone who writes on historical topics, overlooking an old but important study. Any gaps that remain are imputable only to my failure.

It is customary to thank one's family for their support and patience during the redaction of a work. Mine, however, proved helpful in a different way. Their lively curiosity about almost any topic of discussion not related to eighteenth-century French colonial policy and their insistence that meals be served on time allowed me to keep a firm grip on reality. For that, I thank them heartily.

Mathé Allain
Lafayette, Louisiana
April 29, 1988

"Not Worth a Straw"

I

Colonial Policy Before Colbert

I
The Impact of Foreign Affairs

Louisiana was the last Ancien Régime colony established in America. Its exploration, establishment, and development fitted into an overall French colonial policy largely determined by European power politics and France's late entry into the imperial race, the delay being itself a consequence of Gallic involvement in European affairs. From Francis I to Louis XV, from Richelieu and Colbert to Law, Pontchartrain, and Maurepas, colonial expansion was viewed as a facet of foreign affairs, and overseas ambitions were always subordinated to dreams of continental hegemony.

Nevertheless France secured a foothold in North America, establishing Port-Royal in Acadia (1604) and Quebec in Canada (July 3, 1608) thus raising the foundation for New France. Both colonies were far closer to New Netherlands and New England than to New Spain, a fact of minor importance until, in 1688, William of Orange assumed the English throne, forged a national consensus, and gave direction to English foreign and domestic goals. From that time onward, England began to replace Spain as the main opposition to Louis XIV's overvaulting ambitions in Europe and French penetration in America. The English Atlantic colonies, ever pushing westward, northward, even southward, became in time the enemy next door which threatened the very existence of New France. The unfolding French colonial policy and the exploration and establishment of Louisiana must therefore be viewed within the context of Franco-Spanish rivalry, growing distrust of England, and the policy reversal which took place when Louis XIV's grandson, Philip V, ascended the throne of Spain.[1]

Frenchmen were interested in overseas ventures; Breton, Norman, and Basque fishermen plied the Atlantic from earliest days; and the provincial antiquarians have claimed primacy of exploration for local heroes, though most discoveries remain thoroughly undocumented, except for the expedition of Binot Paulmier de Gonneville, who visited Brazil in 1504, bringing back an Indian as proof of his voyage.[2] But these early forays, real or imaginary, were never followed by actual colonization and therefore remained meaningless. The Atlantic trade, except for a few piratical captains, was largely abandoned to the Iberians. The French crown prized far more the traditional Mediterranean trade with the Near East, and the enterprising Spaniards and Portuguese moved quickly to protect their tenuous Atlantic commercial advantage.

After the discoveries of Columbus, Portuguese and Spaniards had divided the Atlantic. Pope Alexander's 1493 bull (*Inter caetera*) had traced a line a hundred leagues west of the Azores and had granted the Spanish sovereign a monopoly on all lands that lay beyond. By the Treaty of Tordesillas, concluded a year later, Spaniards and Portuguese moved the line of demarcation 370 leagues west of the Cape Verde Islands—a change which opened Brazil to the Lusitanians. This reciprocal recognition of privileged zones, however, firmly banished non-Iberians from the Atlantic since the monopoly extended to navigation as well as trade and colonization.[3] French penetration of the New World could only result in confrontation with Spain; yet, French seamen ignored the interdiction—as evidenced by the Gonneville expedition of 1503—but the Gallic crown was slow in challenging the Iberians' theoretical right to the New World monopoly. Francis I, who ascended the throne in 1515, sarcastically asked to see the clause in Adam's testament which guaranteed the Spanish rights. More to the point, he undertook negotiations with the Holy See, negotiations which were greatly facilitated by the marriage of his son to the pontiff's niece.[4] This diplomatic foray was inadvertently supported by the great Spanish theologian Francisco de Vitoria who raised serious ethical issues, affirming in the name of the *ius gentium* that physical power alone did not confer sovereignty.[5] In 1533 Francis I obtained from the Holy See an interpretation of Tordesillas which excluded newly discovered lands, and the French king slowly developed a colonial theory which claimed that permanent occupation alone conferred possession.[6] The logical corollary of this theory was the abandonment by the French of Brazil and other warm-latitude colonies already occupied by Spaniards and Portuguese.

France's ambition in the New World would have to turn to the north and the cold latitudes,[7] which in 1524 had been mapped from the Carolinas to Cape Breton by an Italian navigator in Francis' service, Giovanni da Verrazano.[8] Verrazano had sought not the implantation of colonists but the Northwest Passage which would open a quick route to Cathay. His voyage was encouraged by the Lyons financiers who wanted a direct route to the silk which made their city prosperous.[9] Verrazano failed to find the Northwest Passage but mapped the shores of *Nova Gallia*, baptizing one of his newly discovered lands "Arcadia."[10] Ten years later, Francis launched the voyages of Jacques Cartier who set out to find mines and the ever-elusive Northwest Passage.[11] If, however, permanent occupation was, as the Valois argued, necessary for sovereignty, which would give the French control of the northern route to the Far East, a colony would have to be implanted. The need to organize a new province with a governor empowered to lead armies and grant lands led Francis to select a nobleman, François de la Roque, seigneur de Roberval, as a leader of the third colonial voyage (1541).[12]

French colonial policy in its infancy was thus shaped by the country's late arrival on the scene. Moreover, because France lacked the means for colonial conquest, the French king fell upon the tactic of arguing for the theoretical justification of colonial occupation. Indeed, Pierre Crignon, the Dieppe shipowner, could question the Portuguese claim to Brazil because they had "not spread the faith, and are neither loved nor obeyed."[13] Spaniards and Portuguese were not, however, overly concerned with the morality of possession by conquest, despite the questioning of theologians. Spain had conquered vast empires with a handful of adventurers and was not willing to debate the matter. Nevertheless, Francis I continued to forge his theory for the justification of colonial occupation. He now found it convenient to insist that legitimate possession required not only actual occupation of the land but also native acceptance of colonial rule as well as active proselytizing of the natives.

The Valois consequently began developing a theoretical framework for colonization while recognizing the need for a maritime policy and naval development.[14] Francis did not have true colonization in mind and there is no evidence that he ever foresaw colonization as the "expansion of the race" or America as a future extension of France.[15] Colonization was a diplomatic ploy which the French king used as long as his dreams of easy wealth and commercial profits endured. When the gold and diamond mines of Saguenay turned out to be worthless, giving rise to the *dicton* "faux comme un diamant du Canada," the colonization scheme was abandoned, and France dropped all interest in the New World for nearly fifteen years.

In 1555 Gaspard de Coligny, grand admiral of France and leader of the Huguenots, launched the first of a number of colonizing ventures in the New World.[16] Coligny, whom C. A. Julien calls "the founder of French colonial policy," conceived of colonization as a tool of foreign policy. With him, North American colonization became a factor in geopolitics.[17] After Nicolas Durand de Villegaignon's ill-fated attempt to establish a French fort in the bay of Rio de Janeiro (1555), where the admiral hoped to create a Huguenot refuge,[18] Coligny tried three times to establish outposts in Florida. These would serve as bases to prey upon the Spanish galleons in the Caribbean and to watch for an opportunity to intervene in the West Indies. Coligny thus foresaw the possibility of carrying out European power struggles in the New World, of ruining Spanish commerce, and of thereby weakening the Spanish empire. These attempts, like later expeditions to the Azores, were dramatic failures. Yet, they caused considerable concern in Spain,[19] and Urbain Chauveton, publicist and translator, perpetuated Coligny's challenge to the Castillian monopoly long after the admiral's death.[20] Julien affirms that Catherine de Medici's fear of Iberian reprisals was one of the reasons for the St. Bartholomew's Day Massacre of August 24, 1572, which claimed Huguenot Coligny as one of its victims.[21]

Certainly Spaniards and Portuguese celebrated the demise of the admiral with a grandiose *Te Deum.*

Coligny's death precipitated a long, painful series of religious struggles which ravaged France for almost thirty years. Colonial ventures were quite forgotten during this devastating civil war which left France exhausted and ruined. In 1589, with the end of the religious wars and his actual assumption of power, Henry IV and his minister, Maximilien de Bethune, duke of Sully, set about rebuilding the kingdom. For the first time in French history, economic development took primacy.[22] King and minister strove to reestablish French agriculture, develop industries, and facilitate commerce by building roads and canals. Sully, however, an austere moralist, stressed agriculture, believing that the wealth of France came from "*labourage et paturage*" which produced not only material goods but, equally important, moral virtues.[23] It is not surprising that he disapproved of colonial empires which would flood France with gold and useless tropical produce, stimulate luxurious living, and draw peasants, artisans, and nobles away from the kingdom. In a letter of February 29, 1608, he expressed strong doubts about the colonial conquests which suit neither, "the disposition nor the intellect of the French who do not possess . . . the necessary foresight . . . and bend their efforts only to preserve what touches them immediately and [what] they constantly have present before their eyes. . . ." He concludes that "things separated from us [the French] by foreign lands or seas will always be for us burdensome and unimportant."[24] Thus at the very outset of the seventeenth century Sully announced what would become dogma in some circles: The French are not interested in colonies.

Henry IV was considerably more favorable than his minister toward colonial enterprises, though priority had to be given to rebuilding the traditional Mediterranean trade with the Levant.[25] It is under Henry's aegis that the earliest permanent French settlement in the New World was established. In 1604, after several abortive attempts, Pierre de Gua, sieur du Monts, founded the colony of Acadia, then moved the post across the bay the following year, to Port-Royal, today Annapolis-Royal.[26]

Throughout the sixteenth century the colonial rival was Spain. Yet the decision to forego colonization in Brazil, Florida, and other warm-latitude locations and to concentrate on the northern regions of the American continent and its actual implementation in the early seventeenth century, would inevitably bring French colonists into conflict with the New England colonies. Thus the policy which colonists and colonial administrators advocated would often be at odds with that of the crown, for European hegemony—and in the seventeenth century that meant supremacy over Spain—would remain all important through the seventeenth century.

For a number of years after the death of Henry IV (1610) French colonial enterprises lagged. Champlain maintained the outpost in Canada, but no new ventures began during the regency of Marie de Medici. In 1624, the advent of Armand du Plessis, later cardinal-duke of Richelieu, as prime minister opened a new era in French politics and French colonization.[27] Marc Lescarbot, the chronicler of Acadia, said that there had been enough talk about the new lands and that it was time to start colonizing them. The cardinal could have echoed these words as he echoed, whether he had read them or not, the mercantilism of early economic thinkers such as Barthélémy Laffemas and Antoine de Montchrestien.[28] Richelieu took the jumble of these ideas and synthesized them into a coherent policy which unified political, economic, religious, and colonial aims. His *Testament politique* explicitly proclaims the prime motivation behind his every decision: *La grandeur du roi et sa gloire.*[29]

The pursuit of *gloire* on the continent unfortunately interfered with colonial development, as it would repeatedly during the Ancien Régime. Richelieu's ministry coincided with the Thirty Years' War, the devastating European conflict which drained all participants of economic and human resources until the treaties of Westphalia in 1648. Yet Richelieu labored despite the war to make his king supreme in France, by breaking the power of the great nobles and the Protestants, and France supreme in Europe, by breaking the power of the House of Hapsburg.[30] The national interest dominated his preoccupation. It was, as states Franklin C. Palm, "the fundamental idea behind his entire administration."[31] Richelieu was convinced that individual or personal interests were secondary considerations at best, and that the economic doctrines he espoused were those which would make France rich, prosperous, and powerful, not necessarily those which would make the people happy.[32] Though Richelieu was, as Palm demonstrates, extremely concerned with economics, it never interested him as an end in itself but as a means to a far greater end, the grandeur and power of the French monarchy and that meant its superiority over other European rulers.[33] On the other hand, as a recent biographer of Richelieu points out, the formation of the Council of Commerce, which raised economic affairs to the same level as religious affairs, indicates the laicizing trend in the cardinal's policies and the importance he attached to trade and colonies.[34]

The German historian of economic thought, Gustav Schmoller, has demonstrated that mercantilism, though often called bullionism, is not primarily a doctrine of money, and that though it is protectionism with a vengeance, it is not primarily a doctrine of tariffs; it is a doctrine of state-building. Its aim is to replace local institutions and policies by those of the central government, to blend the local groups into a larger whole,[35] to build a strong centralized nation-state. Mercantilism was therefore a powerful tool in the process which transformed the feudal monarchy into the modern state, in the creation of a new feudalism "in which the state, or its king, was the actual feudal lord and his subjects were his vassals."[36]

Richelieu found the mechanics of mercantilism in England. Duty-free importation for raw materials, but interdiction to export them; encouragement for manufacture, but prohibition to import finished products, what Hauser calls the "protectionist tetragram," had been practiced by Lord Burghley and was adopted by Richelieu who saw it as a source of wealth and power.[37] It has been pointed out repeatedly that Ancien Régime colonization was commercial or mercantile in outlook.[38] Colonies, which in the sixteenth century had been sought for precious metals or as way stations en route to the fabled East, became valuable sources of raw materials not found in the mother country and as outlets for its manufactured goods.[39]

Colonies had another important role to play in state building, one which was acknowledged in the title Richelieu assumed in 1626: *"grand maître, chef et surintendant de la navigation et du commerce."* Colonial ventures stimulated the development of both merchant marine and navy. And Richelieu had adopted the formula coined by his relative and collaborator Isaac de Razilly: "Whoever has mastery of the seas has great power on land." Admiral Mahan's theory of sea power is already contained in Razilly's lapidary statement.[40] Colonies would thus provide another weapon in his lifelong battle against the House of Hapsburg.[41] A strong navy could harass Spanish shipping, hurting the Hapsburg empire at its most vulnerable point, its exposed lines of communications. Richelieu's maritime schemes were successful enough to worry the English, bent on preserving their supremacy at sea, and thus lead them to support Huguenot unrest.[42] Charles I of England informed Buckingham of his decision to prevent the French king from "extending his monarchy over the ocean and wrenching from England the sovereignty of the seas. . . ."[43]

Most importantly, colonies could contribute to that intangible which the seventeenth century prized above all, *la gloire*. "Colonization was to spread *la gloire du roi* among foreign nations, increase the number of subjects, and counter-balance in the world Spanish, Dutch, and English influences," writes Robert Boutruche.[44] This political ideal which fuses in this single word, *gloire,* national interest, royal prestige, and economic supremacy dictated the settlement policy adopted by the cardinal. Commercial penetration and the founding of trading posts might satisfy the economic aspects of mercantilism, might provide the raw materials necessary for home industries, and might allow the sale of the manufactured goods produced in the home country, but they would not "increase the number of subjects" nor spread the king's name. Permanent possession, settlements, and the establishment of New Frances were needed. Colonization had to create overseas new societies which would be extensions of French society, "living from it and by it, creating truly a greater France."[45]

This vision of colonization is perhaps best seen in Champlain's scheme for the assimilation of the Amerindians into a new half-breed society based "on the same ethics, the same social base of the family, the same concept of order, authority and obedience" as French society.[46] The conversion of the Indians was therefore a priority since, along with the acquisition of the French language, it would transform "savages" into subjects. From the first, Richelieu adopted a settlement policy which called for a strong immigration combined with conversion of the natives who, once christianized and gallicized, would increase many times the population of the kingdom, hence *la gloire du roi*, the principal motivation for early colonial policy.

II

Domestic Factors

Sixteenth- and seventeenth-century French colonial policy may have been shaped primarily by foreign-affairs considerations, but social and economic developments at home frequently impeded its implementation. Two major domestic changes affecting colonial policy took place during the reign of Henry IV. First, the French crown, short of money in the wake of the disastrous civil wars, institutionalized the venality of offices. These had long been "venal," that is bought and sold. As far back as the fourteenth century, Charles VII and Louis XI had sold state charges. Throughout the sixteenth century the kings tried to suppress venality, but, in fact, kept creating and selling new offices to increase their revenues. In 1608, however, the venality of offices was systematized by the declarations of December 7 and 12 which established the *Paulette*. An officeholder paid yearly 1/60th of the value of his office, but upon his death the charge belonged to his heirs who could assume it or sell it, as they wished.[47] Once systematized, the venality of offices insured the slow but inevitable social mobility of the bourgeoisie which, buying ever higher offices, eventually acceded to the *noblesse de robe*.[48] In a society of markedly aristocratic outlook such as that of seventeenth- and eighteenth-century France, offices attracted bourgeois wealth by opening the way to social ascension.[49] Thus capital which in England or the Netherlands was plowed into commercial and industrial ventures, as well as into colonial enterprises, was in France invested in administrative posts,[50] creating a virtual crown monopoly on "the nation's supply of brains, ability, and capital."[51] The venality of offices also insured, it was believed, that important charges would be filled by men of property rather than men of learning but low extraction and that it would prevent the great nobles from filling those posts with their "creatures."[52]

Second, at the same time, the French crown adopted the system of commercial companies that the Dutch were simultaneously developing. In fact, the first Dutch company and the first French company were chartered in the same year, 1602.[53] The system had everything to attract the French crown, perennially short of money. The king entrusted to some affluent subjects, who created a company, the colonization of a new land. In exchange, he granted them a trade monopoly which should enable them to recover their expenses and even make a handsome profit.[54] Thus in 1602, Aymar de Chastes, friend of Henry IV and governor of Dieppe, reorganized the company which two St. Malo traders, Pierre Chauvin and Mr. Pontgravé, had launched in 1600. In 1603 Chastes sent Pontgravé with Samuel de Champlain to explore the coast of Acadia. It was as successor of Chastes, who died in 1603, that de Monts had been granted a ten-year monopoly in exchange for which he was to build "a New France which would not cost the king a penny."[55] Throughout the Ancien Régime, companies were to prove indifferent to colonization and eager for immediate profits, yet the French crown turned to them again and again. Between 1599 and 1789, seventy-five companies were chartered, most of them in the seventeenth century.[56]

The two developments were intertwined. The creation of the *Paulette* affected commercial companies chartered to exploit new colonial lands. For in France those companies, unlike the Dutch East India Company, always operated with insufficient capital, furnished reluctantly by the different classes, often only after considerable governmental pressure. Moreover, these insufficiently funded companies always demanded a monopoly. As Chailley-Bert points out, neither the state, ever impoverished, nor individual capitalists, "few in number and prudent," could assume the risk of colonial enterprises. Hence an association of capital was needed. But to attract investors, one had to promise profit; therefore, the necessity of "privilege," that most hallowed Ancien Régime institution.[57] But in turn, the privilege, the monopoly, the *exclusif*, tended to smother colonial commerce and industry to the benefit of the company's shareholders. The Ancien Régime's colonial development would therefore be caught in a vicious circle designed, however unwittingly, under the reign of Good King Henry.

The first example of the competition between office and investment in commercial companies came during Richelieu's tenure. The cardinal's master plan for colonial expansion foundered on the reefs of financial expediency. The French monarchy could not finance ambitious colonial schemes; therefore, the minister turned to trading companies.[58] The success of the Dutch East India Company naturally encouraged hopes that properly organized, well-financed private companies could accomplish as much for France. Under Richelieu's aegis, three companies were chartered in quick succession for colonization projects on the North American continent. The Company of Morbihan, or Company of the Hundred Associates, was founded in 1626, with exclusive trading rights in New France. The resistance of the ports outside of the Morbihan region was such that the Company was quickly dismantled[59] to be replaced in 1627 by the Nacelle de Saint-Pierre Fleurdelisée Company. This one operated for a while, actually sending twelve ships and some 400 families to Canada. Finally in 1628 Richelieu created the Company of New France specifically to colonize.[60] Richelieu's kinsman, Isaac de Razilly, who had had ample experience already with Champlain, was the director, and the cardinal's trusted collaborator, Père Joseph supervised closely the operation of the company which, the two churchmen hoped, would include large-scale proselytizing.

That the crown should turn to a semiofficial corporate body to do a task which in the nineteenth or twentieth centuries would be considered a state function fitted perfectly the Ancien Régime concept of government. Until they were attacked by the physiocrats in the middle of the eighteenth century, corporate bodies fulfilled duties which would seem to be crown prerogatives such as police, taxation, and administration. Such bodies, which included the provincial estates, the guilds, the courts, the universities, and the tax farmers were corporations or intermediate bodies which Montesquieu, for one, considered constitutional safeguards for French liberties.[61] Thus it was perfectly consistent with prevailing thinking that companies be entrusted with the settlement and administration of new lands in exchange for a trade monopoly. In practice, however, the arrangement did not work so well. The companies' stockholders were interested in a large return on their investment, and it always seemed to them that profits could be larger and quicker from trade than from colonizing. Champlain realized quite early that companies were reluctant to send settlers who might become trade competitors of the company's agents.[62] It was useless to remonstrate that settlers would eventually produce the foodstuffs which the company had to import into the colony at great cost and thus, eventually, increase the shareholder's return. The reluctance of chartered companies to live up to their settlement commitment was to be a recurrent trait of Ancien Régime colonization. By the time the Hundred Associates was chartered, Richelieu was conscious enough of the problem to provide that vagabonds, beggars, and petty criminals would be taken into the employ of the company.[63] Forced immigration would provide a cheaper, hence more attractive, alternative to a commercial company.

In any case, the French companies were never sufficiently capitalized: Richelieu quickly found what Colbert would discover again and again, that it was extremely difficult to lure French capital into colonial ventures, even with trade monopoly. The court, beginning with the queen, Ann of Austria, subscribed heavily. Few merchants did. The list of the Hundred Associates is revealing. Who subscribed? First Richelieu himself; then the superintendent of finances, Antoine Coiffier de Ruzé, marquis d'Effiat; and the intendent of the marine, Martin de Mauroy. Some forty civil servants obediently followed the example given by their administrative superiors. Barely twenty merchants were willing to risk their capital. Bourgeois and noblemen showed little enthusiasm, yet they outnumbered the merchants.[64] Noblemen were encouraged to participate. Every charter beginning with that of the Hundred Associates specified that noblemen did not *deroger*[65] —lose caste—by investing in the company or playing a role in its administration. But the financial class did not prove eager to contribute to the capital of later companies. Part of the problem lay with the attraction for the French bourgeoisie to invest in offices rather than in trade, so as to gain entry eventually into the nobility. Richelieu was well aware of the obstacle posed by the venality of charges. In his *Testament politique*, he bewailed the fact that the king's subjects derived their ranks "from vanity."[66] Or, as his friend Jean Eon put it: The French are kept away "from commerce by the states, charges and offices which out of necessity, the state has multiplied and made venal."[67] However, Richelieu could do nothing about the abuse of offices: he lacked the financial resources to buy them back and hesitated, besides, to tamper with the existing order. Venality was for him "a disorder which is a part of the general order" and which therefore could not be removed without endangering the equilibrium of the state.[68]

The chartered companies not only failed to find sufficient capital, they also encountered strong opposition from merchants and ship outfitters who resented the trade monopoly guaranteed by the charters. The chartering of the Hundred Associates aroused such vehement protests in French ports that even Richelieu's vigorous support could not prevent the Company's demise within a few months.[69]

The cardinal was also quite aware that Frenchmen hesitated to immigrate and consequently the same charter provided that Flemings, Hollanders and others who went to the colony would enjoy all the rights of Frenchmen provided, of course, that they professed the Roman Catholic religion.[70] For under Richelieu, domestic factors arose which made exclusion of Protestants an unalterable part of French colonial policy. Historians have pointed out repeatedly how the policy differed from that of England whose American colonies were largely populated by religious dissenters. And, the Ancien Régime has been condemned as shortsighted for depriving its colonies of a potentially rich, hard-working population. The Canadian historian François-Xavier Garneau points out that of nine presidents of the Continental Congress three were descendants of French Protestants: Henry Laurens, John Jay, and Elias Boudinot.[71] Religious pluralism, however, was considered a weakness, one that France had been forced to tolerate since the Edict of Nantes in order to stop the bloodshed of the religious wars, but not a condition to be condoned. The Edict of Nantes while putting an end to an era of bloody disorders had granted the Protestants privileges which, in fact, made them a state within a state, a condition Richelieu had to end if he were to achieve his aim of making royal power supreme in France. He thus set about abolishing the special privileges Protestants enjoyed, particularly the control of fortresses such as La Rochelle which he finally subdued after a long and arduous siege.[72] It is hardly surprising then that the charter of the Hundred Associates specified that the company should "populate the said colony with French, Catholic subjects."[73] Moreover, the Company of the Hundred Associates replaced an early Company of Caen whose directors, Calvinists in the majority, were suspected of intending to make Canada a Huguenot principality which would eventually secede from the French commonwealth and ally itself with its English and Dutch neighbors.[74] Perceiving the Protestants as a threat to unity and as a threat to the very continuation of French dominion over Canada, Richelieu, naturally enough, took steps to exclude them.[75]

Moreover, the social policy to which he had committed himself, that of creating a new society formed by the intimate union of French settlers and "Frenchified" natives, required active missionary activities. Only by conversion to Christianity (and mastery of the the one civilized language!) could Amerindians be brought into the fold. The presence of dissenters would have hindered the missionary work. Historians have disagreed about the importance Richelieu really attached to missionary activities. Many doubt the sincerity of the charter articles which proclaimed the spread of Christianity as a primary aim of colonization.[76] It is often difficult, expecially for American scholars, to take seriously the Catholic convictions of a churchman who did not hesitate to ally himself with the Protestant king, Gustav Adolphus, not to mention the infidel Ottoman Porte, when such alliances suited his foreign policy. Bernard Schnapper, on the other hand, goes so far as to argue that the conversion of Indians was, in fact, the mainspring behind Richelieu's policy, not because of the cardinal's religious faith, but because *la dignité du roi,* his *gloire,* was thought to come as much from the moral element, his Christian virtues, as from the temporal element, his might.[77] Richelieu, he argues, did not need colonies to fight Spain, since he could attack her trade through privateers; nor to enrich the national treasury, since French agricultural exports brought in gold. But he did need them for political and religious reasons, to increase the king's "dignity."[78]

Certainly, missionary activities in the colonies were a necessity if a new society was to emerge and if the number of the king's subjects was to increase. Article 16 of the articles signed before La Rochelle in 1628 provided that converted Indians would be considered French citizens and could settle in France with all the rights of native-born subjects.[79] Political expediency this time was on the side of piety. The chartered companies, however, proved as little interested in Christianization as in colonization.[80] Their narrowly conceived aims put them at odds with the cardinal who was nevertheless forced to resort to them because he lacked the finances to back his grandiose schemes.

Thus Richelieu recognized the need for colonies within a mercantilist economic system intended to bolster royal absolutism. He laid down the principles of the social policy that Colbert would adopt, that colonies were extensions of French society where the natives, once converted and "civilized," would enjoy all the rights of *régnicoles.* His imperial dream of a New France which would mirror France and increase the king's dignity and prestige foundered on the lack of cooperation of financiers who on one hand hesitated to invest in colonial ventures and on the other opposed the granting of privileges, here trade monopoly, to those willing to risk their capital. He also found the church unwilling to commit large numbers of missionaries to the New World. Thus the cardinal-duke could never convince merchants or clerics to serve the needs of France's *gloire.* The merchants invested only reluctantly in the Atlantic trade—the Levant trade with its rapid profits and its well-established routes was far more attractive.[81] The church invested only cautiously in priests—only the Society of Jesus could be said to have provided large numbers of missionaries, and even that compared to the Jesuit effort in the Far East was niggardly. The discrepancy between the minister's policy and its implementation is most revealing of a political system no longer attuned to the economic realities of the nation.

II

Colbert and the Colonies

Jean-Baptiste Colbert has been generally acknowledged as the architect of the economic growth which enabled the *Roi-Soleil* to achieve preponderance in European affairs and as a major force in establishing Ancien Régime colonial policies. Recent revisionist studies, however, have strongly questioned Colbert's motivation, pointing to the protection he extended relatives and clients, and his effectiveness, pointing to the economic woes of seventeenth-century France. As far as colonies are concerned, Colbert established the administrative structures and drew up the legislation which enabled France to build a strong navy, but also found that issuing ordinances and chartering companies did not guarantee implementation.[1]

For a long time the only question raised concerning Colbert's colonial policies had been the credit to be given to Louis XIV himself on the one hand, and to the minister on the other. Certainly Louis took his king's craft seriously and supervised all aspects of French policies.[2] But some aspects were closer to his heart than others, and colonial ventures were not the dearest. Louis displayed, according to reports of the Venetian ambassador, "a natural disinclination toward far-flung ventures."[3] His natural bent lay in the direction of European domination and he disliked entrusting his prestige to an element as unpredictable as the sea.[4] Colbert therefore had to plan highly visible operations to win royal support for colonial aspirations. For example, the minister encouraged the construction of the celebrated "globes de Marly," two *mappemondes* four meters in diameter, one representing the earth and the other the heavens, which Cardinal d'Estrée ordered from Vincenzo Coronelli, a Venetian astronomer, as presents for the king.[5] The globe representing the earth took into account the latest geographic discoveries, including the La Salle explorations at the mouth of the Mississippi, and was designed to arouse royal pride in past French accomplishments as well as to kindle a burning desire to preside over the destinies of as much of the world as possible. The historians of French colonization agree that the grand design of French colonial policy did not originate with the king[6] but with the minister who excelled at flattering his royal master's vanity so as to convince him that he had initiated ideas which, in fact, were Colbert's.[7] Deschamps quotes two interesting letters that Colbert addressed to his son, Jean-Baptiste Colbert, marquis de Seignelay, who accompanied Louis during the Flanders campaign. One of them contains fulsome praise of the king's "glory," "application," "prodigious talents." The second, a most private letter, advises Seignelay to maneuver the conversation so as to be able to give Louis a reading of the pertinent (i. e. flattering) passages, thus gaining favor for both father and son.[8] Thus the minister was ever the courtier, the seventeenth century not seeing courting royal favor as demeaning.[9] Though both minister and king sought French hegemony, Colbert was at odds with his royal master on some basic issues: the king's aim was military conquest, the minister's economic prosperity.[10] But both looked upon financial success as a means to build a strong army and a strong navy, always seeking "la gloire du roi."[11]

Colonies were secondary in Louis's thought though he never relinquished one willingly, even when it proved of limited value. He carefully monitored his negotiations at Ryswick, for example, to make sure no colony was forsaken, and abandoned Acadia at Utrecht only because he could no longer fight the coalition which had formed against him. Colbert valued colonies as elements of his economic policies. He did inherit Richelieu's policy, but while the cardinal thought mainly in political terms,[12] Colbert thought also in commercial terms[13] and looked upon colonization as a mercantile venture, and colonies as "lieux de commerce."

In 1661, when Colbert engineered Fouquet's downfall, the powerful finance superintendent, he knew little about colonies beyond what he had learned managing Mazarin's investments in Guyana and Madagascar. But he studied the Fouquet archives, recruited advisers, and gradually developed a real competence in colonial affairs.[14] He did not simply adopt Richelieu's policies. He refined them and amplified them. Richelieu had striven for conquest and settlement to increase the king's glory, with economic profit as an incidental fallout. His policies belonged to the early stages of mercantilist state building. Colbert aimed at profit: colonies would provide the raw materials and tropical products which France otherwise purchased abroad.[15] Better informed than the cardinal about climate, productions, and populations—he spent the first three years of his administration studying the available documentation—Colbert distinguished between those areas where French interests needed only trading posts and those where actual colonization was necessary. In other words, he understood the distinction between settlement colonies and trade colonies.[16] Therein lies Colbert's contribution, and in its corollary, that a settlement colony needed to produce so as to export and needed to be populated so as to produce.[17] Eventually another corollary would follow: while the trading colonies, *colonies d'exploitation commerciale,* could be entrusted to companies, the *colonies de peuplement* would be administered directly by the crown since they were to be overseas extensions of the mother country.[18]

The areas suitable for settlement colonies, Colbert thought, were Canada, Ile Bourbon (Reunion), Guyana, and Senegal, all of which were considered inhabitable by Europeans.[19] The only one that he truly developed was Canada, New France, which he visualized, in terms borrowed from Razilly and Richelieu, as an extension of the mother country populated by a few French settlers, their half-breed offsprings, and countless converted, Gallicized natives. In Colbert's days, geopolitical factors had not yet come into play in North America; La Salle's 1684 exploration was the first to be primarily motivated by the desire to prevent a rival from occupying the area. The choice between settlement or trading colonies consequently was determined by economic factors. New France, for example, became a settlement colony so that it might grow enough food to feed itself and, later, supply the West Indies. But at all times commercial colonies and settlement colonies were judged by a single criterion, the interest of France and the French monarchy. Colonies existed by and for the mother country.[20] In some cases, such as Canada, that meant developing home industries and making the colony self-sufficient;[21] in other cases an economically dependent military establishment would suffice. The preferences of colonies and administrators did not weigh in the balance.[22]

This indifference to colonial preferences formed also the colonial policies associated with Colbert's name, the *exclusif* and the *pacte colonial,* which determined the role overseas establishments should play within the mercantilist system. As Schmoller points out, in the seventeenth century, the opening of world trade in India and America, the influx of bullion, the development of fleets and trading companies, the creation of a system of bills of exchange and other credit machinery, the use of the press with the concurrent birth of public opinion, the geographical division of labor within countries, the appearance of domestic industry, all these forces "impelled society to some large economic reorganization on a broader basis, and pointed to the creation of national states with a corresponding policy."[23] Thus the central government engaged in a constant struggle against special-interest groups, be they the great nobles, the towns, the corporations, or the provincial estates, a struggle against privilege which in France would be resolved only by the Revolution of 1789. Mercantilism in France, as in the rest of Europe, was as much a "matter of transformation and union at home as of barriers against the world outside."[24] Colbert's administration and his great series of laws—the civil ordinance of 1667, the edict on waters and forests of 1669,[25] the criminal ordinance of 1670, and the commerce ordinance of 1673 (not to mention the Black Code promulgated in 1685, after his death)—aimed at unification, economically as well as politically.[26] Economic activity and especially speedy circulation of money within the state was considered essential to national well-being.[27] The circulatory theory of money assumed that the flow of specie from abroad supported rural life, fostered increased production and concomittantly increased state revenues in the form of indirect taxes. Unfortunately foreign specie could only be obtained at the expense of other countries.[28] As early as 1615 Montchrestien had compared international trade to the "transfer from one full jar to a dry one."[29] Mercantilist thought, after all, developed during that deflationary period which stretches from 1650 to the French Revolution, following the inflation caused by the influx of American precious metals. France's rich resources enabled her to get along without foreign trade, and exploitation of this "God-given economic superiority" would insure French preponderance in Europe as well as domestic prosperity.[30] Domestic prosperity, made possible by vast amounts of foreign treasure, would enable the state, acting on mercantilistic principles, to sweep away local structures and special privileges, all obstacles to centralization and to establish a Cartesian society, a clockwork mechanism, "governed according to principles of order and utility."[31]

Within this system, colonies would contribute to rural well-being by providing the few raw materials France did not have, by absorbing surplus production, and by providing employment for surplus population. Instead of importing sugar, coffee, indigo, dye woods, cotton, beaver pelts, codfish, France would be supplied by its colonies.[32] But naturally the regime designed for those colonies subordinated their well-being to the mother country's. The *pacte colonial* claimed to be two sided: the mother country established and administered the colonies which paid no taxes and contributed nothing toward their defense or administration; they, in turn, made the mother country wealthy by foregoing, in particular, any trade with foreigners. This arrangement could look like a contract, hence its name *pacte colonial*.[33]

Monopoly, however, was not an inextricable part of the system. On the contrary, within the *exclusif* Colbert again and again pronounced himself in favor of freedom of trade, but among French merchants only. In February 1670 he refers to "liberty, the soul of trade, which alone can foster commerce." Any trade hindrance would slow progress in the West Indies and, as he wrote the intendant at Rochefort, "I am rather opposed to anything which can hinder trade, it must be extremely free."[34] In 1670, he sums up his thought in a letter to de Baas, governor of the Antilles: "Total exclusion of foreigners, freedom for all Frenchmen."[35] The *exclusif* which really begins with Colbert was less restrictive than the Spanish system since it was open to all French subjects (except where trading companies held a monopoly).[36] One consequence of *l'exclusif* was Colbert's acceptance of the slave trade which not only furnished workers for colonial plantations but also encouraged shipping in the Atlantic ports and brought in large profits.[37]

The colonists, as unruly and as attached to their "privileges" and special interests as their metropolitan counterparts, protested, even rebelled against the *exclusif.* The revolts were especially endemic in the West Indies which had traded freely with foreigners, particularly the English colonists, before 1660 and needed to exchange their sugar and molasses for wood, flour, and fish.[38] The many Antillian white revolts recounted by Charles Frostin were economically motivated.[39] The protests of the harassed planters fell on deaf ears, and they consequently became quite good at smuggling.

It is, however, going too far to state, as does Varille, that in the mercantilist system, colonies were in bondage to the mother country.[40] There were relaxations of the system, for Colbert was nothing if not pragmatic and his decisions were not monolithic. Colbertism should, for example, have prohibited any industrial development in the colonies which, theoretically, were intended only as sources of raw materials and markets for manufactured goods. Yet Colbert encouraged, for example, sugar refining in the West Indies, despite protests by French manufacturers, and beer brewing in Canada though it would compete with the produce of French vinyards.[41] Canada was also allowed to manufacture consumer goods such as shoes, hats, and cloth. But the Indies, on the other hand, were prevented from trading with the Dutch though the interdiction hindered the sugar industry which needed cheap foodstuffs to feed the slaves.[42] The interpretations of the occasional laxness have varied. Chailley-Bert sees it as a temporary enticement to attract settlers, and Vignols stresses that Colbert would consider such derogation only as a stopgap measure to be used in infant colonies.[43] Weber, the learned historian of the Company of the Indies, on the other hand, argues that the *pacte colonial* was only a school where France would learn commerce and industry and maintains that, once industry developed, Colbert intended to break the shackles and turn private enterprise loose.[44] Nothing in Colbert's letters or memoirs really supports Weber's assertion. On the contrary it is clear that Colbert's dream was a totally autarkic French empire growing ever fatter and richer as foreign bullion swelled its coffers. Freedom of trade was to prevail within the empire (and that freedom as far as he was concerned extended to freedom of conscience: Colbert protected Protestants and Jews in the colonies), but it did not extend to trade with foreigners, unless absolutely necessary.[45]

For colonies which were to be only commercial outposts and for settlement colonies at their beginnings, Colbert borrowed Richelieu's old expedient, trading companies, even though they had been notably unsuccessful in France. Companies were for him, as they had been for the cardinal, a way of supplementing state financing.[46] But Colbert visualized grandiose companies which would regroup the small, underfunded existing ones.[47] In 1660 the French had establishments in Canada, Newfoundland, Acadia; in the Caribbean at Saint-Christophe, Guadeloupe, Martinique, Saint-Domingue and Guyana; at St. Louis-du-Sénégal, a colony at the mouth of the Senegal River; in Madagascar, Ile

Bourbon (Reunion) and the Seychelles. Besides, French ships traded with India and the Moluccas.[48] A number of companies managed the colonial trade. The Company of American Isles (founded in 1626, rechartered in 1635 and 1642); the Company of New France (founded in 1628 but ceded to the Knights of Malta); the Company of France Equinoxiale or Cayenne Company (founded in 1651) held the North American trade. The Company of Cape Verde and Senegal (founded in 1657) controlled the West African commerce.[49] Colbert bought them up and melded them into a single company, the Company of the West Indies chartered in May 1664, headquartered at Le Havre, with a capital of six million *livres*.[50] Its monopoly included the North American colonies, the Antilles, Guyana, and the West African coast where it was to establish outposts to "recruit" workers.[51] The eastern trade was to be the monopoly of the French East India Company chartered in August 1664 from the debris of the 1642 Compagnie de France Orientale, itself the successor of companies chartered in 1633 (Compagnie Dumé d'Applemont); in 1616 (Compagnie de France et de Rouen); in 1604 (Compagnie Gérard Deroy); and in 1600 (Compagnie de Saint-Malo, Laval, et Vilré). It incorporated also the short-lived Company of China of 1600.[52] With Lorient as its seat and a capital of fifteen million *livres,* the French East India Company was closely modeled after its Dutch counterpart, object of Colbert's jealous admiration.[53] It was to trade in the Indian Ocean and the Pacific, between Cape Horn and the Cape of Good Hope.

The two companies corresponded clearly to the two types of colonies that Colbert's incisive mind had recognized: The West India Company was intended for settlement or plantation colonies, with either implantation of metropolitan colonists or importation of servile hands supervised by planters; the East India Company would not develop settlements, but found trading posts, thus corresponding to the purely commercial colony.[54]

The financing of the East India Company, on which Colbert founded great hopes, is most revealing of the problems which bedeviled French colonization. Nothing was spared to insure success. The minister even drafted one of the Forty Immortals, François Charpentier, to pen a propaganda pamphlet, "Discours d'un fidèle sujet du roi, touchant l'établissement d'une compagnie française pour le commerce des Indes orientales. . . ."[55] The piece, which appeared fittingly enough on April 1, 1664, praised Madagascar as a veritable Eden, peopled by friendly, kindly natives,[56] thus most suitable for European settlers, and spared no superlative to vaunt the potential riches to be derived from the East in "silk, cinnamon, pepper, ginger, sugar, cotton textiles, wadding, porcelain, dye woods, ivory, incense, bezoar" these tropical luxuries which had become necessities.[57]

The court and the royal family supported the minister's project energetically and generously. A capital of fifteen million *livres* was considered necessary. Louis XIV put in three million; the queen, the queen mother, the dauphin (age three!) sixty thousand each; the princes of blood, Condé and Conti, thirty and twenty thousand respectively. Twenty-one dukes and duchesses dutifully subscribed, along with seven marshals and forty-one members of the great nobility. All in all the courtiers provided two million *livres.*[58] Court officials, financiers and functionaries provided 800,000 *livres,*[59] the Paris *Parlement* some 1,200,000 *livres.*[60] Merchants, bourgeois, and provincial nobility were less than lukewarm in their response and the participation of officials, provincial *parlements,* and municipalities was not obtained without pressure, in some cases overwhelming. The pressures were particularly strong in the central provinces which had no experience with overseas trade and were therefore most reluctant to invest. In Auvergne, the intendant applied severe pressures on the Superior Court,[61] but even in maritime Brittany and Normandy, Colbert's agent had to pursue officials into their homes to wrench subscriptions from them.[62] Colbert was forced to restrain those overzealous agents.

The chartering of the East India Company thus reveals what would remain one of the essential weaknesses of the French system. In the United Provinces, the commercial bourgeoisie backed the Dutch East and West India companies; in England it was the king, the nobility and the great merchants who sustained the colonial effort. In France the companies could not be launched without strong state support and remained "instruments of state ambition."[63] Without support from the mercantile community, Colbert and his successors depended on men inexperienced in business and failed to gain a true adhesion from emerging capitalists.[64] Moreover, French royal support proved undependable at best. Louis XIV did subscribe generously to the East India Company and, unlike most other shareholders, did not fail to produce his second and third installment.[65] (A few months after the due date of the second payment Prince of Condé owed 10,000 *livres* and Prince of Conti the interesting amount of 6,666 *livres*, 13 *sous*, 4 *deniers*!)[66] When the West India Company was liquidated in 1674, the king paid its debts, three and a half million, from his personal exchequer and reimbursed the shareholders to the tune of 1,300,000 *francs.*[67] However, his financial openhandedness did not mean priority, for the first continental war could, and would, draw the king's attention and support away from overseas enterprises.[68]

The failure of the companies to draw support from the private sector came from a variety of reasons. As it had under Richelieu, the French merchant class preferred investing in state offices. Fermanel, Colbert's agent in Rouen, specifically gave venality as a reason for the sluggish response of the merchants. "They are reluctant," he wrote the minister, "to invest large amounts in enterprises which will not yield profit before three or four years when they can on the other hand, put their money in offices which will yield a quick return and frequent profit."[69] The state offices immobilized an enormous amount of capital;

some estimates place it as high as 800 million.[70] In a society where aristocratic values prevailed, money was used to purchase prestige, not to make more money, and besides offices, the financially successful invested in marriage, a quick way to achieve social mobility for their daughters; in land, which often brought titles and thus entry into the nobility; and in *châteaux* in the country or *hôtels* in Paris.[71] Overseas trade was not prestigious.

Moreover, the merchant class did not feel that French companies could compete with the Dutch who were experienced, well capitalized, and possessed an imposing merchant fleet. Colbert's cousin, Colbert du Terron, who pointed out these facts to the minister, was himself only willing to invest 10,000 *livres* in the West India Company.[72] Occasionally, merchants actively opposed the companies which would interfere with their trade. The resistance of merchants, nobles, and magistrates to Richelieu's Hundred Associates has already been mentioned.[73] Even Colbert with the powerful mechanism of Louis's absolutism behind him met with strong resistance along the Mediterranean when he created the Company of the Levant for Near East trade, and from Atlantic merchants when he created the Company of the North for the Baltic trade.

The distrust of the French merchants toward overseas investment was all the greater because of their fresh memory of the financial fiasco of the *Compagnie de la France Equinoxiale*. Chartered in 1651 to develop Guyana, the company was financed by private funds, handsomely enough to outfit an expedition of five or six hundred colonists. The debacle of the highly publicized enterprise permanently disillusioned the French public with colonial affairs, but French administrators never acknowledged the disenchantment of the merchant class and continued seeking support among them.[74] Overseas investments were not profitable: even the wily Mazarin managed to lose 606,000 *livres* in colonial ventures.[75] Thus, French trading companies were doomed to become, as Professor Eccles has written, crown corporations, which under Louis XIV were "created by Colbert, maintained out of the royal treasury, and governed and directed by Colbert."[76]

Many reasons have been given for the failure of French trading companies: Chailley-Bert lists their undercapitalization; the overabundance of hangers-on; their short-term bases; the scarcity of women settlers; and the large amount of land controlled by the church.[77] But even more significant was the profound discrepancy between the aims of the crown and those of the merchant class on the one hand, and between the companies and their agents, on the other hand. The companies for Colbert represented only a transitional state, a first step in the implantation of colonies, especially settlement colonies,[78] an approach which reveals clearly that the minister and the merchants pursued divergent purposes. Colbert expected companies to provide private capital to launch colonization ventures and begin settlements. The reluctance of the merchant class which always had to be pressured to buy shares in the companies made it clear that they were interested in only one thing, a quick return on their investment. The well-established Mediterranean trade, with the Echelles in the Near East and the Bastion at Algiers, assured such profits and attracted their investments far more readily than risky American ventures. India, China, the East Indies also appealed to French shipowners and great merchants. The large native populations of these areas produced goods eagerly sought in Europe. This lucrative trade could be conducted by maintaining minimal, inexpensive establishments, mere *comptoirs.* North America, on the other hand, offered timber, sorely needed for the royal navy but expensive to exploit and to transport, and it yielded furs, the only truly exploitable New France commodity, hence the *raison d'être* of the colony. But the fur trade did not really need settlement to buttress it. Hence, the shareholders and directors showed little interest in founding and establishing colonies, or in developing agriculture or industry. Colonists were often looked upon as potential rivals who would take trade, hence profit, from company representatives. Moreover, women were especially undesirable as colonists from the mercantile point of view because they were considered incapable of turning out as much work; but without females settlement languished. Charters usually specified the number of colonists a company was obligated to bring yearly, but the prescription was seldom observed. For companies, profit came first while colonization required that social purpose predominate over economic benefits.[79]

The minister wanted companies to underwrite the first settlement expenses that the crown might reap the benefit. The companies, however, held the diametrically opposed view: they wanted the crown to bear the expense of administering and defending the colony while they took advantage of the colonial business opportunities.[80] Moreover, as Boulle points out, the companies themselves were plundered by the agents who grew rich while the companies went bankrupt. Boulle argues that the state under Colbert "put up the bulk of the risk capital and paid most of the operating expenses," in the hope of motivating capitalists "to involve themselves more deeply into these risky trading ventures."[81] In some cases, as in Bordeaux, the policy met with success.[82] Most of the time, it did not. The commercial class did not see itself as being in the colonizing business.

Colbert agreed with them to the extent that he considered privileged companies unsuitable for already established colonies such as Canada or the Antilles.[83] In 1668 he was already debating the suppression of the West India Company and instructing the islands' governors to give "the largest possible freedom to the French private traders," a freedom compatible with commercial monopoly.[84] For several years thereafter he used both the company and private traders to accomplish his aim, substituting French traders for the Dutch. By

1674, this purpose had been accomplished and the West India Company was liquidated.[85] In the edict of 1674 Louis XIV roundly condemned colonization companies but what was meant was that the company had served its purpose and could be dispensed with.[86] With liquidation of the company, the islands and Canada became crown colonies.

The change meant that they now had to be given new forms of government. The crown colonies were treated as French provinces and received a typical provincial administration: a governor, usually drawn from the nobility or the military (or preferably both) who represented the king and administered military establishment and native affairs and an intendant drawn from the *noblesse de robe* or bourgeoisie who controlled financial matters.[87] In Canada, only one governor, Joseph Antoine Le Febvre de la Barre, did not belong to the feudal nobility and to the military establishment. The intendant was in fact the key figure in the economic development of a colony[88] though the governor was the king's own representative, hence held first place.[89]

The system of government in the colonies mirrored that of France: absolutist and paternalistic. Representative assemblies were no more encouraged in the colonies than in the mother country where the Estates General had not met since 1614. Canadian settlers had at first elected syndics to represent them at the Supreme Council in Quebec. Colbert would have none of it and ordered Frontenac in 1673 "quietly to abolish the syndic . . . it being a good thing that each man speak for himself and that no one speak for all."[90] The Sovereign Council itself was an appointed body with mainly judicial functions thus resembling more the French *Parlement* than the English Parliament. The one Colbert established for Canada in 1663, superseding an earlier council,[91] was composed of the governor, the bishop, an attorney general and five councillors chosen by the governor and bishop. Elected assemblies were considered dangerous: Colbert reminded Frontenac who had summoned an assembly that in France the Estates General had been dispensed with since 1614, and forbade any further meetings. The absolutist concept of the French monarchy did not end with Louis XIV. Addressing the rebellious Paris *Parlement* in 1776, Louis XV stated unequivocally: "In my sole person resides sovereign power. . . . From me alone do courts derive their existence and authority . . . Legislative power is mine alone, independent and unshared (*sans dependances et sans partage*)".[92] There were to be no elective bodies in French colonies from the beginning of Colbert's administration till 1787 when local assemblies were established in Martinique and Guadeloupe.[93]

In the system favored by Colbert and Louis XIV, the governor represented the king and enjoyed the same absolute authority. But while Louis XIV and his ministers exercised this absolute authority, especially in the early years, with a great deal of moderation and a real respect for traditional liberties and the unwritten constitution of the kingdom,[94] colonial governors were frequently given to abusing their power. Louis de Buade, count of Frontenac, the flamboyant Canadian governor was a case in point.[95] Jean-Baptiste Le Moyne de Bienville, the irascible governor of Louisiana, would later be another. Since good, fair, moderate government was deemed essential if the colonies were to attract settlers,[96] the king was forced to enact legislation limiting the governor's power. In 1679, as Eccles points out, the same year England passed the Habeas Corpus Act, Colbert instructed Frontenac that he was not to have anyone arrested, that function being the privilege of the courts, thus in fact protecting the king's subjects from arbitrary imprisonment.[97] For, it should be pointed out, absolute government in the French mold was far from incompatible with freedom. In fact, Colbert always stressed that he wanted the maximum liberty for all subjects, especially in the colonies: liberty to cultivate their lands, to create industries, to trade, even liberty of conscience for Protestants and Jews.[98] This liberty, of course, had to accommodate itself of Colbert's long-range plans for economic development and was valued less as a good in itself than as an inducement to attract colonists.

The system implanted in the colonies, however, could not be a carbon copy of the home government, even if the crown had not wanted to introduce changes. Some differences, like the constitutional limit placed on the governors' power, resulted from necessity. The enormous distance from the New World colonies to the home country, plus the fact that the Canadian winter isolated New France several months a year, made it imperative that the limitation of the governor's power be codified and institutionalized while in Europe a dispatch from the king could suffice to curb a would-be despot.[99] The freedoms allowed settlers were imposed on the government by the need to make the colonies attractive. The attempt at transplanting the parish organization failed because France's parishes were bound with village life, and New France rejected villages.[100] But some changes such as the absence of lawyers, the refusal to sell offices, and the unified law code were deliberate improvements that Colbert and the king would have liked to introduce in France, but could not because regional and corporate "liberties" and customs formed a complex fabric where they could not pull a thread without unravelling the whole. In the colonies where they started fresh, they could reform the abuses that were, in the Old World, too deeply engrained for redress.[101] Ancien Régime France knew a welter of "*coutumes*," each province having its own laws and often within the provinces, certain *prévotés* or *baillage,* having their own—all in all, over three hundred. Louis would have liked to unify the system and give France "a comprehensive legal code as a lasting monument to his greatness,"[102] but got no farther than the issuance of the ordinances of civil procedure (1667), criminal procedure (1670), commerce (1673) and the Black Code (1685) which did provide some unity. But he was not willing to override the privileges of the provincews to the extent of eliminating the local *coutumes*. In the colonies, however, the *Coutume de Paris* became the sole law of the land.[103]

In France the welter of local laws and the hopeless complications of procedure had led to a multiplication of lawyers who were usually the only ones to benefit from the prolonged litigation. In New France, there were no lawyers. Contracts, sales and wills were drawn up by notaries; in courts, plantiffs and defendants presented their cases and judges drawn from the community conducted the proceedings and rendered judgement, rapidly and cheaply. The highest fee a judge could charge was eight *livres* a day, and that only if he had to go into the country. Of course, that was the official scale. In actual practice, as Jacques Mathieu has found studying the records of the Quebec *prévoté,* for 1667, the judges earned somewhat more than regulations allowed. And at that date, Canadians had become quite litigious: 1667 and 1668, the *prévoté* registered twice as many cases as it did notarial acts.[104] Justice in New France was also lenient. André LaChance in his study of criminal justice under the French regime could find only sixty-seven executions and only thirty instances of judicial torture.[105]

Another abuse that Colbert, following Richelieu's precedent, refused to allow in the colonies, was the sale of offices. Not in New France, the Mascareignes, the West Indies, or in the late-comer Louisiana would offices be bought and sold. There was one exception, in 1702, when Charles de Monseignat, Frontenac's secretary, and François Clairambault d'Aigremont were forced to purchase the offices of *commissaire de la marine.*[106]

Social organization in the colonies also was based on French precedents, with abuses corrected, sometimes by crown decisions, sometimes because the frontier demanded modifications of the metropolitan model. In the case of the seigneurial system, necessities imposed by the colonial reality and deliberate choices made by king and minister combined to produce a regime based on French precedent but vastly different from it. Canada was to have a seigneurial system, derived from the old feudal tradition. It seemed all the more logical to transplant medieval institutions, that, indeed, an analogy could be drawn between tenth-century France and seventeenth-century Canada.[107] Medieval feudalism, however, had been based on the exchange of military service for land and had developed a complex social and political system. The Canadian seigneurial system was mainly a method of settlement, as the concession or land-grant system in Louisiana later, based on the French axiom "no land without a *seigneur.*" The *seigneur* received a land grant from the crown, (during its tenure the Company of One Hundred Associates received the entire territory as its *seigneurie*), just as medieval lords received fiefs and, like his medieval counterpart, proceeded to subinfeodate, to grant parcels to tenants. As such, the system could be called "feudal," but the *seigneur* did not owe military service to the crown, nor did his tenants owe him any. It can be wondered why the system was transferred to New France when on the continent the crown had fought to destroy feudalism until the great nobles ceased to threaten royal supremacy. The fact is, as Trudel points out, that the monarchy had become identified with the economic and social remnant of the feudal system, the seigneurial regime, which disappeared when the monarchy collapsed. Had the settlement of New France been carried out in a different manner, an allodial system, for instance, with land granted without rent or dues, Canada would have lacked the linchpin of Ancien Régime social order.[108]

Outwardly, the Canadian system and its French antecedent had much in common. Like the French *seigneur* the Canadian lord enjoyed special privileges. He received *foi et hommage*; he had the best pew in church; in processions he followed the priest; at mass he received communion first and was sprinkled first with holy water.[109] He also enjoyed civil honors such as having the *mai*, a fir tree trimmed of all branches but the top, planted before his house by the tenants.[110] And he had the right to dispense justice, in most cases high, middle and low. In Canada, however, royal courts were so easily available that few *seigneurs* went to the expense of establishing their own courts. In 1663, Trudel finds that 45 *seigneuries* out of 104, but 34 of these representing 96.8 percent of the land conceded, enjoyed the right of high justice. Only one, the *seigneurie* of Montreal, exercised that right,[111] and it relinquished it in 1727.[112]

The seventeenth-century Canadian *seigneur* enjoyed only moderate prestige. The Canadian *seigneuries* were *fiefs noble,* meaning that they were passed from father to son, like noble lands, but they did not confer nobility (only the *fief de dignité* did this. Thus the *seigneur* was not necessarily a nobleman.[113] It is true that 84.3 percent of the land held by the 62 individual *seigneurs* (as opposed to institutional *seigneurs* such as the religious orders) was held by 32 nobles. Canadian "nobles," however, were either of recent promotion or belonged to families of provincial *hobereaux*. Trudel finds only two of ancient extraction in 1662.[114] Consequently, the New France *seigneur* did not enjoy the prestige that high birth conferred in French society. Nor did he gain prestige from military commandment, the local militia being placed under the power of a *capitaine de milice*.[115] The seigneurial system was introduced into Canada but not the system of "orders" in which the first two—the clergy and the nobility—enjoyed prestige-conferring privileges. Thus instead of a society of orders, New France developed a class society where position was determined by wealth.[116] Social mobility came through trade, especially the fur trade.[117]

In the seventeenth century, seigneurial dues tended to be low.[118] The *seigneur* did receive the *cens*, an annual fee, and *rentes*, rent from the tenants; *lods et ventes*, a fee equal to one-twelfth the value of the property, whenever the land was transferred by sale or inheritance to anyone but a direct heir; *banalités*, or monopoly on the flour mill; and *corvée*, boon work the tenant owed him yearly. All these feudal dues followed closely the French model, but in New France were very light indeed. The *cens* was symbolic and honorific rather than profitable, usually amounted to the equivalent of pennies; the *rentes* amounting to less than sixty *sols* a year (often paid in kind rather than cash) for an average property of three-arpent frontage; the *lods et ventes* often were not collected at all; the *banalité* being an expensive service the tenants demanded rather than a source of income for the *seigneur*; and the *corvée* being limited to a couple of days a year in the few cases it was actually demanded from the *censitaire*.[119] The Canadian *seigneur* could not increase the *rente* because the Custom of Paris forbade servitude without title, or changing the original amounts,[120] consequently he seldom grew wealthy. In the 1730s and '40s, as Cameron Nish has shown, the *seigneuries* became profitable.[121] Louise Dechêne's meticulous examination of the Montreal *seigneurie* shows that the system evolved considerably from 1642 to 1730. While the early *seigneurs* did not demand their full dues, in the eighteenth century they collected quite strictly whatever dues the leases gave them, even enforcing the *corvée*.[122] But in the seventeenth century the *seigneur*'s powers and his demands were limited by the need to attract settlers.

The protection of the *censitaires* was built into the colonial system. In the Old World, tenants had been in competition for land holdings, thus placing the *seigneurs* in a strong position. In Canada, the landowner never had enough hands to clear the wilderness and cultivate the land, and no concession, however large, was worth anything without labor. Competition was therefore, as Diamond points out, "among *seigneurs* for tenants and not among tenants for land." In the seventeenth century, the *seigneurs* remained remarkably stable, few of them divesting themselves of their land, but the *censitaires* moved frequently: in 1663, one-third of the land held in *censive* changed hands. This instability established a mobility which, with land abundant and hands scarce, worked to the advantage of the tenants.[123] Laws and mores were different in the New World, and the *seigneurs* were not allowed to ride roughshod over settlers. In France the hunting lords had driven through the peasants' fields in their pursuit of game and had thrashed the *manant* who dared protest. In Canada, the Sieur de Frédéric, captain of the Carignan-Salières and nephew of the colonel, damaged an *habitant*'s crops. When the injured settler complained, the officer punished him; Intendant Talon swiftly shipped Frédéric back to France: in the New World, an *habitant* had rights.

Consequently, New World *habitants* began to look upon themselves in a different light. They were less respectful of those of the "better sort," becoming by continental standards quite "uppity," in part because the standard of living of the *habitant* was high compared to that of his European counterpart, placing him on a par with minor French noblemen.[124] The prime example of the transformation can be found in the eighteenth century among the Acadians who drove French officials to despair with their independence. The exiles who had been brought back to France after the peace of 1763 found themselves at odds with the rigid class distinctions which prevailed on the continent and refused to behave with the subservience expected of them. "I think really that the Acadians are mad," wrote a metropolitan official in 1772. "They seem offended by the fact that we wish to treat them like our peasants." And indeed, early in the history of New France the *censitaire* rejected the derogatory appellation *paysan* in favor of *habitant.* The independent spirit of the Canadian settlers was such that Harris could conclude that the *seigneur* was largely irrelevant to the social structure, that he did not lead and that "most *habitants* did not want to be led."[125]

The changes which were wrought in the new land did not always conform to the royal wishes. The Canadian settlement pattern was a case in point. French rural life organized itself in villages huddled around the church and endowed with strong local institutions. This system seemed to the crown both desirable and practical. In Canada, however, where the St. Lawrence was the main line of communication, it was desirable for land grants to front the river so as to have easy access to transportation. Tenants also wanted plots along the banks so that the settlement pattern which developed in New France (and which would repeat itself in Louisiana in the eighteenth century) was one of narrow elongated strips along the river, with the houses built close to the water, producing the typical Canadian *rang.* Even there, the settlers' independence showed itself. Serge Courville has studied the spatial organization and concluded that the institutional organization—the elongated quadrangle—was overlapped by an informal internal structuration corresponding to social and human needs which he calls "*aires domestiques.*" He points out that "no sooner is it [the official structure] organized, than colonial society . . . moves away from imposed mode."[126]

This pattern, well adapted to transportation needs, did make defense difficult and discouraged village and community life. Consequently, as early as 1663 royal instructions directed the Sieur Gaudais, a crown commissioner, to set up villages.[127] Again in 1691 New France Intendant Champigny reported that villages would greatly enhance the defense of the colony. In 1699 Jean Louis Bochart de Phélypeaux, count of Pontchartrain, minister of marine and colonies, wrote the comptroller general of Canada Le Roy de La Potherie to regroup the settlers in *bourgs fermés.*[128] But royal and ministerial orders fell on deaf ears. Canada continued obstinately to establish its settlers in *rang* and turned its back on village life. Intendant Jean Talon did create three villages in 1665 and under his influence the Jesuits established Charlesbourg. But of the three Talon creations, one disappeared and the others were absorbed into Charlesburg once the great intendant vanished from the scene, though they can still be distinguished from the air. Even Jean Talon could not impose French institutions upon a rebellious Canadian reality.

Moreover, as Adair points out, even at the end of the French regime, when water transportation had lost some of its importance, efforts to create villages failed because the social and economic needs which would have justified their existence were not there. As Marc Bloch has shown, the foundation of French rural communities was the collective ownership of lands, pastures, woods, sometimes cattle, rights of usage of woods and pastures; communal agriculture, hence communal decisions.[129] And French villages needed to elect officials to administer this communal property and to oversee the effectiveness of the collective *contraintes* upon the settlers.[130] The New France *habitant* did not practice communal agriculture, though the seventeenth-century *seigneuries* allowed for communal pasturage. Moreover, the independent souls who set out to carve out new homes on the frontiers wanted to escape collective constraints, not reestablish them, so that absence of needs added to the frontier mentality condemned the crown policy to failure.

Sigmund Diamond has argued that in America the French crown was deliberately trying to create a new society. He speaks of "planned social action,"[131] but, in fact, all directives to colonial officials indicate quite the contrary: king and minister did not want to innovate but to transplant French society, that is to say civilization, in the New World. But they would improve this near-perfect system by not allowing the implantation of abuses so deeply woven into the Old World social fabric that they could be extirpated without endangering the state. The abuses, however, were viewed as accretions, not as an organic part of the system so that an organization from which they were excluded was not a new one, but, if anything, more faithful to the original model. Thus both seigneurial system and village life were deemed compatible with the improved version of existing French society. The fact that a new social organization arose was not a product of ministerial decision but of modification imposed by colonial realities.

Even when the changes resulted from administrative decisions, the factors leading to the decision were often not personal preference but exigencies. Liberty, tranquility, and prosperity were the advantages held out to entice settlers. Again and again Colbert insisted that freedom and justice would lead to a natural growth of colonial population added to "the natural desire men have to earn a living and live comfortably."[132] Thus Colbert, whose name has become a synonym for mercantilism, did in fact encourage colonial industries. "One of the greatest needs of Canada is to establish industries," he wrote in 1670[133] and he urged both Talon and Frontenac to encourage manufacturing.[134] Thus Canada manufactured hats, even if it had only two hatters in 1736, brewed its own beer, even if it was only spruce beer (*bière d'épinette*), and made an attempt at ship building.[135] To stimulate Canadian shipping Colbert removed the import duty on Caribbean sugars if they were brought to France in Canadian bottoms.[136] Social mobility was also promised settlers, at least implicitly. Not that it did not exist in France, but social ascension in the mother country was much slower, taking often four or five generations.[137] In Canada, where entry into the nobility could follow as well as precede the granting of *seigneuries* (as in the case of the Le Moyne family or of Cavelier de La Salle), class lines between bourgeois and nobles were blurred, with *seigneurs* residing in town and practicing trade even if they had been ennobled.[138] Yet, as time went on, the mobility lessened and "the ethos of the feudal nobility prevailed."[139] In New France, as later in Louisiana, bitter quarrels exploded over *préséances* and other class niceties. Individuals and groups clung to prerogatives of ranks every bit as much as the courtiers of Versailles. In 1694, Montreal was divided into two factions over the rights of the bishop or the governor to occupy the choice pew in the cathedral.[140] Canadian merchants might be as grasping and avaricious as their French counterparts, mercantile motives might prompt the explorers at least as much as the search for glory, but the military ideal was still prized, and heroism and recklessness preferred over thrift and caution. Class lines may have been blurred and passage from one class to another relatively easy, especially in the earlier days, but that did not mean that New France society was egalitarian. In fact, the noble ethos was all the stronger and exerted all the more attraction that entry into the "first order" was possible.[141]

There was one way in which Colbert deliberately strove to create a new society, and that was in urging the intermarriage of French and natives. This policy was pursued in all settlement colonies. The charter of the East India Company specified that in Madagascar the children born to a French subject, male or female, and a native *convert* would be French citizens.[142] Richelieu had formulated the doctrine that baptized natives would be considered French subjects. Following the same principle, Colbert assumed that the New World Indians were potential Frenchmen. "His Majesty believes," he wrote Frontenac, "that it would benefit Religion and the state more . . . at the same time that the Indians are converted, to entice them into civilized society (*une société civile*)."[143] Indian children were to be drawn into the communities by the clergy so that they "may evolve into a single nation."[144] As early as 1633, Champlain had promised a party of Algonquin "our sons will marry your daughters and we will be a single people."[145] The Indians were to be taught French along with Catholicism, and Frontenac bitterly reproached the Jesuits with not teaching French to the natives of Nostre-Dame de Foy, only two or three miles from Quebec, despite frequent contacts. He remonstrated with the religious that "while making the

Indians into subjects of Jesus Christ, they should also strive to make them into subjects of the King." The true way to make Christians of them, continued the governor, "is to make men out of them" and learning French was the obvious path to full humanity.[146] The Jesuits had promised Talon that they would strive to civilize the Indians and would attempt to change "those barbarians" in every possible way, "starting with their language."[147]

Unfortunately this valiant attempt at creating a brave new society foundered on several shoals. First of all, the missionaries quickly discovered that culture contacts resulted in mutual degradation, each race quickly learning the worst traits from the other. The Indians became drunkards and the French became rebels against civil authority.[148] In fact, the Indians seldom became "civilized." Indian children ran away from schools (or died), converts lapsed back into their former religious practices, and squaws returned to the sexual laxity which horrified the missionaries. The Ursulines in thirty years succeeded in converting and educating only seven or eight Indian girls, not one of whom ever took the vows. By 1668, the nuns had only one native student.[149]

On the other hand, the French took readily to Indian ways. Instead of the savages being civilized by the culture contact, the Europeans went native. The propensity of French youth to take to the woods, become *coureurs de bois,* lead a harsh but independent existence in the wilderness, free from the *contrainte* of marriage, religion, or civil authority was to remain a problem throughout the French regime.[150] As Eccles points out, the reckless ethos of the *coureur de bois,* proud, independent, tough, spending a year's earnings on a wild spree and plunging again into the wilderness was perfectly attuned to the Indian view of life. Both cared above all for the respect of their peers and prized their personal honor over material gain. Thus the French adventurers were absorbed into Indian society while Indians were incapable of adapting to the mercantile, acquisitive values of the French town dwellers.

Thus, where a new society was in fact created, in the forest villages along the routes of the fur trade, it was far from being what Richelieu and Colbert had dreamed. They had visualized a New World replica of France composed of French, Indians and their half-breed offsprings, living within a strict political hierarchy, hard-working and thrifty farmers, industrious craftsmen, all speaking French and faithfully making their Easter duties. What actually arose was a disorderly lot of Gallic adventurers and drunken Indians who flouted equally religious and civil authorities.

Colbert's social experiment might be termed a failure, but his colonial ventures cannot, and the policy formulated would survive him, at least in part, until the reversal of 1701. He established the economic policy of the French colonial empire which would be codified as the *pacte colonial* by the letters patent of April 13, 1717, but deviated from the system when the circumstances warranted it. He also determined that settlement colonies would be considered as French provinces with the same institutions, but after 1664, with unified laws. More importantly for the as yet nonexistant Louisiana colony, he decided that the North American French empire had reached in the 1670s all the expansion it needed. As he wrote Frontenac in 1674 "His Majesty does not intend that you should make grand voyages along the St. Lawrence or that settlers should spread as they did in the past. On the contrary, He wants you . . . to draw them closer together and gather them into cities." The king, insisted Colbert, wanted the existing French possessions settled, cleared, cultivated, "even if European affairs were to be changed by a good and advantageous peace."[151] Thus Colbert laid down the law for North America. The French empire was to be kept compact instead of spreading over vast countries which could never be "inhabited or possessed by the French." Only two exceptions did he admit. Expansion was permissible into territories needed to protect French trade or coveted by some other nation which might threaten French trade. The second exception concerned the search for a Northwest Passage. Until 1701, when a radical change took place in French colonial policy, the exploration and settlement of Louisiana would have to be carried out within those limitations and justified on those bases.

III

Colbert's Policy Crumbles: La Salle's Voyages

I
The French and Canadian Contexts

Colbert had laid down the law: there would be no more expansion, and discoveries would be undertaken only to search for a northwest passage (and/or gold mines) or to protect existing French trade. The minister's seemingly irresistible will, however, would shatter against two immovable obstacles, geography and human greed, which made the fur trade not only possible, but essential in New France. The trade, in turn, embroiled the colonists more and more deeply in Indian affairs and multiplied the confrontations with the English settlers of the Atlantic colonies.

Yet Colbert consistently insisted on a compact colony. As early as 1665, he admonished Jean Talon to allow clearing only adjoining lands and to prevent scattered settlements.[1] The king's glory, this ever-present seventeenth-century preoccupation, commanded it. As Colbert reminded Talon, expanding the colony beyond what could be defended might one day mean withdrawal and therefore "some diminution of his Majesty's repute."[2] Numerous letters to governors and intendants stressed the need to keep the colony compact, to regroup the inhabitants into villages, and to prevent voyages of long duration. But intendants and governors, whether pursuing an imperial dream or drawn by the lure of lucre, took advantage of every fissure in the minister's instructions.

Colbert agreed that it was indeed important to find a northwest passage and to prospect for mineral wealth and he acknowledged later that New France desperately needed a warm-water port.[3] This moderate endorsement was all Talon needed to send Louis Joliet in search of the "great river" which the Indians called the Mississippi. That expedition, as Eccles points out, "led to the ruin of Colbert's plans for the Colony."[4] For Joliet did find the river that La Salle would descend to its mouth ten years later, ending once and for all the hope of a compact colony. Colbert continued to bombard Frontenac the governor and Duchesnau the intendant with orders to rein in explorations, but in vain.[5] The small fissure in the levee would widen and eventually flood the plains.

Why this happened is easy to understand. Born of the fishing industry, the fur trade became, in the seventeenth century, the *raison d'être* of New France before becoming, after 1701, subordinate to the French imperial aims in the New World.[6] The geography of the region, traversed in all directions by lakes and rivers and separated by short portages, made far-flung voyages relatively easy.[7] Moreover, birch trees large enough to provide bark for canoes were abundant in the area the French dominated. The fur-trading area teemed with fish and game, and bore large crops of corn, highly nutritious and easy to conserve on long voyages.[8]

Colbert did not want the French to seek the pelts in far-off villages; the Indians should bring their furs to the colonial markets instead. But the fur trade dictated that voyages should be ever longer in search of pelts. The more valuable pelts were the so-called "greasy" beaver, seasoned by body heat and sweat during prolonged wear. Obviously new sources of seasoned pelts had to be found as tribes depleted their beaver fields to supply foreign traders.[9] Hence the *voyageurs* pushed ever westward. The Indians, in the meantime, became increasingly dependent on European trade goods, especially iron—to them, the French were the *gens-du-fer.*[10] They also shifted from trapping for consumption to trapping for exchange, a switch which transformed their economies radically. Resource shortages increased, and economic specialization developed. The Indians who became middlemen often travelled long distances to acquire pelts and spent less time in food gathering, thus increasing their dependence on Europeans, or other tribes, for foodstuffs.[11] They consequently needed to drive harder and harder bargains and play the French against the English. The New France *voyageurs* were often hard pressed, and the Anglo-French trade rivalry became a confrontation over zones of influence.[12]

Colbert was reluctant to give a free rein to the *voyageurs* to avoid confrontation with the British and to avoid spreading French defenses too thin. He also resented the attractions the fur trade exerted on the able-bodied youths who preferred the dangerous but adventurous, reckless and free existence of the forest to the restricted, controlled life of the town dweller. The minister hoped against hope that the men could be kept back to clear the forest and till the land thus making Canada self-sufficient. But in vain. Refusals of *congé* (official trade passports) did nothing to deter the *coureurs de bois.* Fulminations accomplished even less. And the colonial officials, from the governor down, profited too much from the fur trade to carry out the interdiction rigorously.

La Salle's explorations were conditioned by both the minister's will to restrict the spread of French colonists and by the greed of colonial officials, chiefly Frontenac. By the time La Salle comes into the picture, the Iroquois were temporarily subdued, and the fur trade was spreading over a large area as Joliet, Marquette, Duluth, and La Salle himself expanded the area of activity southward and westward.[13] But French military success meant an increasing supply of poorer furs, hence a reduced price, a predicament worsened by the increased cost incurred by traveling longer distances.[14] The answer seemed to be finding new and cheaper supplies of fur.[15] And as the years passed, Canada sent France more and more furs. The circle was made even more vicious by the presence of the English merchants to the south. Fear of the aggressive and dynamic English colonies was another factor urging New France settlers to seek expansion. For, though Spain may still have been the enemy in Louis XIV's eyes, the Iberian colonists were too remote from New France to cause much concern there. On the other hand, England, or rather the English colonies, especially New York, were ever-present. New York loomed large in the preoccupations of New France officials. As early as 1666, Talon had suggested acquiring New York, and Louis XIV entertained quite seriously a 1689 project which called for conquering New York, deporting the English colonists en masse and scattering them through New England and Pennsylvania.[16]

Trade in the Hudson Bay area was at stake, for one thing. As early as 1614 Captain John Smith had purchased 1,100 beaver skins, not to mention martens and otters there.[17] The arrival of the Pilgrim Fathers at Plymouth Rock in 1620 did not help, as their settlement encroached on French Atlantic trade.[18] The English colonists harassed the little French outpost in Acadia, invading it first in 1613, and again in 1654.

A striking contrast exists between the letters of Colbert and those of Talon. The New France intendant's correspondence reflects his growing awareness of the British threat along the Canadian borders. English encroachments on the French fur trade and especially English claims to Acadia, which was formally restored to the French in 1670, were a thorn in his side.[19] But Colbert held to an official policy of Anglo-French friendliness. In 1670 he admonished the governor of the West Indies, Jean-Charles de Baas, not to encroach on the English trade and to welcome into his harbors British ships in need of help[20] The minister expressed surprise at some hostile English action in the Antilles since everywhere else the French got along well with them, and urged his ambassador in London to petition the court of St. James to remedy the conditions.[21] As much as Colbert gloated over the angry reaction of the Dutch when excluded from the French West Indies,[22] he wanted to keep on good terms with the English, at least officially. The England of Charles II was after all almost a client of the French crown, and the heir to the British throne, the Catholic duke of York, promised to be even more malleable. Hence explorations which led to confrontrations with the English colonies was not encouraged as the traders Pierre Esprit Radisson and Médart Chouart de Groseillers discovered to their chagrin. These daring merchants, whom Grace Lee Nute dubbed with some bombast "Caesars of the Wilderness," tried to trade in the Hudson Bay region and frequently fell afoul of both France and England. In 1676, the "renegades" who had been in the employ of the English Hudson's Bay Company thought they could do better in France. Colbert scolded them for "betrayal," then offered them a bonus of "400 Lewi-Dors", plus payment of their debts and good employment.[23] The "employment" never came as such, but in 1681 François Bellinzani, Colbert's commercial director, advised Radisson to draw "all the natives of those Northern parts of America to traffick with and favor the French, and to dissuade them from trading with strangers" (i. e. the English), promising that the Canadian fur trader, Charles Aubert de La Chesnaye, would tender all the help necessary. Colbert obviously did not hesitate to advocate and encourage a trade policy which ran counter to the king's official foreign policy. As Nute concludes, "For Colbert and Louis XIV never saw eye to eye in matters of trade and overseas colonies."[24] But the British, in the minister's eyes, were minor competitors compared to the formidable Dutch traders.

As if the situation was not complex enough, it was further complicated by the rivalry between the Jesuits and Recollets, Black Robes and Grey Robes. For religion had played a major role in French colonization from the beginning. Francis I had insisted that legitimacy of conquest was predicated on missionary activities. Here, he had formidable support in the work of Francisco de Vitoria from whom the propagation of Christianity alone could legitimize the subjection of the Amerindians.[25] And though he did not proselytize, Jacques Cartier affirmed that his only purpose, since he knew there was neither gold nor silver in the new land, was "the conquest of an infinite number of souls for God."[26] Evangelization of the natives was an obligation every charter imposed on companies or individuals granted a colonial monopoly. Thus, one of the reasons the Pierre du Gua, sieur de Monts lost his monopoly in Acadia was, says Pierre Lescarbot that "after three years of enjoying the said privileges, he made no converts as yet."[27] Modern historians tend to discount the religious motive, but seventeenth-century colonizers did not: Jean de Biencourt de Poutrincourt et de Saint-Just drew the obvious conclusion from his friend's loss and when he decided to continue the settlement of Acadia, in 1610, took to Port Royal a secular priest, Jessé Fleché. Having docked on June 17th, he hurriedly summoned the Indians and had twenty-one of them baptized on the 24th.[28] This imposing number, he hoped, would gain him the financial support of the queen-regent, Marie of Medici. She did decide to send him two Jesuits, Ennemond Massé and Pierre Biard, but, to his chagrin, offered no monetary reward. She did however insist on the need to evangelize the Amerindians. Conversions, wrote the little Louis XIII, "will add to the glory of God and my reputation."[29] For Richelieu also the king's *gloire* and the glory of God were inextricably bound and the Christianization of the New World natives was the continuation of temporal prestige by religious means. Again it is his kinsman Razilly who summarized the policy in a lapidary phrase *"La Croix et les Lys."*[30]

The first component of French religious policy in the New World was then conversion of the natives, all the more important that Christianity along with the acquisition of the French language would make them into men, and thus increase the number of the king's subjects. But since the king's glory was the main purpose, the church could never be allowed to become overly powerful, nor could any religious order be allowed to gain too much influence. The delicate balance between promoting religious activities and controlling religious agents was rendered particularly precarious by the activities of the Jesuits in North America, both because the order was highly controversial and because its missionaries were the most self-sacrificing as well as the most efficient of the apostles to the New World north of the Rio Grande.

How controversial the Jesuits were can be seen in their very first appearance in the French colonies. When Frs. Biard and Massé arrived in Dieppe to embark for Port-Royal, two merchants who were part owners of the vessel refused them passage because "the King's death [Henry IV's assassination] was still too recent, they refuse to outfit a ship to take Spaniards [i. e. Spanish agents, i. e. Jesuits] there [the New World]." The merchants offered, however, "if it pleased the Queen to rid herself of all the Jesuits in France to outfit ships and take them across at their expense."[31] The popular imagination held the Jesuits responsible for the assassination of Good King Henry, and the attending distrust (execration even) would plague the order in New France as it did in Europe.

The French crown played therefore a carefully calculated game with the Jesuits and other orders. For though Louis XIII, and Louis XIV after him, wanted missionary activities and an ecclesiastical presence in the New World colonies, they did not want any one religious order to acquire too large a share of influence. Colbert's letters, surprisingly, reveal how seriously he, like Richelieu before him, took the religious aspect of colonization. "His Majesty's principal concern," he wrote the governor of Martinique, "is that you should promote God's service, even before his."[32] But God's service should be spread around. Colbert warned Talon in 1665 that however much the Jesuits had accomplished in Canada, they were to be carefully controlled for they had gradually gained too much authority, imposing their choices not only for bishop but even for governor.[33] Apparently, Talon did not succeed in curbing the Society's power, for Colbert's instruction to Courcelles in 1669 reiterated the minister's concern with "excessive" Jesuit influence. He expressed the hope that as "the population increased, royal authority would predominate over the ecclesiastical and regain *its proper extent.*"[34]

There were several reasons for the "excessive authority" the Jesuits had gained in Canada. First of all, they were extremely good at missionary work.

Highly trained and hard working, they mastered Indian dialects rapidly and their indifference to hardships and physical suffering gained them the Amerindians' respect. Their adaptability enabled them to carry out with great success activities as varied as reclaiming Poland from the Protestants, evangelizing Japan, and proselytizing Canada. Their introduction in New France was a tribute to their missionary skills. In 1617 Samuel Champlain had brought four members of the Recollets, the most austere branch of the Franciscans, to the shores of the St. Lawrence. A few more began work independently in what is today Nova Scotia, New Brunswick and Gaspé. By 1625, the Recollets had to admit to a lack of success and invited the Jesuits as more experienced in foreign missions, to join efforts with them. Charles Lallemant and Jean de Brebeuf along with the veteran Ennemond Massé answered the call immediately and arrived in New France the self-same year.[35] Moreover, the Society excelled at self promotion. Its *Relations*, published yearly between 1632 and 1673 and sporadically afterward, kept Europe well informed of the Jesuits' accomplishments in New France.[36] They may have been "works of propaganda rather than scientific reports," as Chinard claims, but they were effective.[37]

To counterbalance the powerful Society of Jesus, Louis XIV and Colbert promoted the Recollets and Sulpicians. Royal instructions to Frontenac specifically directed him to protect these two orders "in order to counter the power of the Jesuits."[38] The Recollets were also more lenient and would, the king hoped, "give consciences more freedom than they had enjoyed thus far."[39] The Sulpicians came from the Seminary of St. Sulpice, in Paris, founded in 1642 by Abbé Jean-Jacques Olier.[40] Trained as missionaries especially for the newly established Ville Marie de Montréal, the Sulpicians, like the Recollets, enjoyed much support in Versailles. But the Jesuits also had their partisans. Each party intrigued at court to gain appointments and favors for its "creatures" in the New World, and in the New World the officials or clergymen selected by one faction did their best to impede the work of those associated with the opposite party. Explorations because of their close association with missionary activities necessarily became embroiled in these internecine religious squabbles.

The witches' brew of intrigues was kept bubbling by two abbés, both keenly interested in geographic discoveries, both favorably inclined toward La Salle's projects, and both firmly anti-Jesuit, Claude Bernou and Eusèbe Renaudot. A distinguished Orientalist and, at the death of his father, editor of the *Gazette de France*, the newspaper founded by his grandfather Théophraste, Eusèbe Renaudot enjoyed high favor with both Louis XIV and Colbert.[41] Claude Bernou, a friend of Renaudot's who corresponded with many scholars, showed a passionate interest in explorations and an equally passionate devotion to French colonial expansion.[42] They distrusted the ulltramontane Jesuits, whom Bernou called "M.R.N." (i. e., "M. Robe Noire"), and supported the king's Gallican policies though Bernou believed that "M.R.N." could be of great help in explorations.[43] After La Salle's discovery of the mouth of the Mississippi, Bernou developed a grandiose scheme (maybe in jest) for a Mississippi Valley French empire with himself as bishop and, of course, Recollets ministering to the spiritual needs of his flock.[44]

It was a complicated situation that La Salle stepped into when he began advocating the exploration of the Great River. Minister and king were sometimes at odds, though Colbert never openly opposed his master; colonial officials and metropolitan civil servants sought different aims; private interest, though never expressed of course, often ran contrary to the public weal; and missionary orders battled each other for temporal influence and spiritual exclusivity.

II
The 1682 La Salle Voyage

In this tempestuous sea of conflicting interests and policies, La Salle needed to chart a careful course, navigating between the minister's expressedly stated compact colony policy, a foreign policy which from the 1660s to the 1680s advocated a friendly relationship with England and distrust of Spain, the zeal of the Jesuits who wanted to exclude other orders from a fertile missionary field, the greed of his backers eager for quick profit from the fur trade, and finally his own motivations, whatever they were.

La Salle has been called many things. Those Father Delanglez calls "les La Sallotaters" see in him a colonizing genius, a man of vision whose grandiose plans were foiled by petty enemies, chiefly the Jesuits. Others stressing his paranoiac personality have dismissed the conspiracy interpretation of La Salle's final failure, and pointed out that he was not free from mercenary motives.[45] A Norman, educated by the Jesuits, restless and adventurous, La Salle arrived in New France in 1667 at the age of twenty-three. More at ease among the *sauvages* than among courtiers, he learned some rudiments of several Indian tongues, though undoubtably fewer than he claimed, and became involved in the fur trade. He later acknowledged that his personality was not an appealing one, and defended himself against charges of megalomaniac excesses and outright madness. Bernou, whose letters reflect a real fondness for the explorer, defended his brusk manner because, said the kindly abbé, La Salle is "so preoccupied by his grand design that he is frequently melancholy, a bit abrupt, peculiar, not too open, maybe because the machinations of Mr. R. N. [the Jesuits] have accustomed him to be distrustful."[46]

Pioneering Mississippi explorations were going on during La Salle's first Canadian years. French interest in the Great River could be traced back to Jean Nicolet's 1634 westward journey in search of the Northwest Passage. This daring companion of Samuel Champlain learned in the region of Green Lake, Wisconsin, that three days to the south of the Fox River was a "great river."[47] The Jesuit *Relations* continued to chronicle knowledge gained of the river, reporting in 1669-1670 that it was a league wide, in 1670-1671 that it flowed either into the Vermilion Sea (Gulf of California) or the Gulf of Mexico.[48] Talon favored river exploration in high hope that the Mississippi would be found to flow into the Vermilion Sea. Frontenac, the newly appointed governor of New France, approved the intendant's choice of Louis Joliet, an experienced Canadian trader, to chart the river's course. At Michilimackinac (Mackinaw), Joliet joined forces with a Jesuit missionary, Jacques Marquette, who had been offering constant devotion to the Virgin "to obtain the grace of reaching the Mississippi."[49] They ascended the Fox River, carried their canoes through the Fox-Wisconsin portage, reembarked on the Wisconsin and "on the 17th of June 1673, with a joy that I cannot express," says Marquette, the explorers found themselves on "this renowned river."[50] Joliet and Marquette, however, did not go below the latitude 33°40' as it became very clear to them that the Mississippi flowed southward toward the Gulf of Mexico and that continued exploration would bring confrontation with Spanish colonists.[51]

There the matter rested for several years. The explorers wrote a relation praising the newly discovered country which would provide new fields for the propagation of the faith, easy access to the Gulf of Mexico, possibly access to the Vermilion Sea by following the river in a northwest direction, and wonderfully fertile lands for settlement.[52] But settlement was the farthest thing from Colbert's mind in 1673 and 1674. Louis XIV had embarked on his second Dutch war and was more preoccupied with conquering Franche-Comté than settling the area that in 1679 La Salle began calling Louisiana.[53] Not until the 1678-1679 treaties of Nimwegen would the king and minister's attention turn again to colonial schemes, and that on a very limited basis.

Colbert had praised Talon in 1671 for sending La Salle southward in search of a passage, though mines, he said then, were to be priority.[54] He again the next year stressed the importance of finding such a passage.[55] A warm-water port was indeed a necessity for, as he wrote Frontenac, "the worst thing about Canada is the fact that the river's mouth is so northerly that vessels can enter it only four, five or six months a year."[56] It was therefore with understandable pride that Frontenac reported a few months later that Joliet had come to within ten days of the warm gulf waters.[57]

With the news that the Great River flowed south toward a warm sea, but close to New Spain, Frontenac began weaving a complex scheme which would gain him control of the lucrative western fur trade by flattering the minister's hope for a year-round warm-water port.[58] Already in 1673, without royal permission, Frontenac had built a fort, called Fort Frontenac, at the eastern end of Lake

Ontario. He then sent La Salle to France where the explorer convinced Louis XIV the fort had been a good idea and obtained on March 13, 1675, letters patent which named him seigneur of the outpost and ennobled him as well.[59]

For two years La Salle busied himself at Fort Frontenac, clearing forest and planting fields, establishing a Recollet school and building ships to sail Lake Ontario.[60] But Joliet's and Marquette's discovery of the great south-flowing river was all he needed to start dreaming of vast commercial empires. In 1677 he returned to France and began his trek from bureau to bureau to obtain permission to explore the river to its mouth where a warm-water port could be established and year-round trade routes opened. Colbert had just curtly refused Joliet permission to set up an establishment at the Illinois, reiterating in his letter to Intendant Duchesnau the need to "multiply the population of Canada before thinking of other lands."[61]

La Salle, however, had several assets. For one, he bribed the right man, Colbert's "creature" François Bellinzani, who, at the dissolution of the Company of the West Indies, had been put in charge of *Illes Isles françaises d'Amérique,"* including New France. Even more importantly, La Salle knew what arguments to use. The letters patent that he received at Saint-Germain-en-Laye on May 12, 1678, authorized him to explore the west and to build whatever forts he would deem necessary. Over these he would enjoy the same rights granted him by the patents of May 13, 1675, over Fort Frontenac (namely that he be governor). He was also to enjoy a monopoly on buffalo pelts (called *cibola*). The 1678 letters patent clearly spelled out why he received such privileges at a time Colbert clamored for a compact colony and jealously protected the Canadian fur trade. "Nothing is closer to our heart than the exploration of that region where, it seems, one might find a way to reach Mexico (*pour pénétrer jusques au Mexique*)."[62]

The mouth of the Mississippi was sought less as the hope for a year-round warm-water port, which would benefit the fur trade, than as an outpost from which the Spanish colonies to the west could be harassed and, maybe, even conquered. Again, policy was made less to benefit the colonies affected than to support France's foreign policy. As Chesnel points out, in the years following Nimwegen, France was officially at peace with Spain. But in the West Indies and the Gulf of Mexico hostilities never abated. The Spaniards wished to transform the gulf into an Hispanic "*Mare Nostrum.*" A decree from Phillip II had excluded foreigners from the gulf under pain of death,[63] and the year after La Salle's letters patent, 1679, a serious Franco-Spanish confrontation occurred. The Spanish admiral Quintana captured a French frigate in the gulf waters and took the captain and crew to Portobello. Outraged, Louis XIV dispatched Vice-Admiral Jean, comte d'Estrée with a squadron to capture or sink Quintana.[64] The Mississippi was seen as a strategic outpost to harass Spanish shipping and threaten the Spanish empire, England being still viewed, officially, as a friendly power. Officially only, for Colbert, with ever an eye for commercial profit, listened to the lamentations of La Chesnaye who came to court in 1681, while La Salle prepared his expedition ostensibly toward a year-round port, officially against Spain, but, in the minister's heart of hearts, against English expansion. La Chesnaye complained that the Anglo-French entente was ruining the beaver trade, and it was then that Bellinzani encouraged Radisson to raid the English fur trade, promising La Chesnaye's help.[65] In other words, however friendly Franco-English relations in Europe, in America the gloves were coming off, and an exploration down the Mississippi, establishing forts wherever the discoverer thought them advisable, would strengthen French strategic positions when the bell rang for the next bout.

La Salle sailed from La Rochelle in August 1678, taking along Henri de Tonti, an experienced, energetic soldier who would second him faithfully and well to the end. Many trials and tribulations beset him before he was able to pursue his cherished dream of descending the Great River to its mouth.[66] He finally set out on December 21, 1680, leading one party himself and putting the second one in charge of Tonti. In the second group, La Salle, never fond of the Jesuits since his seminary days, included a Recollet missionary, Father Zenobe Membré. On February 6 the explorers entered the Mississippi; on April 6 they beheld the open sea. On the ninth a column and a cross (erected probably near present-day Venice, Louisiana) proclaimed that the Mississippi Valley belonged to *"Louis Le Grand, Roi de France et de Navarre."*

The extravagant claim for all the land drained by the river and its tributaries was backed by nothing more substantial than the cross and the column, for as soon as Frenchmen finished taking possession, they packed up their canoes and returned home. But La Salle meant to come back and come back in force.[67]

III
The 1684 Colony

Returning, however, did not prove easy. La Salle had to convince king and minister that his discovery was worth pursuing, and before he himself reached his Paris lodging, rue de la Truanderie, many negative reports had been heard about *"la Louisiane."* Though the discoverers turned back immediately in May 1682, La Salle's return to Quebec was delayed considerably by ill health (the Norman spent forty days at Fort Prudhomme between life and death) and by the careful negotiations he carried out along the way with the Indian tribes. From Fort Prudhomme, he sent Tonti to bring news to Michilimackinac. A few months later, he sent Zenobe Membré to Quebec. But he himself reached Quebec late in the summer of 1683 and France on December 23, more than a year and a half after taking possession of Louisiana. The court during that time had had only the reports from the governor of New France, and, unfortunately for La Salle, Colbert was dead, replaced on September 6, 1683, by his son, Jean-Baptiste Colbert, marquis de Seignelay; as for the Norman's fur-trading partner and protector, Frontenac, he had been replaced by La Barre who was not favorably inclined toward the discoverer or toward the Recollets. This negative opinion of La Salle the governor learned from La Chesnaye, who as a wealthy merchant feared the fur trade would be diverted down the river.[68] Frontenac did return to France, arriving in December 1682, but definitely did not enjoy royal favor,[69] so that La Barre's critical accounts were given credence.

And these accounts were black indeed. The governor wrote Seignelay, casting doubts on La Salle's sanity, accusing him of announcing "*une découverte fausse*," and complaining that the so-called discovery was drawing settlers at least 500 leagues away from Canada, and all that for an "imaginary kingdom."[70] Not only was La Salle lying about the Mississippi, but he was gathering around him the enemies of the Iroquois so that this powerful confederation was becoming enraged against the French.[71]

In the Recollet-Jesuit controversy, there was no doubt where La Barre stood. "The conducts of RR. PP. Jesuits," he wrote, "is edifying, and perfect domestic peace would reign in New France, were it not for the Recollets and their quarrel with the bishop."[72] La Barre's comments brought the expected result. The king agreed on August 5, 1683, that "the discovery of Sieur de la Salle is quite useless."[73] As soon as La Salle reached France he sent Seignelay a steady stream of memoirs to counteract the accusations. His memoirs, unfortunately, at times seemed to justify La Barre's accusations of irrationality. For La Salle, determined to exploit his discovery and plant a French colony on the Gulf Coast, entered fully into the game of European politics.

In his first memoir to Seignelay, he listed all the standard arguments for founding a colony. Such an act would serve God by enabling missionaries to labor among new Indian tribes; it would increase "*la gloire du roi*"; it would provide a navigable river with three mouths, each of which was a natural harbor; it would make available to France all the products which enriched Virginia and New England, namely timber, salt meat, suet, wheat, sugar, tobacco, honey, wax, tar, hemp, the goods which 200 ships a year load in the English colonies; and it would provide a fertile colony with a mild climate(!). But La Salle knew that in 1683-1684, the crown would not risk any investment, however small, to create a new establishment just for the standard reasons. He therefore resorted to strategic arguments, playing on the age-old rivalry with Spain, with whom war had again broken out in October, 1683, when Louis invaded the Spanish Netherlands. The first memoir gives only a brief outline of what will become the heart of subsequent arguments. From his projected colony, easy to defend since the shores are rendered impenetrable for some 20 leagues by swamps and marshes, hence open only at the river's mouth, it would be easy to march westward to seize the silver-rich Spanish possessions. These, he claimed, lay wide open to invasion and were defended only by weaklings surrounded by Indians who hated them and could be easily gained as allies.[74]

Gradually, from memoir to memoir, the plan to invade New Biscaye grew until it became the main justification for the founding of a colony. A Spanish adventurer, Diego de Peñalosa, had already presented to Louis XIV schemes for establishing French colonies at Espíritu Santo Bay, or at the mouth of the Río Bravo, or at the mouth of Río Panuco, all for the purpose of using this establishment as a base for the conquest of New Biscaye.[75] Peñalosa, a former governor of New Mexico, had become a naturalized French citizen after running afoul of the Inquisition in the New World. The memoirs stressed his being a Creole, the hatred between "Capuchins," Spaniards born in the mother country, and "Criollos," those born on the American continent, being an essential element of the scheme of conquest. In the Spanish colonies, stated one memoir, there are "capuchins, criollos, half-breeds, 'zembos', Indians and Negroes," and only the first will resist the French, all others hating the Spaniards. Thus New Biscaye could easily be conquered with a handful of men.[76] The author of the memoir, probably Bernou, convinced himself so thoroughly that the Spanish empire would crumble before the first French onslaught, that he actually called for conquering it all, in order to ruin Spain by depriving her of her gold mines.[77] The magnitude of Bernou's dreams can be gauged by his historical frame of reference: he admits to a burning desire to see La Salle become a new Cortez.[78]

Under the influence of the ever-active Bernou and Renaudot, La Salle incorporated Peñalosa's arguments into his own and his plan of colonization became a plan of conquest.[79] Bernou pressed Renaudot to intervene with the minister and convince him to "join the New Biscaye design" with La Salle's. The latter's colonization plan, argued the abbé, would arouse less suspicion among the Spaniards because his colony would be more distant from the Spanish settlements than the one Peñalosa proposed.[80] And so, gradually, La Salle's dream (and Bernou's) for a French empire stretching along the entire valley of the Mississippi and into its tributaries was coopted by the pragmatic necessity of getting funding from a granting agency interested not in colonization but in glory and booty. Whether intentionally as Delanglez charges,[81] or by actual ignorance of longitudes as Miller more kindly suggests,[82] the mouths of the River Colbert (Mississippi) and the Río Bravo (Rio Grande) were represented as lying quite close to each other. In fact, the secret dream of many contemporary Louisianians was realized, Texas vanished and Louisiana almost bordered Mexico. In one memoir (not La Salle's) the Mississippi *became* the Rio Grande! As time passed, his memoirs acquired that unmistakable ring that one hears in off-the-wall grant proposals and Chamber of Commerce fliers.[83]

To make his scheme even more palatable to Louis XIV, La Salle asked for very little: ships, two hundred men, permission to raise fifty freebooters in Saint-Domingue. The manpower for the conquest of New Biscaye would come from the Indians who hated the Spaniards and whose support of the French was attested by their gathering eighteen thousand strong, in a single village. Among those, he could raise 15,000 men easily.[84] Of course, the truce of Regensburg interfered somewhat, the Empire and France having agreed on August 15, 1684, to call off hostilities for twenty years. La Salle was optimistic, however. France could take advantage of the first break with Spain to pounce on New Biscaye and in the meantime, "even though a European peace would force delays," it was important to establish the base which would make that conquest easy."[85] La Salle entered so wholeheartedly into the game of power politics that he even suggested that should conquered New Biscaye prove too difficult to hold, at least it could be used as a bargaining chip during peace negotiations.[86] "Peace," he proclaimed, anticipating Clauswitz, "is the time to get ready for war."[87] The wilderness expert was straying far afield, using European power politics arguments to wrench an American commitment from a reluctant king.

It worked, but at a fearful price, for the king took him at his word, and gave him only what he asked, pitifully inadequate to found a colony. Moreover, committed to the conquest of Spanish territories, La Salle established a military outpost. No real attempt was made at implanting a colony, though one marriage did take place.[88] Despite these obstacles, the little outpost might have blossomed into a colony, but, again either by design or by ignorance, La Salle's landfall took place not at the mouth of the Great River along which he had Indian friends and allies, but somewhere on Matagorda Bay, surrounded by the warlike Karakawaks, whom Cabeza de Vaca had encountered much to his dismay over a century earlier. La Salle wandered off in search of his river and was murdered, along with his nephew Crevel de Moranget, by some rebellious followers. The colonists were attacked by the Indians and the few survivors were finally rescued by the Spaniards in 1690.

La Salle's brilliant discovery had led nowhere because his colonization project had been stretched on the Procustean bed of European diplomacy. The founding of a viable French colony had been subordinated to the uncertain conquest of precious metals and to the jockeying for position in the Franco-Spanish rivalry. Meantime, the English colonies were expanding agressively and no one had heeded La Salle's warning. He had pointed out in one of his many memoirs that the mouth of the Mississippi should be seized by the French, for, were the English to occupy it, they would smother New France, which was already squeezed tight by Virginia, Pennsylvania, New England and Hudson Bay.[89] Twelve years after his death, his project would finally take shape, but only because after a life-long agony, Charles II of Spain died, leaving his kingdom to a French prince. With the accession of Phillip V to the Spanish throne, French foreign policy shifted and the official colonial policy finally caught up with that of New France officials, of Frontenac and La Salle.

IV

Colbert's Policy Collapses: Iberville, the Would-Be Talon

The death of La Salle in 1687 put an end to French interest in the Mississippi for a decade. In fact it seemed to herald a return to Colbert's compact New France policy. A certain number of events encouraged the low-profile adopted by the French crown in America between 1687 and 1697. Foremost among these, European wars monopolized Louis's attention. In 1688, William of Orange ascended the English throne and until his death in 1702 devoted his energies and English might to curbing the ambitions of the Sun King and furthering the Protestant cause in Europe and America.[1] The War of the League of Augsburg, of which William was the heart and soul, would occupy Louis from 1688 to the Peace of Ryswick in 1697 and leave Versailles little money and attention for colonial ventures. Moreover, Seignelay followed Colbert to the grave in a relatively short time and was succeeded, on November 7, 1690, by Louis Phélypeaux de Pontchartrain, a man with a vastly different orientation. While Richelieu and Colbert had striven to build up a strong French military fleet, Pontchartrain suggested shortly after taking office that France did not need a navy at all. Fortifications and mobile troops could defend the coastlines more effectively and cheaply than a fleet.[2] His negative attitude toward the navy was reinforced during the War of the League of Augsburg, when he successfully relied on privateers rather than the royal fleet to harass enemy shipping.[3] This ministerial disinterest for the navy threatened to extend to the colonies. Pontchartrain's son and successor, Jerôme Phélypeaux de Pontchartrain, who succeeded him as minister of marine was profoundly influenced by Sebastien Le Prestre, marquis de Vauban, the great military engineer and an ardent imperialist, and the younger Pontchratrain became an expansionist who backed enthusiastically the Louisiana colonization scheme.[4] In the early nineties, however, the elder Pontchartrain turned a deaf ear to the pleas of Tonti, La Salle's faithful lieutenant, who kept bombarding the court with memoirs asking to be allowed to continue his leader's work. Not only was the king too absorbed by European affairs but in the new religious climate of Versailles, now that the aging monarch had married Madame de Maintenon, Tonti, who was branded as a *débauché*, had no chance of getting a commission.[5] The Jesuits, no more friends of La Salle's lieutenant than they had been of his leader, were in high favor now with the king who chose his confessor, François de la Chaize, from their ranks. And Tonti's tolerance of the *coureurs-de-bois'* opposition to missionary activities had branded him as *libertin*.[6]

Pontchartrain's preference for a compact colony policy received additional justification from the condition of the Canadian fur trade. From 1685 to 1687 alone, Canada produced annually an average of 140,000 pounds of beaver while the French market could only absorb between 40,000 and 45,000.[7] By January 1, 1697, there were on hand 850,185 pounds of beaver which it would take ten years for the French market to absorb.[8] The problem was all the more acute that other, cheaper furs were now mixed with beaver to produce *demi-castor* hats, and that, moreover, fashion now decreed that hats should be smaller and lighter.[9] Thus the vagaries of European fashion influenced the course of empire, for Pontchartrain faced with the collapse of the beaver market resorted to extreme measures: on May 26, 1696, he issued an edict closing the trade. All *congés* were abolished and the garrisons were withdrawn from Michilimackinaw, St. Joseph des Miamis and Fort Frontenac. Though Pontchartrain tempered this edict a year later in principle, allowing the garrisons to remain, in fact, since he maintained the interdiction on trade, the men found it impossible to subsist and abandonned the posts.[10] Only a few Jesuit missions remained in the west. Colbert had seemingly won at last. But this apparent victory proved the dead minister's last hurrah.

For Pontchartrain's restrictive policy found itself challenged on two fronts: in the Great Lakes region by a golden-tongued, unscrupulous Gascon, Pierre Laumet, self-styled sieur de Cadillac, and along the Gulf Coast, by Spanish and English colonization schemes.

In 1699 Cadillac convinced Pontchartrain that it would be an excellent idea, despite the closing of the fur trade, in fact because of it, to erect a fort at Detroit regrouping western tribes around it. The strategic location of Detroit would make it possible to restrain the western expansion of the English colonies and to control the as yet unpacified Iroquois (peace would not be concluded till 1701). And the fort would stem the flow of beaver to Canada since for the first couple of years the western Indians would be so busy resettling they would not have time to hunt. Moreover, if the yearly 25 *congés* were revived, as Cadillac asked, since they would be granted to bring furs to Detroit only, they would not stimulate the Canadian fur trade, but would restrain it.[11] Only Cadillac's Gascon *faconde* could sell such a scheme, but it did. Pontchartrain agreed to the foundation of Detroit despite warnings from Intendant Jean Bochart de Champigny and Governor Hector de Callières. In 1700 the minister ordered the fort constructed and in the summer of 1701 Cadillac arrived at Detroit.[12]

Meanwhile on the Gulf Coast, France's colonial rivals, Spain and England, were not standing still. Tonti had pointed out the dangers for years. In one memoir addressed to Colbert de Villermont he had argued that he should complete La Salle's work not only to gain the wealth in furs and mines that Louisiana contained, but because of the strategic importance of the Mississippi's mouth. A colony at that point would enable France not only to harass the Spaniards, as the old argument of La Salle and Peñalosa went, but it would also secure Canada. For, argued Tonti, should the English occupy this location as they wanted, they would be able to subdue all the Indians and gain control of the fur trade with the Miami, Illinois, and Ottawa, thus ruining Canada. This takeover would be facilitated greatly by the fact that the English were established along the river which emptied into the Ohio which itself emptied into the Mississippi.[13]

Tonti, fur trader and discoverer, was attuned to the activities along the Gulf Coast which the ministry in Paris was choosing to ignore. First of all the Spaniards had been frantic when the first confused reports of La Salle's 1684 expedition reached them. Their concern was sharp enough to move even the ponderous Spanish bureaucracy to action.[14] They launched a series of expeditions to ascertain the veracity of the reports and, should these prove true, to discover the location of the menacing French colony.[15] Even when they finally discovered the last survivors of the ill-fated colony and became certain that no French threat persisted in the gulf, they feared another Gallic expedition. Their first response was sending missionaries into the Texas region;[16] the second, more significant, was establishing a fort on the bay of Pensacola, universally recognized as the best harbor along the Gulf Coast. Though the *cédula* ordering the establishment was issued on June 13, 1694, it was not until November 1698 that a fort was erected on the bay.[17] Undoubtedly, the signature of the Treaty of Ryswick in 1697 played a role, for, by its terms, France gained the western part of the island of Hispañola, Saint-Domingue, and the Spaniards entertained with reason, great fears of French aggression against their Antillean colonies and against their ships in Caribbean waters.

At the same time, the English were not idle either. Daniel Coxe, a London medical doctor and colonial promoter, advocated occupying his enormous land grant, Carolana, and settling it with Huguenot refugees. The area he claimed, "the largest grant by the English crown in the New World to a private individual,"[18] stretched from the western boundary of Carolina to present-day Texas, including Florida, except for the Spanish settlement at St. Augustine. Coxe had read French accounts of the Mississippi and became convinced of its potential wealth. He was familiar with the spurious Tonti relation, *Dernières découvertes,* but had particularly studied Father Louis Hennepin's *New Discovery,* a mixture of fact and fiction, intended to encourage English colonization in the gulf. Hennepin, a Recollet from Belgium, had travelled with La Salle and written an account of the discovery.[19] In 1697, he published the notorious *New Discovery* which he dedicated, fulsomely, to William III whom he urged to occupy the mouth of the Mississippi.[20] Coxe having become convinced joined forces with Huguenot refugees and chartered three ships to establish a British colony on the Gulf Coast.

Now, the French knew nothing of the Spanish establishment at Pensacola, but rumors of the projected English settlements were reaching Paris and Versailles, causing much concern. Pierre Le Moyne d'Iberville, a Canadian sailor, fur trader, discoverer, and veteran of Anglo-French confrontations in Acadia, New York, and Hudson Bay, warned Pontchartrain that a company had been organized in London to colonize the Mississippi and that it was readying ships and men "without hiding." "Such as I know the English," he added ominously, "I am sure that if we encounter them on that coast and they happen to be strongest, they will give us a fight."[21] M. de Rémonville, shipowner and friend of La Salle, had heard earlier that William Penn was sending fifty men down the Wabash to reach the Mississippi and establish themselves and he warned that though the road was long and arduous, "the English, who are not easily disheartened when it comes to commerce, will surmount all difficulties, if given time enough."[22] In July the minister heard that the New Holland Company planned to establish a colony at the Mississippi[23] In August he asked again for information on the English colony[24] and in September ordered it investigated.[25]

And thus, as a preventive strike, the Mississippi expedition was launched, Iberville, the "Canadian Cid," at its head. On October 15, mere days before the fleet weighed anchor, the minister was still fretting about an English occupation of the Gulf Coast.[26] After stopping at Cap Français, Iberville reached Mobile Bay on February 1, 1699, and on April 8 began building a fort at Biloxi.[27] In July he was back in France to report on his settlement and receive the king's orders.

And thus it was that Colbert's policy came to end. Almost simultaneously at both ends of the Great River small settlements were established which committed the French crown to an expansionist policy in America. With a strategic fort on the Great Lakes and one at the mouth of the Mississippi plus forts along the river, the thriving, populous English colonies and their Indian allies were contained. In 1672, Dr. Coxe's son, Colonel Daniel Coxe, would deem it "a great INDIGNITY, that Five Hundred Thousand BRITISH Subjects (which are above five times more than the FRENCH have both in CANADA and LOUISIANA put together) . . . should be straitly coop'd up" by the French occupation of Carolana.[28] And he was well aware of the danger which control of the Iroquois would present for the English colonies, "But should the FRENCH be permitted to establish their projected COMMUNICATION, between CAPE BRETON, the GULF and RIVER of ST LAWRENCE, as far as the MESCHECEBE," he warned, they will be able to control the Iroquois, ruin their trade with the English colonies and thus end their friendship. The hostility of the Five Nations would be disastrous for the English provinces with their open frontiers and settled establishments.[29]

By the time Pontchartrain realized the total failure of Cadillac's western policy, it was too late. He did recall Cadillac in 1709, but unwilling to admit the magnitude of his mistakes, sent the Gascon to Louisiana as governor, thus providing an early example of the Peter principle in action.[30]

However, the commitment to expansionism was reluctant at best. Detroit was allowed to stand, but Pontchartrain named as its next commander a mediocre leader, La Forest, hoping the fort would just go away under inept managment without the minister's admitting to error.[31] And as far as Biloxi and the Mississippi colony were concerned, the British had been kept out of the Gulf Coast—it was during Iberville's first return trip to France that his young brother Jean-Baptiste Le Moyne de Bienville turned back Captain William Bond, one of Coxe's officers who had ascended the Mississippi as far as the place still known as English Turn. As far as the minister was concerned, keeping the English out was sufficient. Establishing a powerful striving colony would be entirely excessive. A similar situtation prevailed in Acadia which the French did not want to see in English hands, but which they were not interested in developing either.

The strategic importance of the little Biloxi outpost grew considerably in the months which followed its foundation. Charles II, the ailing king of Spain, made a new will designating Louis XIV's grandson, Philip of Anjou, as his heir. On November 1, 1700, the Spanish monarch died, and Louis XIV supposedly proclaimed "There are no more Pyrenees." With a Bourbon on the throne of Spain, the Spanish-French American empires became allies against the British. The string of posts along the Mississippi[32] was not only intended to contain the English, but also to protect Mexico and the Spanish borderlands.[33] Louisiana's importance, however, remained purely strategic, and crown support remained niggardly. The minister frankly acknowledged his lukewarm attitude. After Iberville departed for the Gulf Coast, the governor of Saint-Domingue, Jean-Baptiste Ducasse, expressed doubts about the value of a colony in Louisiana, unless it could trade advantageously because, he said, it should not be used as a base to conquer the Spanish colonies.[34] The minister reassured him that the king had no intention of "forming an establishment" at the mouth of the Mississippi, but only "to have exact information and to prevent the English from occupying it."[35] On July 1, he reiterated that the king would not occupy Louisiana unless its usefulness became obvious.[36]

Iberville countered royal and ministerial reluctance by presenting elaborate schemes, but always couched in strategic terms. He had to convince them that his colony was worthwhile just as La Salle had had to convince them that his discovery had been worthwhile, and the Canadian had to resort to the same arguments. Iberville began his campaign in a low key. He arrived at La Rochelle on June 21, 1699, and immediately drafted a memoir for the king in which he presented the pros and cons for keeping his colony of Biloxi. He acknowledged that the Spaniards might take umbrage of a colony on the Gulf Coast and that the mouth of the river was hard to navigate. On the other hand, he argued, the French crown needed a colony there to evangelize the Indians and keep them from falling under the heretical influence of the English and Huguenots, an argument often used in the years which followed the Revocation of the Edict of Nantes. Moreover, the proximity of Spanish mines and the high probability that some might be found in the territory itself rendered the establishment most valuable.[37] This modest estimate of the colony's potential was followed by a more enthusiastic tract penned probably on July 28. In this document Iberville cast doubts on the potential of the trade in buffalo hides—a wise move considering the state of the Canadian fur trade in general and the extreme fear New France officials felt at the prospect of competition. The lead mines, he also thought of dubious value. But, he insisted, France had to establish a strong colony on the coast to prevent the English intrusion. He pointed out the phenomenal growth of the British colonies which would enable them to drive all other nations from the American continent within ten years.[38] He also revived the old La Salle dream of using the Gulf Coast as a springboard for the conquest of New Mexico.[39]

The minister, however, pursued his own aims. Despite Iberville's deprecatory remarks about the buffalo hides and mines, Pontchartrain insisted that attempts should be made to exploit the wool and that priority should be given to the search for mines. Iberville was also instructed to look into the possibility of cultivating mulberry and silk worms. And the minister's instructions clearly indicate the shift in dipliomatic winds: Iberville was directed to avoid causing the Spanish any distress. Even if they should be found to have abandoned Pensacola, he was not to seize this most desirable harbor.[40]

Iberville returned to Louisiana, arriving in Biloxi on January 9, 1700, and, as ordered, gathered information that his royal master might decide whether to continue the Louisiana settlement. On May 26, before returning to France to report, he instructed the ensign de Sauvole, whom he was leaving in charge again, to continue the search for dyewoods and pearls, to attempt the domestication of baby buffalos, and to avoid confrontation with the Spaniards.[41] Iberville had clearly understood Pontchartrain's message, the rival was no longer Spain, it was England, and the veteran of Hudson Bay could not have been more pleased.

As he reported to Pontchartrain in September, he had carried out his duties diligently, sending men to prospect for mines and bringing buffalo wool to France that it might be tried in spinning and weaving, though he again called the minister's attention, albeit discretely, to the transportation problem presented by the heavy and bulky buffalo hides. Most of his memoir, however, concerned the English and the Spaniards. He had built a small fort at the entrance of the

Mississippi to ensure that the English would not occupy it. There were rumors about another English colonization expedition to the Gulf Coast, but if they actually went "to the Mississippi," it would be easy to dislodge them, assured Iberville. He recommended occupying Mobile to keep the English out of a bay which would make it all too easy for British traders to penetrate among the Indian tribes and win them away. The Spaniards presented a different problem. They had displayed steady hostility to French implantation on the coast which they considered a serious threat to New Mexico and Quivira. However, they were not strong enough to overrrun the French fort at Biloxi. Obviously Iberville did not trust the Hispanics, however friendly the minister ordered him to show himself.[42]

The minister remained dubious as to the potential wealth of a Mississippi colony but agreed to the building of a fort at Mobile.[43] A few days later, Charles II died, Philip of Anjou accepted the crown of Spain, and the infant colony gained considerable importance as an obstacle to English expansion.

On August 24, the king ordered Iberville to depart immediately and on December 15, the Canadian Cid arrived before Pensacola. With a Bourbon on the Spanish throne, relations should have been harmonious between the French governor of the future Mobile and the acting commander of Pensacola, Francisco de Córcoles y Martínez. Indeed the sadly beleaguered garrisons at Fort Maurepas (Biloxi) and Pensacola had always extended whatever help each could supply the other. It could be expected that the cooperation would be even closer with the advent of Philip V. But the Spaniards remained resentful of the French intrusion into what they considered their monopoly. Already the Junta de Guerra had curtly refused to yield Pensacola to the French crown (who argued it could make better use of it for the protection of both empires). The Junta, moreover, reminded Pontchartrain that the French had no right whatsoever to the Mississippi which had been discovered by Spaniards and lay within the area reserved to Spain by the bull *Inter Coetera*.[44] It is not surprising then that Martínez, on January 1, 1702, asked Iberville, though very courteously, to delay his projected establishment at Mobile.[45] Just as courteously, Iberville explained that his orders were explicit and proceeded to Mobile.[46]

Mobile had been chosen for its strategic value against the English encroachments. The Mobile River would permit easy communications with the interior, especially with the Chickasaw, powerful supporters of the English therefore a tribe which had to be won over or destroyed by French allies to prevent Carolinian traders and colonists from expanding southward.[47] Despite Iberville's efforts, the Chickasaw would remain a serious threat to the colony.[48]

Iberville asked for arms to equip Indian allies to the tune of 24,773 *livres*. He also requested a "few families," which would cost around 18,000 *livres*, as well as "some girls for the Canadians . . . who are asking for them."[49] The answer was not long in coming. On August 3, Pontchartrain granted the 24,773 *livres* to purchase arms and merchandise for the Indians.[50] For settlers, however, the tune was different. Michel Bégon, the intendant at Rochefort, was ordered to give passage to Louisiana to the wives and families of men going over, but no more.[51] The ministerial missive could be translated "millions [or at least thousands] for Indians, not a cent for settlers." Iberville's unfolding ambition for a thriving empire on the lower Mississippi was encountering a chilling administrative response.

His third stay in Louisiana was brief, four months, and he sailed back to France in April 1702 having begun the establishment of Fort Louis de la Mobile which he left in the care of his brother Bienville.[52] Now he really began planning an empire. He requested, on the New France model, a seigneurie along the Mobile River, two leagues deep on each side.[53] This vast land grant, which he wanted erected in *comté*, he proposed to subdivide among "*particuliers*" as the Canadian *seigneurs* had done. He also requested the concession of lead mines, should he find some; the permission to import slaves from Guinea; authorization to draw Indians into his lands as he needed them; and the monopoly on Louisiana beaver furs to be sold, however, only to the Company of Canada.[54] He wanted also a warehouse at the mouth of the Mississippi and the return freight on royal ships sent to Louisiana. He did not obtain his county, nor the settlers to develop his colony.

It was not for lack of trying. Iberville, as time passed, changed from the fur trader, explorer, sailor to a true empire builder. Not that he forgot to feather his own nest,[55] but increasingly he saw himself as at least an epigone of Jean Talon, called to recreate on the shores of the Mississippi what the great intendant had built along the St. Lawrence. He harped on the need for population. "It is necessary to send immediately here families, and especially farmers," he wrote.[56] In 1704 he suggested discharging the Canadians serving in the colony that they might settle in Louisiana and asked for twenty or thirty girls for them. Knowing well his Canadians' preference for a free-wheeling life in the woods he added, laconically, *"qu'elles soient jolies."*[57] Women settlers were a major preoccupation; already the year before he had asked for "a few reasonable and well-made girls," because these are easiest to marry off.[58] From the first he had visualized grouped settlements to avoid the dispersion which prevailed in Canada.[59] And he was most concerned with preventing the Mississippi colonists from scattering their energy on the fur trade. His memoirs insist on the damage the trade had caused in Canada and on the need to control it strictly.

But the very European events which were endowing his little colony with an importance beyond its size, made it impossible to develop it. He arrived in France and began once more his bureaucratic rounds. In May, 1702, however, the War of the Spanish Succession had begun (actually, warfare had begun in 1701 with Prince Eugene's campaign in Italy) and the colonization of Louisiana became a very minor preoccupation for Louis XIV and Pontchartrain. Iberville remained in France as a Mississippi advisor to the minister and planned expeditions against the English to protect the Spanish colonies in Florida and the French outpost at Mobile.[60] He even led one expedition against Nevis and St. Kitt in 1705, but quite ill with *mal de Siam,* put in at Havana where he died on July 9, 1706.

With him Louisiana lost its best advocate. When he died, he had achieved his immediate purpose—implanting a settlement at the mouth of the Mississippi—but not his long-range plan for a thriving, populous empire. The geopolitical arguments he had used, though they convinced Pontchartrain and Louis, doomed the establishment to remain a strategic outpost, valuable chiefly because someone else wanted it. Thus royal commitment to colonization was half-hearted, at best. Philip V's accession to the Spanish throne increased Louisiana's importance as an essential link in the defense of the Spanish possessions, but French support remained niggardly, just enough to keep it out of English hands. In the years which followed Iberville's death, the colony was little more than a small pawn on a large chess board though for a brief period of three years it became the foremost component of French commercial and colonial policy.

V

In Search of a Policy, 1701-1731

From the day in 1515 when Francis I mounted the throne, French foreign policy had been focused on the rivalry with the House of Hapsburg. With the death of Charles II of Spain and the accession of a Bourbon to the Hispanic throne, the Hapsburg empire fragmented, a division recognized by the European powers at Utrecht. This dynastic change should have led to an alliance between France and Spain, especially in light of the fact that during the War of the Spanish Succession England had emerged as a formidable European power.[1] Instead, for some twenty odd years, France cultivated closer ties with England, actually joining her former enemy in 1719 in waging war against Philip V. [2] On the American continent, however, confrontation persisted between French and English colonists, in fact becoming more bitter as a result of changes on the colonial map wrought at Utrecht.

The War of the Spanish Succession and the Utrecht treaties marked a turning point in the history of European overseas expansion. Colonies had played an important role in the War of the League of Augsburg, but during Queen Anne's War, overseas possessions and trade, for the first time, became as central an issue as continental expansion and prestige gains. Louis XIV himself acknowledged in 1709 that "the principal purpose of this war is the trade with the Indies and the wealth they produce."[3] The importance attached to trade was evidenced in the chartering of institutions such as the Bank of England (1694), the English Board of Trade and Plantations (1699), and the French Council of Commerce (1708) as well as the appointing of Nicolas Mesnager, of the Chamber of Commerce of Rouen, as French plenipotentiary at Utrecht.[4]

In the fall of 1701, English commercial interests had become quite concerned about the alignment of Spanish and French customs policies in the Indies,[5] where the Spaniards were taking steps to prevent the illicit trade of their Caribbean possessions with Jamaica and Curaçao. Until then, they had tolerated the contraband, but now their change of policy was obviously aimed at excluding English and Dutch trade from the Spanish colonies. This action therefore aroused fears that the French and Spaniards would now move to adopt a united policy. The regents who were ruling Spain until the new king arrived took a step which seemed to confirm that indeed there were no more Pyrenees: they asked Louis XIV to take charge of the Spanish government and commanded that the French king's orders be obeyed as if they came from Philip V.[6] London feared

Louis's domination of the Peninsula, but the English feared even more Gallic control of the vast Spanish overseas empire and the lucrative trade it commanded. The French had dominated the Cadiz trade for half a century, though the contraband trade in the Spanish Indies was in the hands of English and Dutch merchants. The fear of exclusion from the Caribbean turned British public opinion from indifference to hostility and earned the war, declared on May 4, 1702, overwhelming popular support.[7]

The War of the Spanish Succession was waged as much over the slave trade as over the throne of Spain. At the death of Charles II, the highly profitable contract for slave importation to the Spanish colonies, the *asiento*,[8] was held by Portuguese merchants, but Philip V lost no time in negotiating with his grandfather its transfer to the French Company of Guinea (which immediately added to its name "*et de l'asiento*").[9] English and Dutch traders protested because for the first time the *asiento* was a state instead of a private contract.[10] England wanted the *asiento* for the slave trade, of course, but even more because it served to cover extensive smuggling operations. Much contraband could be placed in the holds of the *négriers* ships besides black gold. In fact, *asiento* traders often crowded their captives in smaller and smaller spaces so as to reserve maximum room for smuggled merchandise, certainly not improving the conditions though Herbert Klein's analysis of slave deaths in the Middle Passage reveals no correlation between "light packing" and high mortality.[11]

Louis XIV, on the other hand, valued the *asiento* not just as a profitable venture for French merchants but also as a way to rebuild Hispanic power now that the Spanish satellite was entering his orbit. The American colonies were the center of Spanish wealth and might: "The kingdom of Spain, stript of the Indies, would be too inconsiderable," he had written Tallard during negotiations which preceded the death of Charles II.[12] But a large work force was needed to restore their former greatness to his Catholic Majesty's dominions,[13] and French slave traders could supply the Spanish colonies efficiently and cheaply with the needed laborers. Scelle believes that at the time the contract was negotiated, Louis intended to protect Spanish commercial interests and prevent French subjects from using the slave trade as a blind for contraband. The Spaniards believed he was only interested in gaining control of their empire, and events tended to prove them right.[14] The need for money to pursue the war forced the French king to tolerate infractions of the Spanish monopoly, and the Council of the Indies reacted more to the infractions than to the intentions, however pious. At Utrecht, England obtained the *asiento* and, with it, permission to send a yearly vessel to the Spanish colonies. The *vaisseau de permission* opened Iberian ports to British commerce and served to cover huge, profitable smuggling operations.

Another major area of contention between France and England had been the fur trade in Hudson's Bay. In 1670 Prince Rupert had obtained a charter for the Hudson Bay Company to exploit the vast resources of the area. In 1682 the French Canadians retorted by establishing the Company of the North or Company of Hudson's Bay, a well-capitalized venture which rapidly gained control of the fur trade in the bay region. The French company harassed the scattered English outposts along the bay,[15] drew away their Indian suppliers, and greatly weakened their trade. Utrecht excluded French fur traders from the Hudson Bay region, though French interlopers continued trading in the James Bay area, taking advantage of the hazy delimitation of the area ceded.[16] More dangerous for French commercial interests, Utrecht recognized English "dominion" over the Iroquois and the right of the Indians to trade with either French or British.[17]

In Newfoundland, another area of conflict, French fishermen had been active since the sixteenth century. Owing to their Newfoundland catch, the French dominated the Mediterranean cod market, and the new Franco-Spanish unity threatened to make the trade a Gallic monopoly. The agreements at Utrecht excluded French establishments in Newfoundland, except for drying platforms. The French, however, retained their fishing rights on the so-called northern "French shore," from Bonavista Bay on the east to Pointe Roche on the west. This right, which the French quickly claimed belonged to them exclusively, enabled them to exclude English fishermen from the rich cod fishing grounds and to retain Newfoundland as a training ground for sailors. Thus for a nation whose thoughts centered on the Atlantic Ocean rather than the American continent, the Utrecht settlement which surrendered Acadia but kept the fishing rights was in fact a success.[18]

The prize territorial plum England picked up at Utrecht was Acadia, the cession of which began the encirclement of New France.[19] France did not abandon Acadia willingly: Pontchartrain instructed negotiators to procrastinate on this issue, and only agreed to cession when threatened with a collapse of the peace negotiations.[20] The loss of Acadia made imperative French development of new lines of defense. Their response, the erection of a chain of forts from Louisbourg to Mobile, produced constant friction between the French and English colonies for the next half century.

In the Caribbean, England only picked up St. Kitts, an island rich in agricultural potential but exposed to attacks from Martinique.[21] In the Mediterranean, the English acquired Minorca and Gibraltar, both territorially unimportant, but strategically placed for the control of trade. It was becoming clear that English negotiations were carried out with commerce in mind and were directed as much by the Board of Trade as by the diplomats.

The influence of the Board of Trade fully revealed itself in the matter of the trade treaty between France and England. Articles VIII and IX would have given

France most-favored-nation status. Under pressure of the Board of Trade, Parliament refused ratification, thus dealing a serious setback to French commerce and endorsing, in fact, a strict mercantilist approach to trade, colonial traffic included.[22] As a consequence, the overseas trade found itself more than ever in the hands of smugglers, a situtation which multiplied confrontations among subjects of the colonial powers.

The Bourbons had paid dearly for the Spanish throne. New France was, as Priestley puts it, caught in "the jaws of a nutcracker;" [23] the changes wrought in the colonial map carried the seeds of future conflict; and the Spanish alliance was less than dependable.

During the war years, Franco-Spanish relations remained amiable enough, Philip signing himself in letters to the French king "your loving grandson." But with the death of the Sun King the situation changed. Utrecht had guaranteed that the French and Spanish crowns would never be united, but Philip, a Frenchman at heart, looked longingly across the Pyrenees at the throne occupied by a five-year-old nephew whose sickliness seemed to presage an early death.[24] Moreover, Philip took as his second wife a willful Italian princess, Elizabeth Farnese, who focused her considerable (if unintelligent) energy on securing thrones for her sons who were barred from the Spanish succession by heirs from the first marriage. Oversexed and moral, Philip was completely dominated by a wife who conducted Spanish foreign policy for purely dynastic aims. She thus baffled European diplomats who labored under the misapprehension that a Spanish queen should defend Spanish national interests.[25]

Their erratic conduct of foreign affairs and the lack of dependability of the Spanish alliance brought about a French diplomatic reversal. In January 1717, the earl of Stanhope sealed an alliance with the regent, Philip, duke of Orléans, who governed France during Louis XV's minority.[26] The Triple Alliance—France-England-Holland—was born. At a time when English presence to the north and the east menaced New France, when rapidly growing Atlantic colonies encroached on French territories, when on all fronts France faced the colonial and commercial rivalry of England, the regent bound himself to an alliance which guaranteed English naval hegemony.[27]

It should be pointed out, however, that the duke of Orléans faced a most difficult situation. His coming to power was questioned in France because he had acceded to the Regency by having the Parlement break Louis XIV's will, and it was questioned abroad because Philip V seriously considered claiming the Regency himself.[28] Should the sickly boy king die, as was generally expected, Philip of Orléans would need English help to secure the French crown against the claims of Philip V.[29] Moreover, after a war which had united Europe against her, France was economically drained as well as isolated diplomatically. For Abbé

Guillaume Dubois, architect of the policy, the English alliance was indispensable to give France "the superiority she could not acquire otherwise."[30] Eventually, the peace and the alliance would enable French traders to supplant the English in the Levant, in Africa, in North America, and in the Antilles where, despite the Molasses Act, Gallic West Indian merchants monopolized the sugar trade with the American colonies.[31] On his side, Stanhope needed French help against the Jacobite risings.

The English alliance should have meant that, in the immediate future at least, France would return to its traditional land orientation, leaving the sea and colonial enterprises to the English, foregoing colonial expansion in America. Instead, the Regent espoused a New World colonial policy at odds with his foreign policy, on one hand cultivating the friendship of England, on the other backing the building of posts to contain British expansion and encouraging Law's grandiose colonization scheme in Louisiana, thus threatening the entire English seaboard settlement.[32] But at the same time he dismantled the channel fortifications and allowed the French navy to grow ever weaker, thus insuring the eventual loss of the American continent.[33]

These years of policy vacillation took a heavy toll in the infant colony at the mouth of the Mississippi. With the death of Iberville it had lost its strongest advocate, the one who had the ear of Versailles. Moreover, the scandal which followed Iberville's death, when Pontchartrain ordered an investigation of the discoverer's financial shenanigans, discredited the Le Moyne family and the colony itself.[34] A colony established as a strategic outpost changed naturally in importance as European alliances shifted. During and after the War of the Spanish Succession, though its strategic value was recognized, the colony was not only neglected but downright denigrated and found itself the butt of doubts in Paris, antagonism in Madrid, constant harassment by English colonists and their Indian allies, and frank hostility in Quebec.

The crown had had its doubts about the colony since La Salle's discovery. "I am convinced the discovery of sieur de La Salle is quite useless" had written the king to La Barre in 1683,[35] and La Salle had only been able to justify his discovery by dangling the hope of harassing the Spaniards "in the very place from which they draw their wealth." [36] Iberville had been sent to exploit La Salle's discovery only "for fear that another nation should take it from us and occupy it." [37] "I know not what the Court will decide with reference to the Mississippi," the Jesuit missionary Jacques Gravier was writing at the same time, "if no silver mines be found there; for they seek not lands to cultivate." [38]

Even the grudging support Iberville had received faded into nothing when the Canadian disappeared from the scene, and in 1707 Louis XIV threatened to abandon the outpost. He requested information "as to the use it may be for the kingdom" because if it proves itself of little value, he would "abandon the colony without committing any more resources." [39] Pontchartrain chimed in: "only in order to oppose English expansion and stop it, would the King go to the expense of maintaining Mobile." [40]

But it was not French policy, especially not Louis's or Pontchartrain's, to relinquish colonies willingly, and the minister was too well aware of English growth to give up Louisiana. Even in war years, Pontchartrain projected a solidly established French presence on the Gulf Coast whenever conditions became peaceful again.[41] After the Treaty of Utrecht, Louis would resume an expansionist policy in America, and Louisiana would become the last link in the chain of outposts along the great river intended to contain the aggressive British colonists. This containment policy could have been realistic had France committed the settlers and money to develop populous colonies, as she had done in Canada in the 1660s and had built a large, powerful navy. But Versailles believed that fortresses would suffice, and Queen Anne's War was to prove that judgement mistaken.[42]

In the meanwhile, the Louisiana colony languished. Entirely dependent on France for their food supply, the colonists came close to starvation (at least by French standards which did not acknowledge corn as food). In 1703 the *Loire* brought some foodstuff; in 1704 the *Pélican*. In 1706 the *Aigle* provided some meager stores, then in 1708 the *Renommée,* which did not return till 1711, three years during which the soldiers were sent to live in the woods with the Indians and the colonists survived on sagamité and boiled corn.[43] Pontchartrain was concerned, but the depleted treasury forbade excessive generosity. "I hear the settlers are quite naked," he wrote Bégon in 1708. "See if we can purchase suitable merchandise with the money the king pays those in his service." [44] He intended for the soldiers and officials to sell these goods, paid to them in lieu of cash, to the colonists. No suggestions anywhere in that letter that the king may supply food or clothing to the impoverished settlers from his own exchequer. As the *Renommée* was being outfitted for its 1711 voyage, Pontchartrain haggled over the number of persons to be sent ot Louisiana with rations, "the food being too expensive to allow his Majesty to supply a large number,"[45] and ordered the passengers' food cut back from a ration and a half to one ration only. [46]

The end of the war should have brought relief to Louisina whose strategic importance could no longer be doubted. To offset the loss of Acadia, the French were undertaking on Cape Breton the construction of the great fortress of Louisbourg which was intended to protect the entrance of the St. Lawrence and threaten Newfoundland.[47] The line of French strongholds thus stretched from the Gulf of St. Lawrence to the Gulf of Mexico, through Quebec, Trois-Rivières, Montreal, Fort Frontenac, Detroit, Fort St-Louis (ordered evacuated in 1702, but actually maintained, though weakly), Fort Crevecoeur, Cahokia, Kaskaskia, not to mention Michilimakinac to the north. Fort St-Joseph would be added in 1717.

Fort La Baie in 1718, Fort Niagara in 1720, Fort de Chartres much later in 1750. The colony at the mouth of the Mississippi had thus become strategically indispensable.[48] After Utrecht, there were no more suggestions that Louisiana be abandoned, though in 1712 Louis XIV was still trying to negotiate the exchange of the Mississippi colony for the Spanish half of Hispañola.[49] But the recognition of its strategic importance did not bring large-scale crown investment. On the contrary, with their treasury bankrupt, Louis XIV and Pontchartrain looked to private initiative to take the colony off their hands. On September 14, 1712, the king signed the letters patent which granted Antoine Crozat, the wealthy Paris financier, proprietary rights over Louisiana for fifteen years.[50]

From Louis XIV's point of view, the Crozat Company represented a most admirable solution which ensured continued French presence in a strategically important outpost at little cost to the crown. Crozat, whom Giraud calls "*âprement intéressé*," saw Louisiana as an investment.[51] He had been convinced to assume the proprietorship by Cadillac who vaunted the mineral wealth of the region and the potential trade with Spanish colonies, displaying true Gascon eloquence and unabashed mendacity. With remarkable cynicism he boasted to the minister "I have enthralled him, and others, about the trade in that country . . . I have discoursed about the immense wealth of Louisiana, its gold and silver mines, its pearls. . . ."[52] But as he pointed out to Pontchartrain, "I have done these things at your command."[53] The minister could not be exonerated of participation in the deception nor of the betrayal of the Spanish alliance. For the search for mines could only lead to Franco-Spanish confrontation, and Spanish mercantilism, stricter than Colbertism had ever been, jealously guarded for its own nationals the trade with the colonies. A Spanish company, the French well knew, had the "exclusive privilege of trading in all of Mexico."[54] Thus Louis XIV's parsimonious support of Louisiana and his eagerness to shift the financial burden to a private individual resulted in a contradiction between his foreign policy which cultivated the Spanish alliance and his colonial policy which flouted Spanish interests.

The Spaniards reacted to French encroachment and saw the Louisiana colony, supposedly founded to protect the Iberian empire against England, as a threat to both their possessions and their trade. From the first, Spain had considered the establishment of the French on the gulf as an infringement of its monopoly, a threat to its galleons, and a gun pointed at Mexico. The governor of Pensacola had protested again the founding of Mobile[55] and turned a deaf ear, at least in his official correspondence, to the Canadian's protestations of friendship. "The King, my master," wrote Iberville,"has no other purpose in the establishment he has ordered me to make at Mobile than the interests of both crowns."[56] The French post, he argued, would enable both garrison's to support

France's and Spain's Indian allies against the "English of Carolina" and their Chickasaw clients. As a matter of fact, the interest of Spain demanded that Pensacola be yielded to the French. As Iberville explained to Pontchartrain, this excellent harbor would open up the inland trade and would enable France and Spain to harass the English through the *nations sauvages*.[57] He stressed the general weakness of the Spaniards, their lack of men, the indifference of the governor, Andrés de Arriola, and the inadequacy of the fortifications.[58] As he wrote Pontchartrain on July 30, 1701, "If the Council of the Indies does not want to give us Pensacola, it is sheer stubborness, or ignorance of the country, for they cannot defend themselves against the English."[59]

Not unexpectedly the Spanish War Junta did not take kindly to the proposal. They protested French presence on the coast, denied the weakness of their establishment, belittled the English menace, and instead of agreeing to relinquish Pensacola, demanded immediate departure of the French "usurpers."[60] Quite miffed, Pontchartrain wrote a refutation pointing out the growth of the English colonies, but to no avail.[61] The close alliance between French and Spanish crowns did not lead to colonial cooperation.

Locally, however, cooperation was indispensable, and trade thrived between Mobile and Pensacola, neither beleaguered garrison being able to survive without help from the other though neither trusted the other. The French lent a *traversier* to the Spaniards who needed to secure supplies from Veracruz, succoured Arriola when he shipwrecked, even feasted the Spanish official on occasion.[62] The Spaniards, on the other hand, fed the French during the starving times.[63] Trade flourished between the outposts, and had it not been for the vegetables and poultry they sold Pensacola, the Louisiana colonists would rarely have seen any specie.[64]

Yet distrust lingered, and French activities, limited though they were, did nothing to alleviate Spanish suspicions. Trade with the Spanish colonies was supposedly closed to foreigners. But contraband trade flourished, and Louisiana frequently served to cover these illegal activities. Passports would be delivered to ships bound ostensibly for the Mississippi but actually for Veracruz or another Spanish harbor.[65] In the eyes of the French Caribbean officials especially, Mobile was valuable as a port of call and as a blind.[66] Trade with the Spanish colonies was one of the inducements dangled before Crozat to convince him to assume the Louisiana proprietorship, and the royal instructions to *Ordonnateur* Jean-Baptiste du Bois du Clos, were cynically explicit. "The present union between the crowns of France and Spain requires that sieur du Clos pay careful attention to keep peace between both nations and to avoid anything which might disturb their good intelligence," the monarch points out piously. But, continued the king, "it must not be so extreme as to damage French interests."[67]

Cadillac, governor of Louisiana during Crozat's proprietorship, reported a few months later: "Sieur du Clos was supposed to send [to Veracruz] a brigantine under the pretext of getting foodstuff, but, in fact, to bring Brittany cloth, other merchandise and 3,000 deer skins which sell well among the Spaniards." [68] Duclos recommended that the French in Mobile "be given leave to trade merchandise with the Spaniards anywhere they wish." [69] He complained to the minister that the Spanish chartered Company of Veracruz confiscated contraband French merchandise. France should therefore send to Mexico a Spanish-speaking agent who would show the Iberian colonists that it was to their advantage to purchase the cheaper French goods.[70] No wonder the Spaniards distrusted the French of Louisiana and that the viceroy of Veracruz, the duke of Linares, "very civilly" begged Cadillac to keep merchants out of any French ships he sent to Veracruz, otherwise he would be forced to confiscate the cargo.[71]

The distrust was all the greater that the French were pushing westward toward Spanish territories. As early as 1708 an expedition had been sent to the Missouri area to search for mines;[72] even worse, Cadillac had organized an expedition toward the Red River and the Rio Grande. Louis Juchereau de St. Denis crossed Texas in 1714, after establishing Fort St-Jean-Baptiste at Natchitoches, and reached the presidio of Rio Grande.[73] The expedition which threatened New Mexico revived Spanish fears, never fully allayed since La Salle's 1684 attempt. Aware that Louisiana officials dreamed of conquering their mineral-rich possessions, the Spanish saw in St-Denis's expedition the first step of a general offensive.[74] Their fears were not lessened when Louis XIV, on December 27, 1714, ordered the building of Fort Rosalie at Natchez.[75] How justified was their distrust can be judged from the memoir written in 1717 by *Ordonnateur* Marc-Antoine Hubert: Reviving the La Salle-Peñalosa scheme, Hubert advocated seizing New Mexico and conquering the continent all the way to the Pacific.[76]

Moreover, the French advances northward from Mobile and the alliance negotiated with the inland tribes were interpreted by the Spaniards as a prelude to the encirclement of Pensacola.[77] The brief war with Spain in 1719 in which Pensacola was seized by the French would soon exacerbate that mutual distrust and antagonism.

French policy was no more coherent in its dealings with England. During the War of the Spanish Succession, of course, England was the enemy, and the French took advantage of the dynastic alliance between the two Bourbon crowns to displace English commerce. Ships from St-Malo eagerly plied the so-called "South Seas," i. e., the west coast of South America. At Concepcíon, in southern Chile, the French colony of traders and merchants reached 2,000. This profitable contraband drained so much wealth into the French coffers that at the time of Utrecht, Spanish statesmen declared that the loss of the Indies was preferable to opening them to French traders.[78] The exclusion of English traders from the trade with the Caribbean colonies, which though forbidden had been tolerated, until now, was another provocation,[79] as were the Company of Guinea's plans to exploit the *asiento.*"[80] These major complaints, as well as those directed at the activities of French fur traders in Hudson Bay and fishermen along the Newfoundland shores, were settled, in principle at least, by the Utrecht treaties. The Malouins were driven from the South Seas, bringing about the decline of St-Malo, Hudson Bay was closed to French fur traders; French fishermen were forbidden to build fortifications or establishments in Newfoundland; and England secured the *asiento* and the yearly " *vaisseau de permission.*"[81] But the Utrecht treaties did nothing to end the small-scale, but constant, confrontations between French and English colonists.

In fact, the treaties of 1713 exacerbated the hostility by reinforcing the sense of insecurity on both sides. New France, caught between English trading posts to the north and settlements to the east, sought security in the chain of forts from Quebec to Mobile. But the English colonies, looking at the formidable citadel of Louisbourg and the easy lines of communication the waterways gave the French, felt defenseless "like a rope of sand . . . loose and unconnected" as was stated in 1753.[82] The British colonists felt all the more helpless knowing that they were left to assume their own defense and that their mutual jealousy prevented them from uniting against the French and their Indian allies.[83] Their disunity contrasted with the centralized government of the French colonies. The phenomenal demographic growth of the Atlantic colonies would more than offset these disadvantages—in 1714 there were 250,000 American colonists, 20,000 New France settlers, and Louisiana numbered 215 inhabitants, including the 160 soldiers.[84] But the British were not aware of their advantage.

The Louisiana colony, weak as it was, alarmed English colonists, particularly those in South Carolina. Agressive in their westward expansion, the Carolinians took a dim view of a French presence which would reinforce the Spanish colony of Florida. Moreover, from Mobile the French "had direct water communication with the Alabama, Talapoosa, and Abihka."[85] The Carolinians feared that French occupation of the Gulf Coast heralded a Franco-Spanish invasion and in 1700 Carolina settlers were discussing moving to safer grounds should a French prince ascend the throne of Spain.[86] After 1700 an alliance with the Chickasaw greatly strengthened the English position. The French responded by allying themselves with the Choctaw, the Chickasaw's traditional enemies, so that South Carolina and Louisiana became hostile outposts carrying on their warfare "by proxy."[87]

Iberville's policy, however, was based on Indian peace and trade so that he needed to end the Choctaw-Chickasaw conflict. Tonti travelled through Choctaw and Chickasaw country, impressed the Indians most favorably despite his lack of presents and convinced them to meet the "Great Chief" himself at Fort Louis.[88] Iberville warned the Chickasaw not to trust the English who only courted them to get slaves and he threatened, if they did not make peace with the Choctaw and become French allies, to arm their traditional enemies against them.[89] Choctaw and Chickasaw smoked the calumet. Peace was made, but not for long: the English were not going to allow their trading partners to be seduced away from them. English traders constantly moved among the Chickasaw, offering gifts and buying slaves.[90] Again and again the French wrenched promises from the Indians to exclude English traders. "The chief of the nation promised me to chase the English out," wrote Bienville in 1706.[91] But the English offered "considerable presents" while the French seldom had any to give.[92] Despite the presents, the exactions of the English traders led to an uprising known as the Yamasee War. Creek, Cherokee, Choctaw and Alibamon converged on the English[93] who accused the French of having provoked the revolt. Bienville certainly took advantage of the situation, but with little money for presents could not hold the alliance of the tribes. The Council of the Marine which presided over colonial affairs during the early Regency, had acknowledged the need for generous gifts to the Indians,[94] but was less open handed with Louisiana than with Canada. The English, however, tended to overestimate French control over the interior tribes. The French, on the other hand, were convinced the British were winning back their allies.[95] The conclusion of the Triple Alliance did little to ease the Louisiana-Carolina tension: European power politics weighed but little on the frontier. In 1721 the Chickasaw harassed French ships on the Mississippi, and Bienville responded by arming the Choctaw to attack them.[96] The Chickasaw sued for peace and promised, as usual, not to receive any more English traders. For the colonists at Mobile, England or at least English settlers remained the enemy.[97]

Thus neither the close union between French and Spanish crowns nor the friendship treaties with England affected much the colonial reality. After Utrecht, Louis XIV committed himself to an expansionist American policy, ordering the building of new forts, reopening the fur trade, sending reinforcements, and the Regent continued this policy which could only antagonize England and Spain. But, as always, the French crown committed itself parsimoniously so that the colonies were not given the means to hold at bay their antagonistic neighbors.

Louis's cautious expansionism did not please Canada either. The Canadians wholeheartedly endorsed westward expansion, provided they controlled it. Louisiana founded as a last link in the protective chain down the Mississippi threatened their lifeline, the fur trade, for the *coureurs de bois* now had an alternative outlet for their pelts. In 1700 when only twenty *coureurs* from Michilimackinac obeyed the order to return to Montreal, the governor and the intendant of New France knew where to lay the blame: the other eighty-four, they said, were heading down river for Louisiana.[98] Callières and François de Beauharnois protested the exodus of their young men: the king's intent, they said, was "to establish the Mississippi, not to destroy Canada." [99] The New France merchants petitioned the court to forbid the sale of Canadian beaver in Louisiana.[100] These were the years when the price of beaver collapsed, the Canadian fur trade was in the hands of the "Company of the Colony," and merchants and New France officials believed the colony "in danger of perishing if things remain as they are."[101] Iberville complained of their jealousy: "They are so prejudiced against me in Canada and against anyone who has anything to do with the Mississippi that any man who answers to me is suspect."[102] He would have preferred to relinquish the post of governor but the minister left him in charge.[103]

The court did nothing to alleviate the hostility. On the contrary, by erecting Louisiana into a separate government, it confirmed the fears of the Canadians. And these became even sharper when the letters patent chartering Crozat's company gave him governance of the Illinois region.[104]

This was the situtation in 1717 when Crozat relinquished with great relief his costly monopoly. Spain and France were ruled by the same family, but drifting into hostility soon to culminate in war. The Triple Alliance bound French foreign policy to England. On the American continent French settlers in New France and Louisiana feuded with Spanish and English colonists. Louisiana, valued only for its strategic situation, was jealously kept but received only niggardly support. Then everything changed.

Neither mineral wealth nor the prosperous Spanish trade he had been led to expect having materialized, Crozat begged the Regent to relieve him of his costly "privilege."[105] He recommended entrusting the colony to a company, the expense of developing it being too much for a *particulier,* but vaunted the wealth of this land "where there are many gold, silver, lead and copper mines which belong to the same mountain chain as those of Mexico."[106] The copper and lead were not only plentiful but "offered themselves almost on the surface of the ground," so much so that "the settlers pick up daily."[107] The great wealth of timber, the abundance of cattle with a wool "as fine as vicuna," and especially the climate, "gentle and temperate" (!), which favored agriculture, made the colony infinitely desirable. Dyewoods would undoubtedly be found also. "Nature having lavished [on Louisiana] all its other gifts, that one could not be absent." [108]

The financier proposed a company with 500 shares at 3,000 *livres* each payable in state notes. The company would take charge of the development, the king would keep the responsibility of defense.[109] On January 13, 1717, the Council approved the organization of a new company, but it was not till August 26, 1718, that the king accepted Crozat's resignation.[110]

In the meanwhile, the Council had been preparing to transfer Louisiana to the care of the Scottish financier, John Law, whose bank created on the model of the English and Dutch banks was flourishing. On May 19, 1717, the Council had received a draft of letters patent for a Company of the West; the final letters patent were issued in August.[111] By their terms, the Company of the West received the monopoly of Louisiana trade for twenty-five years; of the Canadian beaver trade in perpetuity; the ownership of lands and mines; the right to build fortifications and to nominate both company directors and colonial officials. The king would assume the upkeep of the forts and garrisons and furnish Indian presents. The Company of the West soon enlarged its scope, incorporating the Company of Senegal (December 1718), the Company of China and the East Indian Company (1719), and finally both the Company of St-Domingue and the Company of Guinea (September 1720). Colbert's East and West Indian companies were thus fused into one and the Company of the West (renamed Company of the Indies) having taken over also tax and customs collection controlled all of France's commercial and colonial activities.[112]

Louisiana with its vast agricultural and mineral potential was central to the development of Law's system. Settlers were to be brought to exploit the resources which would enrich the Company, the undertaking to be financed, of course, with state notes issued by the bank. The Company was to enrich the state through trade and the retiring of the public debt; the bank would lend the Company the money it needed, and would issue notes to individuals that they might buy stock in the Company, the entire operation being sustained and fueled by the wealth from Louisiana.

The first name, Company of the West, had been chosen to hide the importance Louisiana assumed in this emerging scheme.[113] England and Spain had displayed such hostility to the Crozat Company and its very limited activity that the Regency feared violent reactions on their part to Law's grandiose system. This was the period in which France, as part of the Triple Alliance, was cultivating close ties to the English.

With Spain, however, relations were rapidly spoiling. Elizabeth Farnese pursued her dynastic aims, seeking thrones for her sons in Italy. In 1717, while the Hapsburg emperor's attention was absorbed by war with the Turks, Spanish forces were dispatched to Sardinia. Besides, the Spanish first minister, an Italian adventurer who had gained the queen's favor for his unusual culinary talents, Giulio Cardinal Alberoni, joined in a plot against the life of the Regent organized by the Spanish ambassador in Paris, Antonio Judice Cellamare.[114] He also encouraged Jacobite activities against the Hanoverian dynasty.[115] In consequence of Hispanic adventurism, Great Britain declared war on Spain on December 27, 1718; France followed suit on January 9, 1719. A year later, the war was over. Philip V sued for peace and on January 26, 1720, joined France,

England, and Holland in the Quadruple Alliance.[116] The Treaty of Madrid, on March 27, 1721, restored amity between Philip V and Louis XV, the alliance being sealed six months later by the betrothal of the twelve-year old French king to a three-year old Infanta.

But from 1717 to 1720 Spain had not been an ally to be placated, and the Company of the West, turned Company of the Indies, launched grandiose schemes in Louisiana, unfettered by foreign policy considerations. As soon as war was declared, the Louisiana officials seized the opportunity they had so long awaited. In May 1719, Bienville captured Pensacola.[117] Retaken by the Spaniards, captured again by the French, Pensacola was finally returned to Spain by the peace treaty so that no lasting territorial gain resulted from the limited military operation.

Law's immigration policy had far more lasting results. The means were not always commendable. When the eloquent, if somewhat mendacious, propaganda which painted Louisiana as a cross between the Garden of Eden and the Land of El Dorado failed to arouse the enthusiasm of voluntary colonists, the Regent and Law turned to forced immigration.[118] Salt smugglers, vagabonds, beggars, "libertines," thieves, murderers, prostitutes drawn from jails and hospitals crowded the ships of the Company.[119]

The results seemed spectacular. Early in 1718 Charles Legac, newly arrived director of the Company of the West, counted between 350 and 400 inhabitants, including the soldiers.[120] In 1718 there arrived 741 immigrants; in 1719, 1,367 (and 450 slaves); in 1720, 2,576 (with 126 slaves); in 1721, 360 (with 868 slaves).[121] But ill-prepared for the rough life of the frontier, weakened by the crowded unsanitary conditions during the long crossing, most forced immigrants died from fevers, exhaustion, and privation. Some real demographic growth took place from the influx of voluntary immigrants, especially Alsatians, who came as concessionaires and *engagés*. An anonymous memoir of 1721 counts 119 concessionaires and 2,462 *engagés*.

Thus for the first time since its founding, Louisiana became more than an outpost and for the first time since 1701 colonial policy and foreign policy did not work at cross purposes. But these halcyon days did not last long. Conflicts between French and English settlers simmered on the New France frontier and on Louisiana's northeastern confines.[122] The Board of Trade, worried about the encirclement of English colonies, (all the more that it exaggerated the realities of the Mississippi establishment),[123] made South Carolina a crown colony to improve its defense.[124] The governor of Virginia clamored for forts to be built on the Great Lakes to cut off communication between Louisiana and Canada.[125] And finally, the War of the Austrian Succession (1740-1748; in America, King George's War) brought the tension into the open again, paving the way for the final confrontation of the Seven Years' War. The first Family Compact, in 1733, brought the two Bourbon monarchies in close alliance once more. Never again would the expansionist colonial policy adopted by Louis XIV after Utrecht be aligned with French policy in Europe. Colbert's compact colony policy had been definitely abandoned; in its stead France pursued a politics of compromise and half-hearted expansion, on one hand allowing its North American colonies to build their prosperity on contraband trade with the Spanish and English colonies, on the other hand negotiating alliances and treaties with no regard for colonial needs. The Peace of Aix-La-Chapelle, at the end of the War of the Austrian Succession which restored the status quo in America and left the causes of conflict intact was a prime example of this disregard. The establishment of Louisiana had embroiled France in an aggressive policy which might have been successful had the crown vigorously committed its resources to the development of an empire but which, pursued hesitantly, eventually led to the loss of Canada.

VI

Colonial Policy and Colonial Society

Colbert's colonial territorial policy may have been buried with him, but much of his social thought lingered, probably because, unlike his grand projections for chartered companies, it corresponded to social realities in the mother country and to deeply ingrained attitudes the settlers carried to the New World. But, like his policy, much of his social planning was designed by capable bureaucrats, including himself, who pored over voluminous reports but had no first-hand experience overseas. Consequently, ministerial intentions were sometimes at odds with colonial reality.

The social assumptions which shaped the thought of Richelieu and Colbert were that colonies should be extensions of the mother country, "New Frances," very much like old France, but improved. Thus the colonies were to have the same administrative institutions as continental provinces, be ministered by the same church, and develop the same social structure, with proper subordination of inferiors to their betters. These Frances which would flourish across the Atlantic would therefore closely resemble their continental model, except that they would blend into a harmonious, orderly whole, white settlers, converted Indians, and, in the case of Louisiana and the Indies, contented black laborers.

Of course, the scheme did not work out quite so neatly. Transposing European institutions wholesale to the frontier proved more difficult than the Paris bureaucrats ever dreamed. It was simple enough to order that the Customs of Paris be sole law in force in the colonies and to ban lawyers from their confines. On the other hand, the bipolar administrative system, governor and intendant, which functioned smoothly enough in France[1] broke down when torn from the social framework which sustained it in Europe. Theoretically, the governor, a high-ranking member of the *noblesse d'épée,* directed military affairs and personally represented the king (much as a French consul today represents the president of the Republic and therefore takes precedence over any official, save the ambassador). The intendant, drawn from the *noblesse de robe,* administered the finances and supervised the courts of law. The intendant's powers were meant to curtail, but not supplant, the governor's. In France where the governors enjoyed great social prestige because of their birth and wealth, the balance of power seems to have been maintained.[2] Moreover, Paris and Versailles were close enough to enable the minister to squash quickly any squabbles arising over jurisdiction. In New France, where all the governors except Lefebvre de la Barre were noblemen, the bipolar system generally worked, though occasionally, as in the case of Frontenac, the pretensions of the governors could lead to conflict.[3] But in Louisiana where except for one, Philippe de Rigault, marquis de Vaudreuil, the governors came from recent nobility such as the Le Moynes; bogus aristocracy, like Cadillac; plain middle class like Etienne Périer and Charles-Philippe Aubry; or minor provincial gentry, like Jean Michel de Lépinay, Louis Billouart de Kerlérec or Jean-Jacques Blaise d'Abbadie, the system broke down. The intendant (in Louisiana, *commissaire-ordonnateur*) did not feel outranked and challenged the governor's authority at every turn. The resulting divisions have led Charles O'Neill to comment that during the Crozat years "Louisiana was as healthy as any normal two-headed infant could be expected to be."[4] The instructions to governor and *ordonnateur* regularly commanded them to rule in harmony and regularly attempted to set out clearly the responsibilities to prevent encroachment.[5] But it was useless, and the dissensions continued into the administrations of the last governor, d'Abbadie and his *ordonnateur*, Denis-Nicolas Foucault.[6]

Similarly the theory envisioned that the spiritual needs of the New World would be exclusively ministered by the Roman Catholic church, in its Gallican form, of course. No heretics or Jews would be allowed to mar the harmony of the American colonies which would finally realize the ancient dream of "*un roi, une foi, une loi*."[7] The Huguenots gathered by Daniel Coxe to settle Carolana asked to be allowed in the newly established Mississippi colony. In Charleston, they explained, they faced a language barrier which meant either assimilation into anglophone society or a marginal existence at best. But Louis XIV replied indignantly that he had not driven those who confessed the *Religion Prétendue Reformée* from his kingdom to build them an empire in America.[8]

On the other hand, in the colonies as in France, a beautiful fiction made *de facto* toleration possible. As Gilbert and Sullivan's Lord High Executioner phrased it "When Your Majesty orders a thing done, it is as good as done." The king had ordered Protestants to convert, hence, since the royal word was law, there were no more heretics in France or in the colonies.[9] Similarly, there had been no Jews in France since Louis XIII had expelled them in 1615, though of course the Bordeaux Israelites in particular prospered into the twentieth century.[10] Though Louisiana, like other colonies, was closed to Protestants who were steadfastly refused admission when they requested it, a number of them in fact lived in the Mississippi colony. Charles O'Neill estimates their number at some ten percent of the population.[11] The official exclusion of dissenters has been much criticized, but in an age when nationalism had not yet replaced religion as a motivating force, the religious unity was considered essential for social cohesion. Just as the ultramontane Jesuits had been distrusted as tools of Spain, so the Protestants were feared as instruments of English designs as well as sources of domestic dissension.[12]

Moreover, the Catholic church was expected to help in establishing and maintaining social order with a proper subordination of the lower classes to their superiors. There was no notion of creating in the New World an egalitarian utopia. A few observers, tainted with the new "philosophic" ideas, might praise the independence of Indians vis-à-vis their chiefs, most Frenchmen saw in this absence of hierarchical degrees confirmation of the savages' barbaric nature.[13] "Degree," which Shakespeare said made society as harmonious as music, was greatly valued by the eighteenth-century French. It proved as easy to transfer social stratifications to the gulf shore as it proved difficult to transplant administrative organization: the colonists were not coming to create a brave new classless society, but to re-create their old world, with themselves as the privileged.

Marriages provide the most obvious example of the persistence of European attitudes. It has already been mentioned that as far back as La Salle's colony, officers had been forbidden to marry "beneath" their station. Joutel allowed a soldier to marry but refused the marquis de la Sablonnière permission to take a commoner wife.[14] Bienville was most irritated with the conductress of the *Pélican* girls, Marie Françoise de Boisrenaud de Roisneau who refused to marry, because she claimed there were no bachelors of compatible station in the colony. She remained adamant and even the authoritarian Canadian could not overcome the social taboo against *mésalliance*.[15] Another officer found himself stymied in his advancement because he had married Mandeville's half-breed illegitimate daughter.

The niceties of court etiquette had absorbed much of the emotional and intellectual energy at Versailles. The king himself would take time away from state affairs to decide fine points of precedence, such as who should pass the plate during Good Friday services. On the Louisiana frontier, in the wretched hut which served as a church, the same quarrels were repeated when the hapless Capuchin curate auctioned off his pews to the highest bidder thus dispossessing some ladies of their front seat in favor of base-born rivals.[16] The disputes over precedence may appear ridiculous in twentieth-century eyes, but Ancien Régime France was a society of "orders" in which rank and prestige, the highest accepted values, were inseparable from their outward manifestations.[17] Thus Louisiana colonists clung to their transplanted old France social values.

But the soil into which they were transplanted could not always sustain the social institutions which had thrived in the mother country. The attempt to implant a modified feudalism in Canada is a case in point. The large seigneuries granted along the St. Lawrence were not exploited as king and minister had hoped, and Louis XIV came to the conclusion that the Canadian seigneurial system was a failure.[18] He decided to grant concessions only in *roture*,[19] that is to make simple land grants.[20] By the time the Mississippi colony was established, the failure of the feudal experiment was so universally acknowledged that there was never a question of trying it in Louisiana.[21] Iberville's request for a "county" was promptly turned down as were later petitions for "marquisates" along the Mississippi.

Nowhere does the New France ideology break down more completely than in defining the role of the Indians in Louisiana society. By the time French explorers, missionaries, and settlers reached the Gulf of Mexico, there had developed in Canada attitudes which made implementation of the Colbertian vision impossible. The *Jesuit Relations* had set the general tone: they stressed the Indian's fierceness so as to elicit support and admiration for their heroic missionaries, but on the other hand, pointed out their *bon naturel* to avoid the conclusion that evangelizing the savages was doomed to failure and should be abandoned.[22] At the same time, French administrators learned to look at the Indians from a strictly utilitarian point of view, with the Indians acting as suppliers of furs and pelts and as allies containing English settlement.[23]

Missionaries also played a role. By Christianizing the Indians, encouraging them to settle in permanent villages, teaching them French (thereby making them into men), they were to transform barbarians into good, loyal subjects of his Most Christian Majesty, subjects who, like their metropolitan counterparts and their colonial brethren, the settlers, would harness their energy for the greater glory of the crown.[24]

The methods used were simple. Gaining the support of some tribes by flattery and generous presents, the skilled administrators used them against the English and their Indian allies. Louisiana officials who were often Canadian born and bred, would turn to the same techniques and their correspondence resounds with frequent and often desperate requests for Indian presents. There was one major difference, however, between New France and Louisiana. The great brandy controversy which divided New France had been generally settled by the time the gulf colony was established.[25] While in New France the missionaries and some officials tried to prevent traders from supplying liquor to the Indians, in Louisiana the missionaries were too few and too scattered to weigh much in policy making. Moreover, the religious fervor born out of the Catholic Reformation which suffused the activities of Jesuits and Recollets in Canada, had generally spent itself by the end of the seventeenth century. Lieutenant Louboey transmitted without qualms a request from the sieur Azur, commander of the Alibamon fort, who needed brandy, which is "at the heart of any negotiations with red men."[26] In Louisiana, the prevalent attitude was that of the administrator and the trader seeking political control and commercial advantage. Often the missionary's utterances could not be distinguished from the official's.

Maybe because most Louisiana documentation comes from official letters, memoirs, and orders, there is little philosophizing. Cornelius Jaenen enumerates a number of broad concepts which had helped shape French views of America and the Indian. He cites,"recurring world cycles, geographic and climatic determinism, colonial degeneration, and infinite perfectability of the gradual progress of mankind," all singularly absent from Louisiana documents.[27] Nor is there any suggestion of other themes Jaenen lists, such as a Millenial Kingdom where Indian mass conversion would prepare the Second Coming of Christ.[28] Neither was Louisiana ever seen in the light of an Infant World whose Indians were children of nature, wards to be cared for until they reached adulthood.

Other constructs discussed by Jaenen such as the Terrestrial Paradise, Utopianism, and the Golden Age, though encountered frequently in the Law propaganda, are not found in the accounts written in the colony. In Upper Louisiana, explorers were uniformly impressed by the great stretches of virgin prairies where the grass grew tall as a man, and they all commented on the abundance of game in the plains, fish in the rivers, fruits in the forests. Lower Louisiana, however, with its mosquito-infested marshes and swamps was seen in a different light. The relations of La Salle's voyage down the Mississippi all stress the scarcity of food; in 1699, Iberville, and his men survived solely on *sagamité*.[29] In 1726, Father Paul du Poisson found that the Mississippi presented "nothing beautiful, nothing exceptional, save itself; nothing mars it but the continuous forest on both sides, and the frightful solitude. . . ."[30]

In this anti-Paradise, one could not expect to find heroic figures out of the Golden Age. Père Marquette, who did not go beyond Upper Louisiana, spoke admiringly of the beauty, strength, and grace of the Illinois Indians.[31] Iberville described the Bayagoula men as "alert, well proportioned and agile," but of the women, he noted, "I have not seen any of them who are pretty."[32] The ugliness of Indian women, and their stench, would become a recurring theme in Louisiana relations.

The Louisiana Indian tended to be seen as libertine, perfidious, treacherous, cruel, and mercenary, all common Canadian views carried south by discoverers, officials, and settlers. Because natives served either as tools of European expansion, or as foils to European decadence, the same trait could be viewed in a totally different perspective depending on the observer. The sexual freedom observed among Indians, for example, is called infamous, lewd, lubricious by the missionaries who found the Louisiana Natchez particularly libertine. "Among them," comments Charlevoix, one of the more restrained critics, "a woman is not the less esteemed for being public."[33] The chief's eldest sister's son succeeds him, explains Father Le Petit, because knowing the wantoness of their women, they want to insure that the next leader will have some royal blood.[34] On the other hand, Lahontan and the friend of the Abbé de

Gallinée, praised Indian men for divorcing their wives when they wished a change and the wives for repudiating their husbands when they tired of them or found them faithless.[35] The Illinois, unlike the Natchez, drew universal praise for cutting off the noses of adulterous women, male jealousy being apparently a sign of advanced civilization.[36]

Similarly, the loose social and political organization of Indian nations was seen as a superiority over decadent Europeans or as a proof of backwardness depending on one's point of view. A forerunner of the *philosophes* such as Lahontan admired them for knowing neither "mine nor thine neither judges nor priests"[37] and praised them for refusing to "bend their knee before the demi-gods we worship under the fine name of State Minister."[38] The Louisiana accounts, seldom written from a philosophical point of view, reflected dismay at such egalitarian, anarchical society. The explorers breathed a sigh of relief when they reached the Taensa or the Natchez where "the chief has much authority . . . and exacts obedience . . ." Tonti and Membré report approvingly the respect Taensa chiefs receive from their subjects. "They command and the others obey," says the good father.[39] For soldiers and missionaries, social subordination was a *sine qua non* condition of civilization. It also made control by a handful of colonizers easier.

New France accounts had related, often in gory details, the refined torments the savages inflicted upon their prisoners. Indian cruelty was thus one of the intellectual categories that the Canadians brought into Lower Louisiana. The Louisiana tribes were considerably less fierce than the Sioux or the feared Iroquois. Some, like the Houmas, were actually so gentle that they not only coddled their prisoners but refused to kill even their chickens. "There are few villages in France with as many chickens and roosters as the Houmas," writes Father Gravier in 1700. "They never kill them and will not eat those their dogs kill. . . ."[40] Yet the Houmas' gentleness drew less attention than the Natchez and Choctaw's fierceness which corresponded better to the stereotype and to the propaganda needs. The systematic slow burning of prisoners practiced by those tribes is frequently described, often quite matter-of-factly. In fact, it becomes praiseworthy when the victims are enemies of the French.[41] After the Natchez uprising, Father Le Petit approvingly wrote his superior: "They had abandoned to the *Tchactas* three Negroes who had been most unruly, and who had taken the most active part in behalf of the *Natchez*. They have been burned alive with a degree of cruelty which has inspired all the Negroes with a new horror of the savages, but which will have a beneficial effect in securing the safety of the colony."[42]

Indian cruelty is often associated with revenge "which is their dominant passion" said the sieur de Belestre, a New France settler testifying in a brandy-trade hearing.[43] What some saw as vengeful spite, more experienced colonial officials recognized as a harsh but fair *lex talionis* which lay at the heart of the Indian sense of justice. "The justice I demanded for the Choctaw . . . for a man and woman of their nation murdered by two young creoles," wrote Bienville to the minister, "did us honor in the Indians' mind."[44] Similarly, the more successful French officials demanded justice when their nationals were murdered. Bienville nearly annihilated the Chitimacha when a party of their warriors killed the missionary Jean-François Buisson de St. Cosme on the banks of the Mississippi, and Bernard Diron d'Artaguiette boasted that he had refused to give the Choctaw their presents until they brought him the head of the Indian responsible for the death of a Frenchman. Governor Périer, inexperienced in Indian ways, compensated the warrior's parents, "against my sentiment," complained d'Artaguiette, and "against the law reciprocally acknowledged between us and the Indians."[45]

Similarly the officials with Canadian experience recognized present giving as a reciprocal exchange which represented more than simple mercenary greed, at least during the early contacts between Louisiana Indians and Europeans. Lamothe-Cadillac might write the minister that "one could never place any trust in these perfidious nations,"[46] but a man like La Salle who had long lived and traded among the Amerindians knew that presents were not bribes, but tokens of good faith. "Presents," he explained, "are so necessary in these occasions that if words are not accompanied by gifts and not related to them, they are considered as meaningless (*discours en l'air*)."[47] And the presents had to be symbolically relevant to the negociations.[48]

Far from being greedy, the Indians were originally recklessly generous: "It is customary for the Indians to respond by other presents worth at least as much as the first," says La Salle.[49] The Abbé de Gallinée's friend echoes the discoverer: "They make a point of giving more than they receive."[50] In early fur-trade days, French *voyageurs* took shameless advantage of the Indians' generosity, exchanging trinkets for priceless beaver pelts.[51]

As the tribes became aware of the traders' dishonesty, they began driving hard bargains, playing the English against the French. Not unnaturally, French officers concluded that their loyalty belonged to the one who gave them the most."[52] A memoir presented to the Council of Regency of 1716, expresses regret that, "in this New World where one might have hoped to find the simplicity and innocence of the early centuries, men behave as they do in the Old World: self-interest is the mainspring of action."[53] Missionaries also became convinced that Indian conversions were for sale. "They do not love us and find us of the same spirit as themselves, except when we are giving them something," wrote Father Le Petit.[54]

The Indian's casual tolerance of religious differences, which delighted the philosophically inclined, scandalized the religious. Gallinée's friend points out complacently that though firm in their own beliefs, the Indians think it "perfectly normal that other nations should believe otherwise."[55] To devout men this tolerance was culpable indifference. Recollets and Jesuits alike lamented the tepid religiosity of the Louisiana Indians. Father Gravier rejoiced at the gentleness and docility of the Houma, but after saying mass, was surprised at their lack of curiosity.[56] Frequently, baptized Indians differed from the pagan only by having "the name, a medal, and a rosary."[57] Membré found among the savages "a mind so brutal, so closed, and morals so corrupt and opposed to Christianity that much time will be needed to harvest any fruit."[58]

Indian tolerance and politeness could easily be misunderstood for acceptance. Native etiquette forbade contradicting a speaker, so that what was often mistaken for acquiescence was simply good manners. La Salle who viewed the Indians with cool realism noted that "they are quite indifferent to life after death and listen willingly to anything one wants to tell them about it, without, however, believing any of it, taking the same pleasure in hearing about it as we take in reading a novel. . . ."[59]

This lack of success, however, mattered but little, the Louisiana missionary being chiefly seen as an arm of secular colonization. In the New World, the French had always used evangelization as a means of penetration and control. In Louisiana, the missionaries accepted that role, sometimes with unconscious cynicism. Father Nicolas-Ignace de Beaubois wrote a significant memoir: "The Indians respect a missionary and listen to him," he stated, "and even should he not succeed in converting them, he does at least win their allegiance to the French."[60] As the good father pointed out, Louisiana was a vast territory, sparsely settled and garrisoned, where the Indians could "be attached to the French side by no bonds stronger than those of religion."[61] Even Pierre F. X. de Charlevoix, a Jesuit of impeccable rectitude and religious devotion, accepted to subordinate religion to secular aims: "The salvation of these tribes was always the main object which our kings kept in view before all else, wherever they extended their dominion in the New World," he said, but, he added in the next breath, "the experience of nearly two centuries has taught us that the surest means of binding the natives of the country to us, was to gain them to Christ."[62]

With missionaries so thoroughly gained to the colonizer's perspective, one could not expect settlers to distinguish themselves by their generosity and understanding. Faucon-Dumanoir, a large concessionaire, poured out his anger in a venomous *Requête* addressed to the Council in May 1723. He detailed the misdeeds of the Indians who had harassed settlers, their slaves, and their cattle. The War Council called by Bienville later in the same year concluded that "the French caused the trouble . . . by their ill-treatment of the natives which went so far as having them beaten and put in irons upon a simple refusal."[63] But Faucon-

Dumanoir blamed the weakness of the Council who concerned itself with rendering justice to the Indians instead of avenging French blood spilled by the savages. Before peace was made, "as far back as they saw us, they got out of the way to let us pass. Now, since that fatal peace, they look at us threateningly and no longer yield us the right of way." Indians could only be controlled by a display of force, and the arrest and imprisonment of the chiefs and their retinue was imperative. Obviously convinced, as other frontiersmen, that the only good Indian was a dead Indian, Faucon-Dumanoir dreamed of a *Pax Romana* where French colonists would "enjoy a happy tranquility," the Indians having received "the just punishment due their crimes."

The Louisiana Indian, then, was seldom observed with disinterested curiosity. Discoverers and officials looked upon the Indians as weapons in the Anglo-French struggle; colonists saw them as obstacles to settlement; and missionaries, discouraged by the natives' tepid responses, accepted to serve French aims rather than religious ends. It was not in Louisiana that Colbert's great half-breed society would see the light of day. "The experience of two centuries," as Charlevoix called it, had taught the good fathers that the dream of a Franco-Amerindian society made up of European settlers and converted natives had been scuttled by the Indians' rejection of French mores and constraints, by the adventurers' enthusiastic embracing of Indian independence, and by the races' distrust and contempt toward each other.

The Louisiana missionaries did work, without conviction, to convert the Indians, and they did perform a few of those mixed marriages on which earlier French administrators had founded great hopes. But mixed unions produced the same result in Louisiana as in New France. The native women did not accept western civilization; instead their European husbands adopted the Indian lifestyle. Consequently, unions with Indian women, whether legitimate marriages or concubinage, came to be seen as a major impediment to colonial progress. "We must bring back all the Frenchmen who are among the Indians and forbid them to live there as libertines simply because they have wives among them," complained Bienville in 1706, protesting against the missionaries who performed marriages between Frenchmen and Indian girls.[64] Du Clos, *commissaire-ordonnateur* from 1712 to 1717, pointed out that Indian marriages would not help populate the colony, quite the contrary, because the women preferred the dissolute life they led in their villages where they could change husbands at will and because they often left their French husbands to go back to their people. Moreover, the only Frenchmen willing to marry Indians were those who preferred to live like Indians.[65]

Indian marriages had proved such a disaster, from the administrators' point of view, that the prevention of these unions was one of the most frequently enunciated reasons for wanting Frenchwomen. Unless French girls are sent, "It will be difficult to prevent concubinage," writes one official. "The Indian women are easy, the air is stimulating, and the men are young, mostly Canadians, that is to say, very vigorous."[66] Fond of the roving life and indifferent to creature comforts, the Indian women would not, either as wife or concubine, tie down a backwoodsman.

Finally, the Council of Marine forbade these unions[67] though they continued to take place; in 1729 Périer still chaffed at the clergy for celebrating them.[68] But the number, as in Canada, remained small and they never bore the fruits Richelieu and Colbert envisioned.

With the colonists so scarce, *engagés* so unfrequent, and Indians so refractory to work and settled living, the French turned to Negro slavery to provide Louisiana with a laborious class, indispensable base of a well-ordered society. The first slaves were imported in 1719[69] and by 1724 had become numerous enough to warrant legislation.

The Louisiana Black Code, closely patterned after the one issued in 1685 for the West Indies, reflects the French monarchy's preoccupation with order, centralization, and unity, as well as its belief that the American colonies should pattern themselves after the mother country. Historians have viewed the Code as a proof of French humanitarianism or as an instrument of coercion designed to establish a "master race."[70] Colbert and his epigones in the Council of Marine who shaped French colonial policy after his demise would have marvelled at these judgements passed on what they considered practical bureaucratic measures, intended to protect property and to fit into an overall reorganization of French administration. It was, in fact, as its title indicates, a *police* measure, using "police" in the very precise meaning the seventeenth century attached to the term—"measures making work both possible and necessary for those who cannot survive without it."[71] The provisions of the Code followed well-established French precedents regulating vagabonds, beggars, apprentices, children and wives, in other words, members of the lower orders or persons unfit to act for themselves.

It is not surprising that the French monarchy should have had no qualms legislating about slavery. Stanley Elkins has pointed out that the Spaniards, unlike the English, had a tradition of slavery so that the African slaves who reached the Iberian peninsula in the fifteenth century found "a legal and social setting incredibly complex, thick with the experience of centuries, and peculiarly fitted to receive and absorb them."[72] To a lesser degree, this was true of the French. The Parlement of Bordeaux, in 1571, freed the slaves a Normandy trader was trying to sell in the city with the dictum: "France does not recognize slavery."[73] Legal commentators agreed that "France, the mother of liberty, knows not slavery." Yet, household slaves were sold and bought in southern France as late as the fifteenth century,[74] and until the Revocation of the Edict of

Nantes, French consuls in the Near East routinely purchased slaves for the Mediterranean galleys.[75] In the eighteenth century, serfdom persisted in French provinces such as Burgundy and Nivernais, and though the jurist Robert Pothier insisted that serfs who had a civil status and property rights could not be equated with slaves who enjoyed neither,[76] serfs and slaves had much in common.

The French, moreover, acquired a certain experience in Canada where Indian slavery, though never very important numerically, maintained itself throughout the French regime.[77] The crown, which had quite early participated in the African slave trade, had little qualms about accepting the institution and legislating about it, though its legislation embodied pre-existing ambiguities.

Louis XIII, the only French king to have had moral doubts about the institution, had finally consented to the introduction of Negro slavery in the colonies, and to the participation of the French in the slave trade, when Richelieu convinced him the West Indies would never be viable otherwise.[78] And he salved his royal conscience by convincing himself that enslaving Africans would promote Christianization. From the first the institution was therefore linked to religion, and the ambiguity Frank Tannenbaum describes in the Hispanic colonies prevailed also in the French.[79] There also, "the slave had a right to become a Christian, to be baptized, and to be considered a member of the Christian community," so that underlying the real life rapport there remained in the background the fact that slaves and masters had to "recognize their relationship to each other as moral human beings and as brothers in Christ."[80] Thus, the Black Code does not define the slave as chattel; the black bondsman is certainly recognized as a human being who is not to be killed at will and who is not to be subjected to "barbarous and inhuman treatment."[81] Yet, he is defined as "moveable property," and he is denied the right to own property, to hold public office, to testify at criminal trials except in extreme cases, and to be a party in civil matters, to bear arms, or to marry as he pleased.

Of the rights which were denied Negroes, however, only the right to hold property would have been considered a basic, unalienable human right in eighteenth-century France. Even that right was limited in the case of foreigners residing in France who enjoyed property rights during their life, but whose property was forfeited to the crown when they died. Civil functions and public offices are "reserved to men and forbidden to women," writes Pothier,[82] and though women could, in French law, sue and be sued, they could not witness legal documents because, explains the same learned source, "of the solemnity expected from such witnesses."[83] Beggars and vagabonds were forbidden to carry weapons and heavy sticks, just like slaves, with savage penalties provided for offenders.[84] And though it is true that a slave could not marry without his master's consent, neither could the master's children. The difference, was, however, that while sons over thirty and daughters over twenty-five were still bound to request "respectfully" their parents' consent, they could marry without obtaining it.[85] The slave needed it whatever his age.

The power of masters over slaves greatly resembled that of French fathers over minor children: parental power, wrote Pothier, consisted of the right to control the person and property of the children. It included the right of "moderate correction" extending to the authority to have them imprisoned. The power of masters over slaves also resembled that of husbands over wives: "The husband's power over the person of his wife," explains Pothier, "consists, by natural law, of the right the husband has to demand from her all the duties of submission which are owed a superior."[86]

In the same vein, the Code admonished administrators of estates "to govern the said slaves as good fathers of family,"[87] a duty which entailed "moderate correction," as Vaudreuil was to remind slave owners in his 1751 ordinance. The king intended, pointed out the governor, that each master should chastise "his slaves as a good father of family" but since most of them were remiss in their duty, officials might be obliged to usurp the quasi-parental rights of owners and order severe punishment for the over-indulged "children."[88]

The paternalism which permeates the master-slave relationship set up by the Black Code (and one needs to remember Genovese's warning that paternalistic and kindly are not necessarily synonymous)[89] is nowhere more evident than in the provision which regulated the relationship of freedmen to their former owners. The freedman, says the Code, must show "singular respect" to his former master, his widow, and the children.[90] Similarly, parents under French law had the right to "demand of their children certain duties of respect and gratitude," a right which ended only with the death of the father or his children.[91]

The Black Code reflected the concerns of the French crown with absolutism and order. Kings and ministers were determined that the colonies should be subject directly to their authority. Thus it was that slave crimes, be they theft, murder, or maroonage, were to be judged and punished by royal judges and that masters were forbidden to administer judicial torture to their bondsmen or to mutilate them.[92] Beating with rods and ropes, which presumably came under the heading of moderate correction, was allowed. The concern was less to protect the slaves against arbitrary owners than to affirm royal prerogative over the masters.

The preoccupation with royal authority also underlies the prohibition of interracial marriages. The concern is certainly not the preservation of "racial purity."[93] Seventeenth-century France was not racist; its indifference to the color lines can be seen in Article LIV of the 1685 Code which extends to freedmen all the rights of native-born Frenchmen. Interracial marriages, though not numerous, occurred in France into the eighteenth century,[94] and the original

Black Code had authorized such unions. But, between 1685 and 1724, a series of colonial uprisings caused grave concern at Versailles. In 1680, on Bourbon Island, the settlers imprisoned the governor for five years and assumed power. In 1717, Martinique rose against royal officials and talked independence and republic. From 1720 to 1722, Saint-Domingue was in constant turmoil, actually expelling the royal governor.[95] Faced with rebellious colonists, the home government began to fear that freedmen and white settlers should ally to seek independence. An edict of 1731 elaborated that it was "of utmost consequence" to prevent black-white marriages, because, "besides being a stain upon the whites, such unions risk attaching them too much to the interest of their allies."[96] The 1766 instructions sent a new governor of Saint-Domingue were even more explicit: "If by means of such marriages the whites and freedmen came to an agreement, the colony might easily escape royal authority."[97] Hence, in 1724, after the flurry of uprisings, the crown issued an edict forbidding interracial marriage which was not obeyed, but the provisions of which were incorporated into the Louisiana Black Code.[98] Indications are that the prohibition was also violated in Louisiana, at least occasionally.[99]

At the same time, in the early years of the eighteenth century, a certain racism developed in France, with many Enlightenment thinkers clamoring on one hand for the abolition of slavery, while proclaiming the inferiority of the black race on the other. No one would tax Colbert with sentimentality or compassion. The protections which were incorporated in the Code simply aimed at preserving an expensive investment: the crown, after all, paid a bounty for each slave brought into the colonies. Brutal and cruel masters damaged valuable property, which was wasteful, and endangered an institution which, by 1685, was considered indispensable for the development of tropical colonies. The monarchy had to be protected against the shortsightedness and selfishness of its subjects. As Deschamps phrases it, Colbert legislated out of foresight, not concern for human dignity nor feelings of compassion.[100]

Thrift also presided over the drafting of the article which commands a master to feed and care for old and sick slaves: the crown was protecting its purse. The fear of "useless mouths" which the king may have to feed is a recurring obsession in official French correspondence of the seventeenth and eighteenth centuries and permeates the innumerable decrees concerning vagabonds and beggars. The same concern in part informs the requirement that a master should obtain the consent of the Superior Council before freeing a slave. The dread of freedmen-white alliances against the crown is present of course, but so is the fear that mercenary masters would manumit superannuated slaves to avoid feeding them.[101]

How valuable a property slaves were and the care with which that property was protected is obvious in the penalties inflicted for slave crime. The death penalty was imposed for striking a master or his family, for inflicting bodily harm to free persons, and for major thefts. But it was also the punishment meted out to convicts who struck their guards.[102] Minor slave crime such as petty theft was to be punished by flogging and branding with a fleur-de-lys. It is no wonder that Lord Brougham, writing in early nineteenth-century England where juveniles were hanged for stealing a handkerchief, called the Code's provisions "extremely mild."[103] A slave would be flogged for stealing "sheep, goats, pigs, poultry, grain, peas, beans . . ." but a Frenchman convicted of the same offense would have been sent to the galleys. Vaudreuil's 1751 ordinance provides that a slave who sold goods without his master's written permission would be jailed for eight days; the Frenchman who purchased the goods from him would be sent to the galleys for life if he repeated the offense.[104]

The Code enumerates without qualm what would qualify today as "cruel and unusual" punishments—flogging, branding, ear cropping, hamstringing—but eighteenth-century French justice resorted to penalties such as burning at the stake, breaking on the wheel, as well as drawing and quartering; and military criminals in Louisiana had their heads crushed between two stones. The eighteenth century was cruel, brutal, callous in its treatment of the poor, the helpless, vagabonds, beggars, and slaves. Rather than reflecting the development of a racist society, the Black Code reflects the transfer of European patterns to the New World, another effort at creating New Frances across the ocean. However, here again, the legislation so carefully drafted by the home bureaucrats got a mixed reception in the colonies. As Carl Brasseaux has pointed out, "provisions deemed conducive to the efficient management of slaves were obeyed, while articles viewed as unnecessarily restrictive or impractical were ignored." In other words, only as much of the law was enforced as was compatible with colonial realities.[105]

On the other hand, the task of reestablishing French society suited very well the deeply ingrained attitudes settlers brought to the colony, and the women, in particular, seconded the government admirably in this effort. Requests for female settlers had come early. As soon as Iberville established a colony in 1699, he clamored for women (and slaves). On July 2, 1701, he wrote the minister: "If you want to make something of this country, it is absolutely necessary to send this year some families and a few girls . . . who will be married off shortly after their arrival." Memoir after memoir in 1701, 1702, 1703 reiterate the request for wives, preferably pretty, for the Canadians. A shipload of women, sent to the colony on the *Pélican* in 1704, eased the pressure somewhat, but the clamor resumed in 1709 when the Canadians discharged by Bienville, requested "about forty girls as wives."[106] It was to continue unabated until the Company of the Indies sent to the colony women of all sorts, from hardened "blasphemers" to demure "casket girls."

The colonial administrators' reports make very clear why the women were wanted: to populate the colony, of course, but also to tie down the footloose *coureurs de bois* and other adventurers, more addicted to trade and exploration than to agricultural and pastoral pursuits. "The young men need wives," *Commissaire-ordonnateur* d'Artaguiette claimed in 1710: "I know only this way to hold them." And he insisted on "the necessity of girls to pull in the backwoodsmen."[107] A 1709 memoir even more frankly suggested that wives would force the men to work in order to maintain the family social status: "Once married," it stated, "they should work to support their families in mutual rivalry."[108]

Crown and companies complied with the request and women came, some willingly, others in chains, but most seem to have reacted with shock at the hardships and poverty which they encountered in the promised land. Though they have received the most attention, the forced women immigrants were by far the least significant. In the journal he kept during the stormy Regency years, Jean Buvat gave a picturesque, albeit grossly exaggerated, depiction of the deported women. He speaks of 500 sent in August 1719; 180 in September; thirty cartfuls in October; 300 more individuals in November. In March 1720, just before an edict ordered the end of forced immigration, Buvat depicted 600 forced immigrants of both sexes on the road to La Rochelle.[109] His figures accurately reflect the rumors which were flying widely and wildly around France during the Mississippi experiment. But in fact, Professor Giraud's study of passenger lists reveals only about 160 women transported to Louisiana.[110] These women, ranging in age from 13 to 38, contributed little to the colony. Thieves, prostitutes, and assassins (one of them was accused of fifteen murders), they were parasites, accustomed to drawing sustenance from a reasonably thriving social body. Exhausted by long journeys and malnutrition, often in advanced stages of venereal disease, they died off rapidly, proving that toughness and endurance are not necessarily synonymous.

Female *engagées* played only a minor role. In the English colonies, young unmarried women went as indentured servants and remained to become wives and to found families. But the Louisiana passenger lists reveal very few female *engagées*; in 1720, for example, only seven crossed on the *Loire.* The number was probably slightly larger, since when both spouses were *engagés,* the wife was simply listed alongside her husband, without specifying her function.

The small number of female *engagées* is hardly surprising when one considers the contracts they were offered. Giraud has studied the engagement contracts in the Archives du Morbihan and found very few where women were paid wages; usually they could expect nothing more than maintenance during their term of service. One particularly exploitative contract granted a midwife the permission to practice her profession, but she had to give her master two-thirds of her earnings. It is little wonder that female *engagées* remained few.[111]

A more significant contribution to the colony and its nascent society was made by officials' wives and by the *épouseuses,* the marriageable girls. The wives constituted a small group, but quite influential. The wives of governors, such as Mme Cadillac and Mme Périer; of *ordonnateurs,* such as Mme de la Salle; of officers, such as Mme de Mandeville; or of notable *habitants* such as Mme Trudeau or Mme Trépagnier would play a major role in developing a "creole" society. The *épouseuses* came in three waves, if one can use so strong a word for so modest a group. The first group arrived in 1704. Carefully selected by Monsignor Saint-Vallier, the bishop of Quebec, the twenty-two girls who had crossed on the *Pélican* were warmly received. A few died shortly after arrival, but the others were promptly married.[112] The 1699 and 1700 censuses had been all male; the 1706 census, on the other hand, lists only two bachelors, and one of them a mere "boy." Instead, there are numerous families, some already with one child.[113]

The next group of *épouseuses,* which would not reach the colony until 1713, was less successful. Twelve girls crossed with Cadillac and his wife on the *Baron de la Fauche,* but improperly supervised by Mme Cadillac, who spent more time quarreling with the officers than watching her wards, the young ladies landed in Louisiana with sadly besmirched reputations. The Sieur de Richebourg, a colonial captain who crossed on the same ship, a man said to have married two women at the same time and debauched another, seduced some of the girls (some reports say all twelve), as well as Mme Cadillac's maid. The worse of it, however, was that the poor girls were so unprepossessing, "*si laides et mal faittes,*" that after taking one look, the colonial bachelors returned to the woods, declaring that all things considered, they preferred Indians. Du Clos, the *ordonnateur* who reports this fiasco, suggests that in the future it would behoove recruiters to "seek looks rather than virtue," for, he says, the Canadians "who are all well-built men" are not too "particular" about the girls' behavior before marriage.[114]

The last marriageable girls shipped to Louisiana were the celebrated "casket girls" who in July 1720 sailed from Nantes on the *Baleine.* (A few had already gone by two other ships.) These girls were supposed to have been carefully selected among the orphans of the Hôpital Général. Fourteen to fifteen years old, they were given two *"conductrices"* and one "matron" to supervise their conduct.[115] Eighty-eight girls thus reached the colony in January 1721.[116] Bachelors were allowed to come by and make their selection. At night, the girls' living quarters were tightly sealed off. Dumont de Montigny relates that they were soon married, and that two over-eager swains nearly fought a duel over the last one even though that "Helen" looked more like "a guardsman" than "a girl."[117]

Actually, Bienville reported some problems in getting them husbands. Only nineteen were married easily, another thirty-one unions being concluded at a later date.[118] It seems that despite the care supposedly exercised in choosing the girls, the selection had been somewhat slovenly so that a young officer writing Father Bobé complained in 1727: "Officers and those who hold any land cannot make up their minds to marry such girls who in addition to the bad reputation that they bring from France, give reason to fear that some also bring remnants of infirmities of which they have been imperfectly healed."[119]

The women who came to Louisiana, whether forced or lured, were given expectations that reality would dispell brutally. Already the *Pélican* girls of 1704 had been told by the bishop of Quebec that the country was "well provisioned" when in fact the poor ladies arrived in time to participate in Louisiana's "starving times." For the casket girls, who undoubtedly had heard some of the propaganda that Law's agents were tirelessly spreading in Paris, the shock of reality must have been devastating. What the girls found, in fact, was a colony ever on the verge of stavation. The scarcity of meat, a recurring complaint in letters and reports, continued well into the nineteenth century. It was so acute in the colonial period that until the 1740s settlers were forbidden to slaughter their own cattle under pain of corporal punishment. Wheat flour was scarce and expensive, when not totally absent. Even corn was often in short supply. The only vegetables mentioned with any kind of regularity, peas and beans, must have become awfully monotonous. Milk and butter were not to be had, unless obtained from the German farmers, and for cooking and salad dressing, the women were reduced to using bear oil.

Yet, some of the women made it. Many died, of course. Hunger, malnutrition, disease got to them. The "friendly" Indians finished off a few more, particularly in 1729 during the Natchez uprising. But, they tried to adapt, and, wherever possible, to reestablish the French ways to which they were accustomed. Of the few forced immigrants who survived the first year, many, inevitably, went back to their dissolute ways. Others were forced into "libertinism" for lack of other resources. The letters and reports abound with complaints, both generalized and individual, about the immorality of the colony. "On Dauphin Island, there is a married woman who gives herself to everybody,"[120] complained Cadillac. Périer comments, "There are many women and girls of bad life here."[121] Father Raphaël found "a frightful indifference for the sacraments," and horrifying acceptance of "public concubinage."[122]

And it must be recognized that women who survived the first shock exhibited an extraordinary will to live, and to live civilly. For, as soon as they had gathered a gaggle of "ladies," they set about reconstructing French life. Far from the Paris salons, they re-created society. "From now on, life will be most unpleasant in Mobile," wrote one young engineer to another. Madame de

Mandeville, who was the "ornament of Mobile society," was moving to New Orleans.[123] The same young man relates the sad adventure of Mme Olivier, who in proper eighteenth-century style decided to visit friends in Pensacola, in Spanish territory. Mme Olivier and her party were imprisoned, their belongings were burnt before their eyes, and what should have been an elegant rococo outing turned into a nightmare.[124] Yet, the ladies persevered, and held on to their home country social stratification.[125] When the Capuchin Fathers auctioned off the new pews in the parish church, there was a storm of female protest about the seating. The controversy over the church seating which echoes through the letters of governors, *ordonnateurs,* and missionaries reminds one of the intricate court intrigues reported in Saint Simon's *Memoires*: can a "*président à mortier*" of the Paris *Parlement* remain covered in the presence of a "*duc et pair*"? It is at the same time outrageously ridiculous and extremely touching, to see the ladies (and their husbands) trying to maintain the pecking order, the *préséances,* which, to them, was civilization.

The growing influence of women, and the resulting stabilization of the population, were offset—from the crown's point of view—by the females' failure to populate the colony. The censuses of 1721 to 1731-1732 reveal a rather surprising distribution of children. In 1721, for the whole of Lower Louisiana, there were 53 childless families, 27 with one child, 7 with two, none with three, and 9 with more than three. In 1724, along the German Coast where one would expect high fertility, one finds 27 childless families, 37 with one child, 20 with two, 9 with three, and 5 with more than three (and the numbers, among the Germans, included quite a few adopted orphans or minor in-laws living in the household).[126] The census of January 1, 1726, gives 188 childless families, 145 with one child, 101 with two children, 39 with three, and 28 with four or more.[127] In 1727, there were 82 childless families, 125 with one child, 79 with two, 24 with three, 11 with four, and 3 with five. When at the same time, one studies the burial lists of Mobile, New Orleans, and Biloxi for the same years, in which infant burials are quite rare, the conclusion is inescapable: the women in Lower Louisiana were not bearing children, at least not in large numbers.

A reversal appears in the 1731-1732 census, which shows 91 childless families, but also 76 families with 1 child, 77 with 2, 65 with 3, 25 with 4, 21 with 5, one with 6, and one with 7. There was still, however, a scarcity of women: 159 men were without wives, yet there were not more than 20 unattached women in the colony.[128]

The ladies, then, were ultimately more successful at civilizing the colony than at populating it. By the 1740s, these frontier women had forged a viable society in a wilderness environment. During the initial years of the colony's settlement, women worked to transplant to the new milieu home institutions which improved the less tangible aspects of life. Parties, visits, squabbles over status, while frivolous, served a basic human need. Meanwhile men dominated the struggle to secure a psychologically and emotionally satisfyinjg organization despite famine, disease, Indian attacks, and neglect from the mother country.

Thus in Louisiana, the New France ideal failed where the theories elaborated at Versailles contravened colonial reality, and succeeded where, through some trick of chance, they fitted the frontier experience. Unifying the law code was simple enough, but transferring the bipolar administrative system produced irresolution, inefficiency, and inaction. The hope of creating a great society blending settlers and Indians into a Gallic whole had overlooked the natives' attachment to their mores. Cultural relativism would not dawn in European consciousness until the second half of the eighteenth century, and Richelieu, Colbert, Pontchartrain, as well as the king, assumed, in all innocence, the superiority of European culture in general, of French civilization in particular. The settlers' social outlook, however, formed in the hierarchical framework of the Ancien Régime, favored transferring to the new country the stratification of the old. Thus, they had some measure of success in maintaining *préséances*, and recreating Old-World social intercourse. Even there, the success was limited by the poverty of the colony, the indifferent birth of most settlers, and the dearth of laborers. For a while, Negro slavery worked as a solution, the bondsmen becoming a sort of black peasantry, regulated according to the same principles as the lower orders in France. The fear of slave uprisings and the spread of the plantation system eventually ended even this limited successs, though in Louisiana some of the Code provisions lingered and tempered somewhat the harshness of the institution. The most enduring legacy of the New France ideal has been the persistence of the feudal ethos which suffused Ancien Régime society. Wealth did not purchase social position, as it does in a class society, but instead, prestige and rank were expected to bring one a fortune. This attitude, totally inimical to the spirit of capitalism, would persist into the nineteenth century and doom the French Creoles to disappearance as a political and economic elite.

Chapter VII

Conclusion

French colonial policy in the New World was first determined by her late entry in the race for empires. She had to forego the warm latitudes, preempted by Spaniards and Portuguese and thus found herself from the first in competition with England, also a late comer, also excluded from the southern regions. Francis I, who launched French explorations in America, also developed the earliest colonial policy. Lacking the resources for actual conquest, he argued that no European power could claim sovereignty over newly discovered land unless it established permanent settlement, gained the acceptance of the natives, and spread the Christian faith among them. But his limited colonial vision was dominated by the hope of finding precious metals. Once the mineral riches of Saguenay proved illusory, he abandoned colonization schemes and concentrated his attention on European hegemony.

For Richelieu, colonization was part of a general plan to increase *la gloire du roi.* His king was to be not only supreme in France, but also supreme in Europe, and that meant conflict with the Hapsburgs wherever their power extended, including the Indies. Richelieu needed a strong navy and merchant marine to insure control of the sea which, believed this early advocate of sea power, would insure control of the land. Colonies were therefore valuable because they would stimulate naval activities as well as provide raw materials for the nascent home industries. But more than anything, the colonies would increase *la gloire du roi* by multiplying the number of his subjects. Hence, he saw overseas territories as extensions of the homeland, New Frances, whose natives, Christianized and Gallicized, would become good subjects of his Most Christian Majesty.

From the first, French colonial policy was hampered by the diplomatic problems as well as domestic factors. It was always conceived as a facet, and only a facet, of foreign policy. Hegemony on the European continent remained the primary aim of French policies from Francis I to Louis XIV. Colonies were valued insofar as they served that purpose and were sacrificed, again and again, in the game of European power politics.

Colbert adopted Richelieu's policy, refining it to distinguish between settlement colonies and trading colonies, the first to be New Frances, the other simple counting houses. Colonies served his master plan for French self-sufficiency by providing raw materials not available in the home country: *La gloire du roi* needed to be backed by *la richesse du roi.* But Colbert's grand schemes foundered on the same reefs as Richelieu's: wars on the continent commandeered crown resources which would have been spent for colonial development, and the French monarchy, perennially short of money, entrusted the development of American territories to chartered companies. The French companies, however, were always undercapitalized because the French middle class preferred to invest in state offices which would one day enable them to enter the ranks of the nobility while the nobility invested in colonial ventures only under crown pressure. French society in the seventeenth and eighteenth centuries was still pervaded by a feudal ethos which prized rank and prestige over wealth and looked upon enterprise as demeaning. Besides, the Levant trade with its established patterns and quick turn around was more appealing than the as yet unproved Atlantic commerce. Moreover, the chartered companies sought profit, not development. French settlement colonies were successful only when the crown, as in New France, was willing to absorb the financial burden of providing colonists with administration and defense.

But the crown was not ready to divert large amounts of money from European involvement into American colonization. Colbert, therefore, insisted on a compact colony as easier and cheaper to defend. He tried to halt Canadian westward expansion, through colonial administrators, partly from the hope of great profit from the fur trade, partly from ambition, supported expansionist views. Some, like Frontenac and Cadillac, were given their way and thus committed the monarchy to an expansionism it was not willing to support adequately. The erection of Detroit and the founding of the Louisiana colony doomed Colbert's compact policy and, eventually, brought about the conflict which drove the French from North America. After the War of the Spanish Succession, Pontchartrain embraced expansionism and erected a line of forts which linked New France and Louisiana, made strategically indispensable by the adoption of this policy. But the English seaboard colonies, with their large populations and aggressive traders resented being contained on the east bank of the Mississippi. Any conflict would greatly endanger French control. Their limited resources were spread too thin, their lines of communication too long, their population too sparse to enable them to sustain long an English attack.

La Salle was allowed to explore Louisiana so as to provide a base for an attack on the Spanish borderlands. Iberville was allowed to found an establishment on the Gulf Coast so as to provide a buffer between the English and Spanish empire now that a Bourbon seemed likely to ascend the Spanish throne. In both cases, European power politics dictated colonial decisions. The founding of Louisiana exemplifies the French crown's undercommitment to overseas Frances. Having decided it needed to guard the entrance to the Mississippi, just as it needed a fortress to protect the mouth of the St. Lawrence, the French monarchy authorized a strategic outpost. It never intended to invest more in Louisiana than was strictly necessary to keep it out of English hands.

The ulltimate demise of the French empire in North America came from the discrepancies between the colonial policies formulated at Versailles, to fit in the overall scheme of French foreign policy, and the colonial practice followed by administrators who pounced on every loophole to promote their expansion schemes. The same discrepancy existed in social policies. The New France ideal professed by Richelieu and Colbert overlooked the realities of the terrain and the difficulty of transplanting institutions. The bipolar administration, which functioned fairly well in France, broke down in Louisiana where the social fabric was different. The dream of a half-breed, Gallicized, Christianized society made up of natives, French, and métis was dispelled by the realities of Indian culture and by the contempt that the settlers eventually developed toward natives. The bureaucrats tried to impose an abstract blueprint on concrete reality, but the society which developed, while profoundly marked by the European model, refused to fit the bureaucrats' mold. Yet it is within this context, that of the French colonial empire and of continental French social organization, that Louisiana must be viewed.

Notes

Chapter I

[1]Herbert Ingram Priestley, *France Overseas Through the Old Regime: A Study of European Expansion* (New York, 1939), pp. 146-157.

[2]Charles-André Julien, *Les Français en Amérique au XVIIe siècle* (Paris [1976]), pp. 1-2; Marcel Trudel, "Enfin les fleurs de lis, 1524," *Revue d'Histoire de l'Amérique Française*, XV (1962), 478.

[3]Arthur Girault, *Les Colonies françaises avant et depuis 1815* (Paris, 1943), p. 47.

[4]Introduction by Robert Lahaise and Marie Couturier to Jacques Cartier, *Voyages en Nouvelle-France* (Ville La Salle, 1977), p. 13.

[5]Frederick Charles Copleston, *A History of Philosophy*, 9 vols. (Westminister, Md., 1946-1975), III, pp. 350n, 352.

[6]Julien, *Les Français en Amérique*, pp. 4-6.

[7]Jean-Alexis Néret, *Capitaine Jacques Cartier* (Ottawa, 1949), p. 52. The imperial ambassador wrote Charles V ". . . he [Francis I] said that passing by and discovering with the eye was not taking possession." Quoted in R. J. Knecht, *Francis I* (Cambridge, 1982), p. 340.

[8]Gabriel Gravier, *Les Voyages de Giovanni Verrazano . . .* (Rouen, 1898), p. 18.

[9]Julien, *Les Français en Amérique*, p. 6.

[10]Lawrence C. Wroth, *The Voyages of Giovanni da Verrazzano, 1524-1528* (New Haven, 1970), pp. 82-83; Trudel, "Enfin les fleurs de lis, 1524," 507-508.

[11]Introduction, Cartier, *Voyages en Nouvelle-France*, pp. 15-22.

[12]Jean Jacquart, *François Ier* (Paris, 1981), p. 262.

[13]Quoted in Néret, *Capitaine Jacques Cartier*, p. 50.

[14]Gabriel Louis Jaray, *L'Empire français d'Amérique (1534-1803)* (Paris, 1938), p. 63.

[15]Vincent Confer, "French Colonial Ideas Before 1789," *French Historical Studies*, III (1964), 356.

On the failure of the first colonization scheme, see Jacques Lacoursière, "La Tentative de Colonisation (1541-1543)," in Fernand Braudel and Michel Mollat du Jourdin, eds., *Le Monde de Jacques Cartier* (Paris, 1984), pp. 273-283.

[16]A. W. Whitehead, *Gaspard de Coligny: Admiral of France*(London, 1904), pp. 315-316.

[17]Julien, *Les Français en Amérique*, p. 9; Henri Dubief, "Gaspard de Coligny et Walter Raleigh: Un grand dessein et son échec," *Bulletin de la Société d'Histoire du Protestantisme Français*, 128 (1982), 494; Jeanine Jacquemin, "La Colonisation protestante en Floride et la politique européenne au XVIe siècle," *Bulletin de la Sociéte de l'Histoire du Protestantisme Français* (Oct.-Dec., 1955), 181-208.

[18]Priestley, *France Overseas*, p. 47.

[19]Ivan Cloulas, *Catherine de Médicis* (Paris, 1984), pp. 216-217.

[20]See Maurice Bataillon, "L'Amiral et les 'nouveaux horizons' français," *Actes du Colloque l'Amiral de Coligny et son temps (Paris, 24-26 octobre 1972)* (Paris, 1974), pp. 41-52.

[21]Julien, *Les Français en Amérique*, p. 12.

[22]Franklin C. Palm, *The Economic Policies of Richelieu, University of Illinois Studies in the Social Sciences*, IX, no. 4, (1920; reprint ed., Urbana, Ill., 1970), p. 19.

[23]C. Turgeon, "Les Idées économiques de Sully," *Revue d'Histoire Economique et Sociale*, X (1922), 266. For a rather unflattering evaluation of Sully's economic policy, see George Bordonove, *Les Rois qui ont fait la France: Henri IV, Le Grand*(Paris, 1983), p. 259.

[24]Quoted in Turgeon, "Les Idées économiques," 266.

[25]Priestley, *France Overseas*, p. 58.

[26][Edme] Rameau de Saint-Père, *Une Colonie féodale en Amérique: L'Acadie (1604-1881)*, 2 vols. (Paris, 1889), I, 21-22.

[27]For a summary of Richelieu's colonial policy, see Gabriel Hanotaux, *Histoire du cardinal de Richelieu*, 6 vols. (Paris, 1932), IV, 548-599.

[28]Henri Denis, *Histoire de la pensée économique* (Paris, 1966), pp. 87, 89-92, 97.

[29]*The Political Testament of Cardinal Richelieu. The Significant Chapters and Supporting Selections*. Trans. by Henry Betram-Hill (Madison, Wis., 1961).

[30]G. R. R. Treasure, *Cardinal Richelieu and the Development of Absolutism* (New York, 1972).

[31]Franklin C. Palm, "Mercantilism as a Factor in Richelieu's Policy of National Interests," *Political*

Science Quarterly, XXXIX (1924), 664.

[32]*Ibid.*, p. 660.

[33]Palm, *The Economic Policies of Richelieu*, p. 174. See also Henri Hauser, *La Pensée et l'action économique du Cardinal Richelieu* (Paris, 1944).

[34]Michel Carmona, *Richelieu: L'ambition et le pouvoir* (Paris, 1983), p. 53.

[35]Gustav Schmoller, *The Mercantile System and Its Historical Significance* . . . (New York, 1931), p. 51.

[36]Palm, *The Economic Policies of Richelieu*, p. 18.

[37]Hauser, *La Pensée et l'action économique du Cardinal Richelieu*, p. 62.

[38]Henri Brunschwig, *La Colonisation française du Pacte colonial à l'Union française* (Paris, 1949), p. 9.

[39]*Ibid.*, pp. 9-11; Georges Hardy, *Histoire sociale de la colonisation française* (Paris, 1953), pp. 13-14.

[40]J. Saintoyant, *La Colonisation française sous l'ancien Régime, 2 vols (Paris, 1929)*,, I, 85-86; Henri Hauser, *La Pensée et l'action économiques du Cardinal de Richelieu* p. 41; Léon Deschamps, "Un colonisateur du temps de Richelieu. Isaac de Razilly,"*Revue de Géographie*, (1886), 273-284.

[41]Marcel Dubois, *Systèmes coloniaux et peuples colonisateurs. Dogmes et faits* (Paris, 1895), p. 259. Richelieu did not hesitate to use his charge as *grand maître* to increase his considerable wealth, but then the age saw no contradiction in devotion to the state and pursuit of one's interest and one family's ascension. See Joseph Bergin, *Cardinal Richelieu: Power and the Pursuit of Wealth* (New Haven, 1985), pp. 94-118.

[42]Saintoyant, *La Colonisation française*, pp. 85-87. For the importance that Richelieu attached to the navy, see L. A. Boiteux, *Richelieu: "Grand Maître de la navigation et du commerce de France"* (Paris, 1955). Michel Carmona, *Marie de Médicis* (Paris, 1981), p. 424.

[43]Quoted in Carmona, *Richelieu*, p. 461.

[44] Robert Boutruche, "Existe-t-il une continuité dans la politique coloniale de la France?," *Revue Historique*, CLXXII (1933), p. 263.

[45]*Ibid.*, p. 264.

[46]J. Saintoyant, "Des Politiques religieuses et indigènes des diverses colonisations européennes avant le XIXe siècle," *Revue d'Histoire des Colonies,* XXIII (1935), 299.

[47]R. Doucet, *Les Institutions de la France au XVIe siècle*, 2 vols. (Paris, 1948), I, 406-418.

[48]Roland Mousnier, *La Vénalité des offices sous Henri IV et Louis XIII* (Paris, 1971); G. Pagès, "Le Conseil du Roi et la vénalité des offices pendant les premières années du ministère Richelieu," *Revue Historique,* CLXXXII (1938), 245-282; J. H. M. Salmon, "Venality of Office and Popular Sedition in Seventeenth- Century France: A Review of a Controversy," *Past and Present,* No. 37 (1967), 21-43.

[49]R. B. Grassby, "Social Status and Commercial Enterprise Under Louis XIV," *Economic History Review,* XIII (1960), 23-25.

[50]George V. Taylor, "Noncapitalist Wealth and the Origin of the French Revolution," *American Historical Review,* LXXII (1967), 469-496; Guy Richard, "Un Aspect particulier de la politique économique et sociale de la monarchie au XVIIe siècle," *XVIIe Siècle,* XLIX (1960), 23-25.

[51]William J. Eccles, *Canada Under Louis XIV, 1663-1701* (Toronto, 1964), p. 57.

[52]Michel Carmona, *La France de Richelieu* (Paris, 1984), p. 99.

[53]Emile Salone, *La Colonisation de la Nouvelle-France: Etude sur les origines de la nation canadienne française* (Paris, [1906?]), p. 18.

[54]*Ibid.*

[55]Priestley, *France Overseas,* p. 60.

[56]David K. Fieldhouse, *The Colonial Empires: A Comparative Survey from the Eighteenth Century* (New York, 1971), p. 35.

[57]Joseph Chailley-Bert, *Les Compagnies de colonisation sous l'Ancien Régime* (1898; reprint ed., New York, 1968), pp. 7-18.

[58]Henri Blet, *Histoire de la colonisation française, 3 vols.* (Paris, 1946), I, 99.

[59]Kenneth M. Dunkley, "Trading Companies and Privilege in Richelieu's France: The Hundred Associates of Morbihan," *Proceedings of the Third Meeting of the French Colonial Historical Society, May 5-7, 1977* (Athens, Ga., 1978), p. 10.

[60]Blet, *Histoire de la colonisation française,* pp. 101-102.

[61]Henry Bertram Hill, "French Constitutionalism: Old Regime and Revolutionary," *Journal of Modern History,* XXI (1949), 233.

[62]Salone, *La Colonisation de la Nouvelle-France*, p. 30.

[63]Pierre Grillon, *Les Papiers de Richelieu. Section politique intérieure. Correspondance et papiers d'etats.* 8 vols. (Paris, 1975), I, 311.

[64]Salone, *La Colonisation de la Nouvelle-France*, pp. 40-41.

[65]Grillon, *Les Papiers de Richelieu*, I, 310. On the problem of dérogeance, see Etienne Dravasa, "Vivre noblement: Recherches sur la dérogeance de la noblesse du XIVe au XVIe siècle," *Revue Juridique et Economique du Sud-Ouest, Série Juridique,* XVI (1965), pp. 135-193; and Jacqueline Hecht, "Un Problème de la population active au XVIIIe siècle en France: La querelle de la noblesse commerçante," *Population,* XIX (1964), 267-290.

[66]Quoted in Hauser, *La Pensée et l'action économiques de Richelieu*, p. 66.

[67]*Ibid.*, p. 67.

[68]Pagès, "Le Conseil du Roi et la vénalité des offices," 281. That indifference to colonial trade would plague the early years of the Louisiana settlement. Marcel Giraud, "La France et la Louisiane au début du XVIIIe siècle," *Revue Historique*, CCIV (1950), 193-194.

[69]Kenneth M. Dunkley, "Trading Companies," p. 3.

[70]Grillon, *Les Papiers de Richelieu*, I, 324, 337.

[71]Quoted in Paul Leroy-Beaulieu, *De la colonisation chez les peuples modernes* (Paris, 1886), p. 155.

[72] Marcel Trudel, *The Beginnings of New France, 1524-1663* (Toronto, 1973), p. 171. Even Henry IV, usually hailed as the champion of religious tolerance, only lissued the Edict of Nantes because of the threats of his former coreligionists. See Janine Garrisson, *L'Edit de Nantes et sa révocation. Histoire d'une intolérance* (Paris, 1985), pp. 14-15.

[73]Saintoyant, "Des Politiques religieuses et indigènes," 286.

[74]*Ibid.*, 287.

[75]However, neither Richelieu nor his successors succeeded in excluding the Protestants completely from New France or, for that matter, the West Indies. See Cornelius J. Jaenen, "The Persistence of Protestant Presence in New France, 1541-1760," *Proceedings of the Second Meeting of the Western Society for French History, November 21-23, 1974* (1975), 29-40.

[76]See, for example, Alfred Martineau and Louis-Philippe May, *Trois siècles d'histoire antillaise: Martinique et Guadeloupe de 1635 à nos jours* (Paris, 1935), p. 8.

[77]Bernard Schnapper, "A Propos de la doctrine et de la politique coloniales de Richelieu," *Revue d'Histoire des Colonies,* XLI (1954), 314-315.

[78]*Ibid.*, 319-323.

[79]Hanotaux, *Histoire du Cardinal de Richelieu,* IV, 558.

[80]Chailley-Bert, *Les Compagnies de colonisation,* pp. 183-188.

[81]The Levantine trade, which had been dominated by Marseilles, was supported by a network of counting houses along the Eastern Mediterranean, the *échelles du fond du Levant* with a large staff of officials and commercial representatives. Near Algiers, the French occupied a stronghold, *Le Bastion,* which greatly facilitated trade. See Paul Masson, *Histoire du commerce français dans le Levant au XVIIIe siècle* (1896; reprint ed., New York, 1967), I, 139-184.

Chapter II

[1]On the revisionist side, see Pierre Goubert, "Le Tragique XVIIIe siècle," in Fernand Braudel and Ernest Labrousse, eds., *Histoire économique et sociale de la France,* 2 vols. (Paris, 1970), II, 351-359; and Daniel Dessert and Jean-Louis Journet, "Le lobby Colbert: un royaume ou une affaire de famille?," *Annales Economies, Sociétes, Civilisations,* XXX (1975), 1303-1336; and André Zysberg, "L'Irrésistible Ascension de Jean-Baptiste Colbert," *L'Histoire,* n° 60 (Oct., 1983), 34-42. Marcel Delafosse points out that the commerce of La Rochelle was already quite developed when Colbert created the Compagnie des Indes Occidentales, but acknowledges that the minister's actions contributed to the port's soaring economy. "La Rochelle et les Iles au XVIIe siècle," *Revue de l'Histoire des Colonies Françaises,* XXXVI (1921), 276. For his contributions to the navy, see Etienne Taillemite, "Colbert, legislateur de la Marine Royale," *La Nouvelle Revue Maritime,* n° 380 (1983), 44-70. The most recent summary of Colbert scholarship is found in Klaus Malettke, "Colbert devant les historiens (1683-1983)," in Roland Mousnier, ed., *Un Nouveau Colbert* (Paris, 1985), pp. 13-28.

[2]John C. Rule, "King and Minister: Louis XIV and Colbert de Torcy," in Ragnhild Hatton and J. S. Bromley, eds., *William III and Louis XIV, 1680-1720: Essays by and for Mark A. Thomson* (Toronto, 1968), pp. 213-236; and John C. Rule, "Louis XIV, Roi-Bureaucrate," in John C. Rule, ed., *Louis XIV and the Craft of Kingship* (Columbus, Ohio, 1969). An interesting aspect of the importance attached by Colbert and the king to colonies is treated by L. May in "Nicolas Fouquet et la politique coloniale de Louis XIV," *Revue d'Histoire des Colonies,* XXXIII (1940-1946), 70-83, in which he argues that the Surintendant's disgrace was brought about because he was about to gain a monopoly through chartered companies, of the colonial trade, especially in spices.

[3]Quoted in Monique Pelletier, "Des globes pour le Roi-Soleil: Les Origines des 'globes de Marly'," *Revue de la Bibliothèque Nationale,* I (Dec., 1981), 80.

[4]Louis XIV says in his *Mémoires* "The good of the state does not permit a king to take chances on the capricious sea." Quoted in Inès Murat, *Colbert* (Paris, 1980), p. 267.

[5]Pelletier, "Des globes," 80.

[6]Léon Deschamps, *Histoire de la question coloniale en France* (Paris, 1891), pp. 140-141. See also Paul Walden Bamford, *Forests and French Sea Power, 1660-1789* (Toronto, 1956), pp. 5-7.

[7]Joannès Tramond, *Manuel d'histoire maritime de la France des origines à 1815* (Paris, 1927), p. 338.

[8]Deschamps, *Histoire de la question coloniale,* p. 142.

[9]Charles Wolsey Cole, *Colbert and a Century of French Mercantilism,* 2 vols. (Morningside Heights, N.Y., 1939), I, 288-293; Jean Meyer's *Colbert* (Paris, 1981) illuminates the master-servant relationship which was that of king to minister. In Chapter V ("L'Intendant de Mazarin"), Meyer shows how once "given" to another employer by the original one, a "servant" transferred absolute devotion and loyalty. Meyer stresses repeatedly Louis XIV's determination to remind even his most trusted minister of the limitations of their power.

[10]William J. Eccles, *Frontenac: The Courtier Governor* (Toronto, 1968), pp. 1-2

[11]Jean Meyer, *La France moderne de 1515 à 1789* (Paris, 1985), pp. 310-312. See also François Lebrun, "Le Colbertism a-t-il existé?," *L'Histoire,* n° 60 (Oct., 1983), 52-54.

[12]Roland Mousnier, "Le Testament politique de Richelieu," *Revue Historique,* CCI (1949), 68-70.

[13]Georges Hardy, *Histoire sociale de la colonisation française,* p. 13.

[14]On the formative years, 1660-1664, see Philip P. Boucher, "Comment se forme un ministre colonial. L'Initiation de Colbert, 1651-1664," *Revue d'Histoire de l'Amérique Française,* XXXVII (1983), 431-452. On Colbert's careful engineering of Fouquet's trial and condemnation, see Daniel Dessert, "L'Affaire Fouquet," *L'Histoire,* n° 32 (March, 1981), 39-47.

[15]Tramond, *Manuel d'histoire maritime,* p. 346.

[16]Henri Pigeonneaux, "La Politique coloniale de Colbert," *Annales de Science Politique,* I (1886), 493. Colbert ordered the gathering of enormous documentation, but does not seem to have received answers as complete or as accurate as he wished. See Meyer, *Colbert,* pp. 220-231; Saintoyant, *La Colonisation française,* II, 427.

[17]Deschamps, *Histoire de la question coloniale,* p. 151.

[18]Marcel Dubois, *Systèmes coloniaux et peuples colonisateurs* (Paris, 1895), p. 265.

[19]*Ibid.*

[20]As late as 1779, *L'Encyclopédie* proclaimed that European colonies established after the discovery of America are established "only for the benefit of the mother country." [François-Victor] V. D. de F[orbonnais], "Colonies," *Encyclopédie* . . . , Ed. by Denis Diderot and Jean Le Rond d'Alembert, 36 vols. (Lausanne, 1778-1781), VIII, 521.

[21]Léon Vignols, "La Mise en valeur du Canada à l'époque française," *Revue d'Histoire Economique et Sociale*, XVI (1928), 720-793.

[22]Martineau et May, *Trois siècles d'histoire antillaise*, pp. 37-38.

[23]Schmoller, *The Mercantile System*, p. 47.

[24]*Ibid.*, p. 54.

[25]The edict on waters and forests was in parge part inspired by the naval needs for masts and ship timber. Bamford, *Forests and French Sea Power*, pp. 19ff.

[26]Schmoller, *The Mercantile System*, p. 47.

[27]Lionel Rothkrug, *Opposition to Louis XIV: The Political and Social Origins of the French Enlightenment* (Princeton, N. J., 1965), p. 88.,

[28]*Ibid.*, p. 95.

[29]Quoted in *ibid.*, p. 95.

[30]*Ibid.*, p. 109.

[31]*Ibid.*, p. 129.

[32]Pigeonneaux, "La Politique coloniale de Colbert," 494.

[33]Hardy, *Histoire sociale de la colonisation française*, p. 15. See also, Cornelius J. Jaenen, "La , Colbertisme," *Revue d'Histoire de l'Amérique française*, XVIII (1964), 64-84, 252-266.

[34]To Colbert de Terron, June 24, 1699, in Pierre Clément, *Lettres, instructions et mémoires de Colbert*, 3 vols. (Paris, 1861-1865), II, pt. 2, 473; see also, Stewart L. Mims, *Colbert's West Indian Policy* (1912; reprint ed., New York, 1977), pp. 225-229; Chailley-Bert, *Les Compagnies de colonisation*, p. 88. It should be noted, however, that Colbert was willing to expand freedom of trade to include foreigners when necessary; he, for example, encouraged trade between Acadia and New England because commerce between Acadia and Canada was expensive and difficult. Jean Daigle, "Nos Amis les ennemi : Relations commerciales de l'Acadie avec le Massachusetts, 1670-1711" (Ph. D. dissertation, University of Maine, 1975), p. 84; Allana G. Reid, "Intercolonial Trade during the French Regime," *Canadian Historical Review*, XXXII (1951), 241.

[35]Quoted in Deschamps, *Histoire de la question coloniale*, p. 161; see also orders to "majors and officials of oceanic ports," June 18, 1670, in Clément, *Lettres et instructions*, II, 529-530.

[36]Fieldhouse, *The Colonial Empires*, pp. 43-44. The pacte colonial was systematized by the letters patent of April 23, 1717 which excluded foreign traders and opened colonial trade equally to French merchants.

[37]Tramond, *Manuel d'histoire maritime*, pp. 338-339; Pigeonneaux, "La Politique coloniale de Colbert," p. 494. On the importance of the slave trade for the Atlantic ports, see Pierre H. Boulle, "Slave Trade, Commercial Organization, and Industrial Growth in Eighteenth-Century Nantes," *Revue Française d'Histoire d'Outre-Mer*, LIX (1972), pp. 70-112.

[38]Henri Sée, "Le Grand Commerce maritime et le système colonial dans leurs relations avec l'évolution du capitalisme du XVIe au XIXe siècles," *Revue de Synthèse Historique*, XXXIX (1925), 31.

[39]The revolts were endemic and often quite violent. Charles Frostin, *Les Révoltes blanches à Saint-Domingue aux XVIIe et XVIIIe siècles (Haïti avant 1789)* (Paris, 1975).

[40]Mathieu Varille, "La Politique coloniale de Law," *Revue du Lyonnais, Séries 5*, I (1921), 59.

[41]Eccles, *Canada Under Louis XIV*, p. 55; Rosario Bilodeau, "Liberté économique et politique des Canadiens sous le Régime français," *Revue d'Histoire de l'Amérique Française*, X (1956), 49-68.

[42]Paul-M. Bondois, "Colbert et la question du sucre. La Rivalité franco-hollandaise," *Revue d'Histoire Economique et Sociale*, X (1923), 12-61. On the metropolitan sugar lobby see, Paul-M. Bondois, "Les Centres sucriers français du XVIIIe siècle," *Revue d'Histoire Economique et Sociale*, XVI (1929), 27-76.

[43]Chailley-Bert, *Les Compagnies de colonisation*, p. 119; Vignols, "La Mise en valeur du Canada," 763-764.

[44]Henry Weber, *La Compagnie française des Indes (1604-1875)* (Paris, 1904), pp. 106-107.

[45]Letter to de Baas, May 23, 1671, Clément, *Lettres et instructions*, III, pt. 2, p. 522. See also, Jacques Petitjean-Roget, "Les Protestants à la Martinique sous l'Ancien Régime," *Revue d'Histoire des Colonies*, XLII (1955), 220-265; "Les Juifs à la Martinique sous l'Ancien Régime," *Revue d'Histoire des Colonies*, XLIII (1956), 138-158; Albert Cahen, "Les Juifs dans les colonies françaises aux XVIIe siècle," *Revue des Etudes Juives*, IV (1881), 127-145, 235-248; V (1882), 68-92, 258-272; "Les Juifs à la Martinique au XVIIe siècle," *Revue des Etudes Juives*, II (1879), 93-122.

[46]Deschamps, *Histoire de la question coloniale*, p. 145.

[47]Pigeonneaux, "La Politique coloniale de Colbert," 495.

[48]Xavier Yacono, *Histoire de la colonisation française* (Paris, 1969), p. 16.

[49]Chailley-Bert, *Les Compagnies de colonisation*, pp. 22-23; Cole, *Colbert and French Mercantilism,* II, 3; Varille, "Politique coloniale de Law," 61.

[50]The *livre tournois* was a money of account established in 1602. One *livre* was worth twenty *sols* or *sous*; the *sol* was worth a twelve *deniers*. In 1795, the *livre* was replaced by the *franc* which unlike the earlier money was actually minted. Jean Meyer estimates that the 1718 *livre* equals roughly 10 to 15 new francs, or between $1.50 and $2.00. (*Le Régent, 1674-1723* [Paris, 1985], p. 256.)

[51]Blet, *Histoire de la colonisation française,*, I, 122.

[52]Chailley-Bert, *Les Compagnies de colonisation,* p. 27.

[53]Cole, *Colbert and French Mercantilism,* I, 477. On Colbert's Dutch obsession, see Murat, *Colbert,* pp. 210ff.

[54]Chailley-Bert, *Les Compagnies de colonisation,* p. 27.

[55]Philippe Sagnac and A. de Saint-Leger, *Louis XIV (1661-1715)* (Paris, 1949), p. 82.

[56]Pierre Clément, *Histoire de Colbert et de son administration,* 2 vols. (1874; reprinted ed., Geneva, 1980), I, 338.

[57]Quoted in Cole, *Colbert and French Mercantilism,* I, 484.

[58]*Ibid.*, I, 496-497; Weber, *La Compagnie française,* p. 123.

[59]Cole, *Colbert and French Mercantilism*, I, 497.

[60]Chailley-Bert, *Les Compagnies de colonisation,* p. 71.

[61]Weber, *La Compagnie française,* , pp. 129-130.

[62]*Ibid.*, p. 129.

[63]Frédéric Mauro, *L'Expansion européenne (1600-1870)* (Paris, 1967), p. 127; Tramond, *Manuel d'histoire maritime*, pp. 183-184.

[64]Henri Hauser, "Les Caractères généraux de l'histoire économique de la France du milieu du XVIe siècle à la fin du XVIIIe," *Revue Historique,* CLXXIII (1934), 322. Pierre Boissonnade, "Colbert et la souscription aux actions de la Compagnie des Indes specialement en Poitou (1604-1668)," *Bulletin de la Société des Antiquaires de l'Ouest*, VII (1907-1909), 423-451.

[65]Cole, *Colbert and French Mercantilism,* , I, 499.

[66] *Ibid.*, p. 500.

[67] Chailley-Bert, *Les Compagnies de colonisation*, p. 62.

[68] *Ibid.*, p. 75.

[69] Weber, *La Compagnie française*, p. 129.

[70] Colbert tried to curb the sale of offices: by edicts in 1665, 1666, 1667, he bought back thousands of charges. But this effort was ended by the War with Holland. Murat, *Colbert*, pp. 157, 365. The damage done by the venality of offices had been recognized from the first. The Paulette had barely been established that the Estates General of 1614 clamoured for its abolition. At the cloture of the Estates, young Louis XIII solemnly promimsed to do away with the sale of offices. The Paulette was effectively abolished on December 5, 1614, but the expenses of the civil war between Louis and his mother forcedthe crown to reestablish it in February 1619. Carmona, *Marie de Medici*, pp. 279-280, 284, 381.

[71] See Grassby, "Social Status and Commercial Enterprise under Louis XIV," 19-38; Julian Dent, *Crisis in Finance: Crown, Financiers and Society in Seventeenth-Century France* (Newton Abbot, 1973).

[72] Eccles, *Canada Under Louis XIV*, p. 21.

[73] Dunkley, "Trading Companies," 3-15.

[74] The fiasco and its deleterious impact on French colonization efforts are treated fully by Philip Boucher, "A Colonial Company at the Time of the Fronde: The Compagnie de la Terre Ferme de l'Amérique ou France equinoxiale," *Terrae Incognitae*, XI (1979), 43-58.

[75] Clément, *Histoire de Colbert*, I, 51-52.

[76] Eccles, *Canada Under Louis XIV*, p. 21.

[77] Chailley-Bert, *Les Compagnies de colonisation*, pp. 98-99, 107, 108-111.

[78] Saintoyant, *La Colonisation française*, I, 97.

[79] Hardy, *Histoire sociale de la colonisation française*, p. 26.

[80] Pierre H. Boulle, "French Mercantilism: Commercial Companies and Colonial Profitability," in *Companies and Trade*, ed. by Leonard Blussé and Femme Gastra (Leiden, 1981), p. 105.

[81] *Ibid.*, p. 107.

[82]Webster, "Colbertism and Colonial Commerce," 30.

[83]Varille, "Politique coloniale de Law," 61.

[84]Mims, *Colbert's West Indian Policy,* pp. 153-154.

[85]*Ibid.*, pp. 235-236.

[86]Chailley-Bert, *Les Compagnies de colonisation,* p. 52; Mims, *Colbert's West Indian Policy,* p. 181.

[87]Fieldhouse, *The Colonial Empires,* pp. 37-38. In seventeenth century Canada, relations were often tense between governor and intendant, the worst being of course between Frontenac and Jean Bochart de Champigny. H. M. Thomas argues that "left to their own devices," the officials managed better than when closely supervised by Louis XIV's "efficient" bureaucracy ("The Relations of Governor and Intendant in the Old Regime," *Canadian Historical Review,* XVI (1935), 40.

[88]Eccles, *Canada Under Louis XIV,* p. 30. The power of the governors, whether in France or in the colonies remained very great, all the more that they enjoyed the enormous social prestige attached to nobililty. See Maurice Bordes," Les Intendants de Louis XIV," *Revue Historique,* CCXXIII (1960), 45-62; Roland Mousnier, "Notes sur les rapports entre les gouverneurs de provinces et les intendants dans la première moitié du XVIIIe siècle," *Revue Historique,* CCXXVIII (1962), 339-350.

[89]*Ibid.*

[90]Colbert to Frontenac, June 13, 1673, *Lettres de Colbert,* III, pt. 2, p. 559.

[91]Gustave Lanctot, "Un Parlement colonial au temps de Louis XIV (1647-1663)," *Revue d'Histoire des Colonies,* XLII (1955), 277-290. In 1665, Colbert changed the appelation of the French *Parlements* from "sovereign" courts to "superior" courts, an indication of his desire to keep them closely reined. Georges Bordonove, *Les Rois qui ont fait la France: Louis XIV, Roi-Soleil* (Paris, 1982), p. 139. In Canada also the "Sovereign" Council was demoted to a mere "Superior" Council in 1703. Guy Fregault, *Le XVIIIe Siècle canadien. Etudes* (Montreal, 1968), p. 181.

[92]Quoted in Georges Bordonove, *Les Rois qui ont fait la France: Louis XV, Le Bien-Aimé* (Paris, 1982), p. 257.

[93]Fieldhouse, *The Colonial Empires,* p. 39. See also, Jean Tarrade, "L'Administration coloniale en France à la fin de l'Ancien Régime: Projets de reforme," *Revue Historique,* CCXXIX (1963), 103-122.

[94]The intendant Bochart de Champigny recommended in 1700 that Canada be given a deliberative body with control over money matters, but nothing came of his project. Allana G. Reid, "Representative Assemblies in New France," *Canadian Historical Review,* XXVII (1946), 25-26.

[95]Eccles, in *Frontenac: The Courtier Governor*, relates in detail the governor's many abuses of power.

[96]To de Baas, governor of Martinique, July 3, 1670, in Clément*Lettres et instructions,* III, pt. 2, p. 489; to de Baas, April 9, 1670, *ibid.*, p. 477; Instruction to Talon, March 27, 1665, *ibid.*, pp. 389, 394, 395; to Frontenac, April 7, 1672, *ibid.*, p. 535.

[97]Eccles, *Canada Under Louis XIV,* p. 86.

[98]Pigeonneaux, "La Politique coloniale de Colbert," 503.

[99]Eccles, *Canada Under Louis XIV,* p. 79.

[100]Jean-Charles Falardeau, "La Paroisse canadienne-française au XVII, No. 7e siècle," reprint from *Cahiers de l'Ecole des Sciences Sociales, Politiques et Economiques de Laval* II (n.d.), 41.

[101]Sigmund Diamond, "An Experiment in 'Feudalism': French Canada in the Seventeenth Century," *William and Mary Quarterly,* 3rd series, XVIII (1961), 3.

[102]William F. Church, "The Decline of the French Jurists as Political Theorists, 1660-1789," *French Historical Studies,* V (1967), 4.

[103]Clément, in his introduction to the second volume of Colbert's *Lettres et instructions,* criticizes king and minister sharply for trying to impose upon the frontier laws developed for more settled conditions. The intent, however, was less to legislate from afar than to unify. (II, clxiv-clxv.) The *Coutume de Paris* had been introduced into the colony by the Compagnie des Cent Associés in 1640, along with the *Coutume de Normandie* and that of Vexin-Français. After 1664, the *Coutume de Paris* was sole law of the land. Yves F. Zoltvany, "Esquisse de la Coutume de Paris,"*Revue d'Histoire de l'Amérique Française*, XXV (1971,) 367.

[104]Eccles, *Canada Under Louis XIV,* p. 33; Jacques Mathieu, "La Vie à Québec au milieu du XVIIe siècle. Etude des sources," *Revue d'Histoire de l'Amérique Française,* XXIII (1969), 411, 422.

[105]André LaChance, *Le Bourreau au Canada sous le régime français* (Québec, 1966), pp. 43-44, 48.

[106]Peter N. Moogk, "Charles de Monseignat," *Dictionnaire biographique du Canada* (Toronto and Quebec, 1969), II, 505.

[107]Julien, *Les Français en Amérique,* p. 99.

[108]Marcel Trudel, *Les Débuts du régime seigneurial au Canada* (Montreal, 1974), p. 7.

[109]E. R. Adair, "The French Canadian Seigneurie," *Canadian Historical Review,* XXXV (1954), 194.

[110]Marcel Trudel, *Le Régime seigneurial* (Ottawa, 1971), p. 11; Jean-Pierre Wallot, "Le Régime seigneurial et son abolition au Canada," *Canadian Historical Review,* L (1969), 371.

[111]Trudel, *Les Débuts*, pp. 41-42.

[112]Louise Dechêne, "L'Evolution du régime seigneurial au Canada: Le Cas de Montreal aux XVIIe et XVIIIe siècles," *Recherches Sociographiques*, XII (1971), 163.

[113]Trudel, *Les Débuts*, p. 5.

[114]*Ibid.*, pp. 58-59.

[115]Adair, "The French Canadian Seigneurie," 193.

[116]Dechêne, "L'Evolution du régime seigneurial," 182.

[117]Marcel Trudel, "Les Débuts d'une société: Montreal, 1642-1663. Etude de certains comportements sociaux," *Revue d'Histoire de l'Amérique Française*, XXIII (1969), 205.

[118]Fernand Ouellet, "Liberé ou exploité! Le paysan québécois d'avant 1850," *Histoire Sociale/Social History*, XIII (1980), 346.

[119]Trudel, *Le Régime seigneurial*, pp. 12-15. Studying the seigneurial income for 1662, including *cens, rentes, lods et vente*, and others, Trudel found that 27 *seigneurs* received a total income of 2,889 *livres*, 7 *sols*, and 3 *deniers*. The highest income derived from feudal dues for that year, 375 *livres*, 8 *sols*, 10 *deniers*, went to the Jesuits; the lowest, 2 *livres*, 2 *deniers*, to the Hotel-Dieu of Quebec. Marcel Trudel, "Les Obligations du censitaire à l'époque des Cent-Associés," *Revue d'Histoire de l'Amérique Française*, XXVII (1973), 37-41; Pierre-Georges Roy, "Le Moulin banal dans la Nouvelle-France," *Le Bulletin des Recherches Historiques*, XLIX (1943), 3-9. Trudel cites several instances in which *seigneurs* are ordered to build a mill. In France the dues ranged from non-existent or very light in Lower Provence, Languedoc or Beauvais, to heavy in Brittany or Bourgogne. On the *corvée générale* for the building of royal roads, see Roland Sanfaçon, "La Construction du premier chemin Quebec-Montreal et le problème des corvee," *Revue d'Histoire de l'Amérique Française*, XII (1958), 3-29.

[120]Trudel, *Le Régime seigneurial*, p. 12.

[121]Cameron Nish, *Les Bourgeois gentilhommes de la Nouvelle France, 1729-1748* (Montreal, 1968), pp. 99-124.

[122]Dechêne, "L'Evolution du régime seigneurial," 172.

[123]Diamond, "An Experiment in 'Feudialism,'" 21.; Wallot, "Le Régime seigneurial," 373; Trudel, *Les Débuts*, 76-78, 237-253. Fernand Ouellet considerably tempers the traditional interpretation of New France society as idyllic, but admits that before 1763 the *censitaires* did not frequently express resentment of the *seigneurs*. He points out that they mostly resisted anything which drew manpower from farming, such as *corvées*. "Libéré ou exploité!," 348.

[124]Marcel Trudel, *La Civilisation de la Nouvelle France, 1713-1744* (Ottawa, 1969) points out that though poor the Canadians had "driven away the inhuman specter of destitution." (p. 92)

[125]Richard Colebrook Harris, *The Seigneurial System in Early Canada: A Geographical Study* (Madison, Wis., 1968), p. 192. A very different interpretation is given by Fernand Ouellet who surveys both French and English historiography pertaining to Canadian social history and concludes that the seigneurial regime and the military ethos united to create a "société d'ordres" dominated by the nobility and the clergy. For him, France succeeded in exporting its social organization. "La Formation d'une société dans la vallée du Saint-Laurent: D'une société sans classe à une société de classe," *Canadian Historical Review*, LXII (1981), 407-450.

[126]Serge Courville, "Espace, territoire et culture en Nouvelle France: Une Vision géographique," *Revue d'Histoire de l'Amérique Française*, XXXVII (1983), 421.

[127]Adair, "The French Canadian Seigneurie," 188.

[128]*Ibid.*, p. 189.

[129]Marc Bloch, *Les Caractères originaux de l'histoire rurale française*, 2 vols. (Paris, 1964).

[130]Albert M. Soboul, "The French Rural Community," *Past and Present*, X (1956), 82.

[131]Diamond, "An Experiment in 'Feudialism,'" 4.

[132]Letter to de Baas, July 3, 1670, in Clément, *Lettres et Instructions*, III, pt. 2, p. 489.

[133]Quoted in Roland Lamontagne, "L'Influence de Colbert sur l'oeuvre de Jean Talon," *Revue d'Histoire de l'Amérique Française*, VI (1952), 59. Colbert's successors were much stricter "Colbertists". On the mixed mercantilism of New France, see Bilodeau, "Liberté économique et politique des Canadiens sous le régime français," 49-68.

[134]Lionel Groulx, "Note sur la chapellerie au Canada sous le régime français," *Revue d'Histoire de l'Amérique Française*, IV (1949), 387. In 1736, Maurepas as Minister of the Marine ordered the tools destroyed and the industry terminated. (p. 394)

[135]Cole, *Colbert and a Century of French Mercantilism*, II, 77-80. The Canadian brewery was successful enough to displace Dutch beer in the West Indies. Jaenen, "Le Colbertisme," 260.

[136]Eccles, *Canada Under Louis XIV*, p. 53.

[137]See the entire issue of *Le Dix-Septième Siècle*, No. 122, XXI [1979) devoted to social mobility. As Roland Mousnier points out in the conclusion, it existed, but took place slowly. In contrast, New France offered a rapid ascension.

[138]See, for example, Nish, *Les Bourgeois gentilhommes,* pp. 108ff. After 1685, Canadian nobles were allowed, even encouraged, to engage in trade without *dérogation.* Wallot, "Le Régime seigneurial," 378-379.

[139]Eccles, *Canada Under Louis XIV,* p. 58.

[140]"L'Affaire du Prie-Dieu à Montréal en 1694,"*Rapport de l'Archiviste de la Province du Québec,* (1923-1924), pp. 71-110.

[141]Fernand Ouellet uses the word "mimetism" to describe that attraction. *Histoire économique et sociale du Québec, 1760-1850. Structures et conjonctures* (Montreal, 1971), pp. 559-561.

[142]Weber,*La Compagnie française*, p. 204.

[143]May 17, 1674, Pierre Margry, ed.,*Découvertes et établissements des Français dans l'ouest et dans le sud de l'Amérique septentrionale (1614-1754). Mémoires et Documents originaux,* 6 vols. (Paris, 1876-1886), I, 249.

[144]Eccles, *Frontenac: The Courtier Governor,* p. 56.

[145]Quoted in Silvio Dumas,*Les Filles du Roi en Nouvelle France* (Quebec, 1972), p. 31.

[146]Frontenac to Colbert, November 2, 1672, in Margry,*Découvertes,* I, 247-248.

[147]Talon to Colbert, October 27, 1607,, in *ibid.,* I, 79.

[148]Eccles, *Frontenac: The Courtier Governor*, p. 57.

[149]Olive Patricia Dickason, *The Myth of the Savage and the Beginnings of French Colonialism in the Americas* (Edmonton, 1984), p. 261.

[150]On the appeal of the *voyageur's* free-wheeling life, see Grace Lee Nute, *The Voyageur* (1931; reprint ed., St. Paul, Minn., 1955).

[151]Colbert to Frontenac, May 17, 1674, in Clément,*Lettres*, III, 62, 578. See also the documents quoted in Kenneth A. MacKirdy et al., *Changing Perspectives in Canadian History* (South Bend, Ind., 1967), pp. 3-4.

Chapter III

[1]Clément, *Lettres,* III, pt. 2, pp. 393-394.

[2]Colbert to Talon, April 5, 1666, in Margry, *Découvertes*, I, 77-78.

[3]Colbert to Frontenac, May 17, 1674, in Clément, *Lettres*, pt. 2, p. 579; Colbert to Talon, June 4, 1672, *ibid.*, pt. 3, p. 540.

[4]Eccles, *Canada Under Louis XIV* (Toronto, 1963), p. 65.

[5]See, for example, Clément, *Lettres*, III, pt. 2, pp. 578-579.

[6]William J. Eccles, "The Fur Trade and Eighteenth-Century Imperialism," *William and Mary Quarterly*, XL (1983), 342. H. P. Biggar, *The Early Trading Companies of New France* (New York, 1965), pp. 17ff. Before Cartier's explorations and the establishment of the Canadian fur trade, beaver had already become a luxury item much used in France to trim clothing. The beaver pelts were then imported from Russia. The Russian supply became depleted in the late sixteenth century, thus making Canada very attractive as a source of furs. Daniel G. Glenday, "French Mercantilism and the Atlantic Colonies, With Specific References to New France, 1494-1672" (MA thesis, McGill University, 1975), pp. 26-27.

[7]Eccles, *Canada Under Louis XIV*, p. 60.

[8]*Ibid.*, p. 61.

[9]Harold A. Innis, *The Fur Trade in Canada: An Introduction to Canadian Economic History*,(1956; reprint ed., New Haven, 1973), p. 56.

[10]*Ibid.*, p. 18.

[11]Arthur J. Ray, "Periodic Shortages, Native Welfare, and the Hudson's Bay Company, 1670-1930," in Shepard Krech, III, ed., *The Subartic Fur Trade: Native Social and Economic Adaptations* (Vancouver, 1984), p. 3.

[12]The traditional interpretation derived from Innis was that the Indians preferred English goods because they were cheaper and better. This view was attacked by Eccles ("A Belated Review of Harold Adams Innis, *The Fur Trade in Canada*," *Canadian Historical Review*, LX [1979], 428-435.) Eccles maintains that the Indians continued trading with the English, despite a marked preference for French goods, in order to keep the prices competitive (fn. 20, p. 425). He staunchly maintains his revisionist position in the same journal (LXII [1981], 323-329) despite a violent attack by Hugh M. Grant, ("One Step Forward, Two Steps Back: Innis, Eccles, and the Canadian Fur Trade") in the same issue, pp. 304-322.

[13]Innis, *The Fur Trade*, p. 51.

[14]*Ibid.*, pp. 82-83.

[15]*Ibid.*, p. 110.

[16]Marcel Trudel, "Louis XIV et son projet de déportation, 1689," *Revue d'Histoire de l'Amérique Française*, IV (1950), 157-171.

[17]Biggar, *The Early Trading Companies,* p. 96.

[18]*Ibid.,* p. 119.

[19]See *Rapport de l'Archiviste de la Province de Québec pour 1930-1931,* which is entirely devoted to Talon's correspondence.

[20]Colbert to de Baas, October 1, 1670, Clément, *Lettres,* III, pt. 2, p. 499.

[21]Colbert to Colbert de Croissy, August 5, 1670, *ibid.,* p. 492.

[22]Colbert to de Baas, July 3, 1670, *ibid.,* p. 487.

[23]Grace Lee Nute, *Caesars of the Wilderness: Médard Chouart, Sieur des Groseillers and Pierre Esprit Radisson, 1618-1710* (1943; reprint ed., St. Paul, Minn., 1978), p. 168.

[24]*Ibid.,* p. 177.

[25]Francisco de Vitoria, "De Indiis Noviter Inventis," in James Brown Scott, *The Spanish Origins of International Law. Francisco de Vitoria and His Law of Nations* (Oxford, 1934), p. xliii.

[26]Quoted in Dickason, *The Myth of the Savage,* p. 172.

[27]Marc Lescarbot, *Histoire de la Nouvelle France suivie les Muses de la Nouvelle France,* 3 vols. (Paris, 1866), III, 593.

[28]Lucien Campeau, "Introduction générale," *La Première Mission d'Acadie (1602-1616),* vol. 23 of *Monumenta Missionum Societatis Jesu* (Quebec, 1967), p. 194.

[29]"Documents," in *ibid.,* p. 326.

[30]Hanotaux, *Histoire du Cardinal de Richelieu,* IV, 557.

[31]"Factum du procès entre Jean de Biencourt et les P. P. Biard et Massé, 1614," in Campeau, "Documents," *La Première Mission,* pp. 330-331. See also Marcel Trudel, *Histoire de la Nouvelle France,* II, *Le Comptoir, 1604-1627* (Montreal, 1966), pp. 94-100.

[32]Colbert to Clodoré, May 7, 1665, Clément, *Lettres,* , III, pt. 2, p. 397.

[33]Colbert to Talon, March 27, 1665, *ibid.,* p. 389.

[34]Colbert to Courcelles, May 15, 1649, *ibid.,* p. 451. My emphasis.

[35]Trudel, *Histoire de la Nouvelle France*, II, 317-351.

[36]See Reuben G. Thwaites, *The Jesuit Relations and Allied Documents. Travels and Explorations of the Jesuit Missionaries, New France, 1610-1791,* 73 vols. in 36 (New York, 1959).

[37]Gilbert Chinard, *L'Amérique et le rêve exotique dans la littérature française au XVIIe et au XVIIIe siècles* (1913; reprint ed., Geneva, 1977), p. 64.

[38]Colbert to Frontenac, June 13, 1673, in Clément, *Lettres*, III, pt. 2, p. 559.

[39]The king to Frontenac, April 22, 1675. BN, Mss. fr., N.A.., 6288:170.

[40]Thomas Guthrie Marquis, *The Jesuit Missions* (Toronto, 1916), p. 118.

[41]"Eusèbe Renaudot," *Nouvelle Biographie générale . . .* (Paris, 1866), XLI, 998-999.

[42]Bernou speaks of "the inclination I have had all my life and which I cannot overcome, toward French colonization." B.N., Mss. fr., N.A., 7997:116vo; see also, Marcel Giraud, *Histoire de la Louisiane française*, Vol. I, *Le Régime de Louis XIV* (Paris, 1953), p. 17.

[43]Jean Delanglez, *Some La Salle Journeys* (Chicago, 1938), p. 12.

[44]B.N., Mss. fr., N.A., 7497:81; B.N., Mss. Clairambault 1016:633.

[45]The best and most recent summary of La Salle historiography is Carl A. Brasseaux, "The Image of La Salle in Patricia K. Galloway, North American Historiography," in *La Salle and His Legacy: Frenchmen and Indians in the Lower Mississippi Valley* (Jackson, Miss., 1982),pp. 3-10. La Salle's vision is evaluated by Glenn R. Conrad, "Reluctant Imperialist: France in North America," in *ibid.*, pp. 93-105.

[46]See "Relation de l'abbé de Gallinée, 1660-1670," in Margry, *Découvertes*, I, 12, 117; B. N., Mss. fr., N.A., 7497:142vo; B.N., Mss. Clairambault 1016:81vo.

[47]Frederic Austin Ogg, *The Opening of the Mississippi: A Struggle for Supremacy in the American Interior* (New York, 1968), pp. 46-49.

[48]*Ibid.*, pp. 60-61; John Gilmary Shea, *Discovery and Exploration of the Mississippi Valley* (New York, 1852), xxvii.

[49]Shea, *Discovery*, xxix.

[50]"Narrative of Father Marquette," in Shea, *Discovery*, p. 18.

[51]John Anthony Caruso, *The Mississippi Valley Frontier: The Age of French Exploration and Settlement* (New York, 1966), p. 156.

[52]"Découverte du Mississippi par Louis Jolliet," 1674, in Margry,*Découvertes*, I, 260, 267, 268.

[53]"Concession d'une île . . . à François Daupin," June 10, 1679, in Margry,*Découvertes*, II, 21.

[54]Colbert to Talon, February 11, 1671, in Clément,*Lettres*, III, pt. 2, pp. 516-517.

[55]Colbert to Talon, June 4, 1672,*ibid.*, p. 540.

[56]Colbert to Frontenac, May 17, 1674, in Margry, *Découvertes*, I, 257.

[57]Frontenac to Colbert, November 11, 1674,*ibid.*, I, 258.

[58]On Frontenac's complex wheeling and dealing, see Eccles, *Frontenac*. See also, Edmund R. Murphy, *Henry de Tonty: Fur Trader of the Mississippi* (Baltimore, 1941).

[59]Margry, "Voyage du Comte de Frontenac au Lac Ontario, en 1673,"*Découvertes*, I, 203-216.

[60]Caruso, *The Mississippi Valley Frontier*, p. 161.

[61]Colbert to Duchesnau, April 28, 1677, in Clément,*Lettres*, III, pt. 2, p. 618.

[62]March 12, 1678, B. N., F.fr. N.a., 9293:55.

[63]Francis Parkman, *La Salle and the Discovery of the Great West* (Boston, 1902), p. 373.

[64]P. Chesnel, *Histoire de Cavelier de la Salle: Exploration et conquête du Bassin du Mississippi* (Paris, 1901), pp. 179-180.

[65]Nute, *Ceasars of the Wilderness*, pp. 176-177.

[66]The most balanced account to date is Edmund B. Osler, *La Salle* (Don Mills, Ont., 1967). The most exciting remains Parkman, *La Salle and the Discovery of the Great West*. Gabriel Gravier, *Découvertes et établissements de Cavelier de La Salle de Rouen dans l'Amérique du Nord* (Paris, 1870), and Pierre Leprohon, *Le Destin tragique de Cavelier de La Salle* (Paris, 1969) are so hagiographic as to be practically useless.

[67]"Relation officielle de l'entreprise de Cavelier de La Slale, de 1679 à 1681," in Margry, *Découvertes*, I, 435-544; "Récit de Nicolas de La Salle," *ibid.*, pp. 547-570; "Narrative of the Adventures of La Salle's Party" by Father Zenobius Membré, and "Narrative of La Salle's Voyage Down the Missisisippi by the Same," in Shea,*Discovery*, pp. 151-188.

[68]Justin Winsor, *Cartier to Frontenac* (New York, 1977), p. 300. Frontenac was formally recalled on May 9, 1682. La Barre received his instructions on May 10, 1682. AC, C 13c, 3:31.

[69]Eccles, *Frontenac,* pp. 153, 155.

[70]La Barre to Seignelay, November 54, 1683. AC, C 11a, 6:137vo.,

[71] *Ibid.*

[72]*Ibid.*

[73]Margry, *Découvertes,* II, 310.

[74]Memoir, 1684. AC, C 13c, 3:53-59.

[75]Robert S. Weddle, *Wilderness Manhunt: The Spanish Search for La Salle* (Austin, 1973), pp. 18-19. Peñalosa wanted to use filibusters, from the islands, despite Louis XIV's strong objections to the institution. Léon Vignols, "Les Antilles françaises sous l'ancie\. Régime. Aspects économiques et sociaux. Un Produit social de la guerre. Filibuste et boucane (XVIe-XVIIIe siècles)," *Revue d'Histoire Economique et Sociale,* XVI (1928), 151-155.

[76]Clairambault 1016:197vo.

[77]B.N., Mss. Clairambault 1016:194-198vo. This memoir deals in great detail with the objection that the conquest of America might depopulate France as it had depopulated Spain. It argues that Spain had been depopulated not by emigration to the New World but by the arridity of its land, the sterility of its women (caused by the dry, hot air and their improper diet of fruits and herbs), the debauchery of both men and women, the wars against the Moors, the expulsion of the Moors, and the wars against the Turks. Moreover, Spain could not repopulate itself by attracting immigrants because of its isolation, because of the Inquisition, and because of Spanish arrogance. France, on the other hand, a fertile land with fecund women, attracted foreigners because it treated them well and left them free to practice their religion. The concern with depopulation will remain an objection to colonization during the eighteenth century.

[78]B. N., Mss. fr., N.A., 7497:86-87.

[79]Osler, *La Salle,* pp. 160-172; E. T. Miller, "The Connection of Peñalosa with the La Salle Expedition," *Texas State Historical Quarterly,* V (1901), 97-112.

[80]B. N., Mss. fr., N.A., 7497:89-090.

[81]Delanglez, *Some La Salle Journeys,* pp. 81ff.

[82]Miller, "The Connection," carefully assesses the evidence and concludes that the landfall was a result of error. (p. 110)

[83]For a full treatment of the development, see William Edward Dunn, *Spanish and French Rivalry in the Gulf Region of the United States, 1687-1702: The Beginnings of Texas and Pensacola* (1917; reprint ed., Freeport, N.Y., 1971).

[84]AC, C 13c, 3:68.

[85]*Ibid.*, 67vo.

[86]*Ibid.*, 68.

[87]*Ibid.*, 69.

[88]*Joutel's Journal of La Salle's Last Voyage, with an Introduction by Darrett B. Rutman* (New York, 1962), p. 80.

[89]Memoir to Seignelay, 1684. AC, C 13c, 3:57.

Chapter IV

[1]Equated by some historians with the defense of European freedom. See Stephen B. Baxter, *William III and the Defense of European Liberty, 1650-1702* (New York, 1966).

[2]Tramond, *Manuel d'histoire maritime*, p. 288.

[3]*Ibid.*, p. 294.

[4]John C. Rule, "Jerôme de Phélypeau, comte de Pontchartrain and the Establishment of Louisiana, 1696-1715," in John Francis McDermott, ed., *Frenchmen and French Ways in the Mississippi Valley* (Urbana, Ill., 1969), pp. 180-181.

[5]O'Neill, *Church and State in French Colonial Louisiana*, pp. 25, 27.

[6]*Ibid.*

[7]Innis, *The Fur Trade*, p. 70.

[8]*Ibid.*, p. 71; Frégault, *Le XVIIIe siècle canadien*, p. 245-246.

[9] *Ibid.*, p. 74.

[10] Yves F. Zoltvany, "New France and the West, 1701-1713," *Canadian Historical Review*, XLVI (1965), 301-303.

[11] *Ibid.*, pp. 305-306.

[12] *Ibid.*, p. 307.

[13] Henri de Tonty to Cabart de Villermont, September 11, 1694, Margry, *Découvertes*, IV, 4.

[14] Dunn, *Spanish and French Rivalry*, pp. 24-30, relates in detail the slow progress of one memorial through the Byzantine complications of the Spanish colonial administration.

[15] See Weddle, *Wilderness Manhunt.*

[16] Dunn, *Spanish and French Rivalry*, pp. 110-145.

[17] *Ibid.*, pp. 171-181.

[18] William Coker, "Introduction," to Daniel Coxe, *A Description of the English Province of Carolana, by the Spaniards Called Florida, and by the French La Louisiane* (1722; facsimile reprint ed., Gainesville, Fla., 1976), pp. xx-xxi.

[19] Louis Hennepin, *A Description of Louisiana*, trans. by John Gilmary Shea (1880; reprint ed., Ann Arbor, 1966).

[20] Louis Hennepin, *New Discovery of a Vast Country in America. Reprinted from the Second London issue of 1698 . . .*, ed. by Reuben Gold Thwaites (Chicago, 1902), pp. 3-8; Henry Folmer, *Franco-Spanish Rivalry in North America, 1524-1763* (Glendale, Calif., 1953), p. 200.

[21] Iberville to the minister, June 18, 1698. Margry, *Découvertes*, IV, 58-59.

[22] Memoir of Rémonville, December 10, 1697. AC, C 13a, 1:76.

[23] July 9, 1698. AM, B2, 136:27.

[24] Pontchartrain to Dantin, August 6, 1698. AM, B2, 136:84.

[25] Pontchartrain to Dantin, September 2, 1698. AM, B2, 136:159.

[26] Pontchartrain to Dantin, October 15, 1698, AM, B2, 136:253.

[27]See Carl A. Brasseaux, trans. and ed., *A Comparative View of French Louisiana, 1699 and 1762: The Journals of Pierre Le Moyne d'Iberville and Jean-Jacques-Blaise d'Abbadie* (Lafayette, La., 1979).

[28]"The Preface" to Hennepin, *A Description*, no pagination.

[29]*Ibid.*

[30]Zoltvany, "New France and the West," 313.

[31]*Ibid.*

[32]Eccles, *The Canadian Frontier*, p. 130.

[33]Charles E. O'Neill, ed., *Charlevoix's Louisiana: Selections from the History and Journal* (Baton Rouge, 1977), pp. 12-13.

[34]Ducasse to Pontchartrain, January 13, 1699. AC, C 9a, 4:n.p.

[35]"Le Ministre de la Marine à M. Ducasse," April 8, 1699. Margry, *Découvertes*, IV, 294.

[36]Pontchartrain to Ducasse, July 1, 1699. AC, B, 21:372.

[37]Memoir, June 21, 1699. AC, C 13c, 2:12-13.

[38]Memoir, July 28, 1699. AC, C 13a, 1:188.

[39]*Ibid.*

[40]Instructions to Iberville, September 22, 1699. AC, B, 20:281-281vo.

[41]Instructions to Sauvole, May 26, 1700. AC, C 13a, 247-253.

[42]Iberville to Pontchartrain, September 7, 1700. Margry, *Découvertes*, IV, 371-377.

[43]Pontchartrain to Iberville, August 3, 1701. Margry, *Découvertes*, IV, 495.

[44]Mémoire de la Junta de Guerre, July 5, 1701. Margry, *Découvertes*, IV, 553-568.

[45]Martínez to Iberville, January 1, 1702. AC, C 13a, 1:361-362.

[46]Iberville to Martínez, January 3, 1702. AC, C 13a, 1:357-360.

[47]Memoir to Iberville, 1701. AC, C 13a, 1:333-348.

[48]See Michael J. Forêt, "Irresolution and Uncertainty: French Colonial Indian Policy in Louisiana, 1699-1763" (MA thesis, University of Southwestern Louisiana, 1982).

[49]Mémoire sur le Mississippi. Margry, *Découvertes*, IV, 482-485. Margry gives the date as July 20, 1701, but Surrey calendars that memoir as July 12. The detail of his request is given in AM, B4, 21:544-545vo.

[50]Minister to Iberville, August 3, 1701. AM, B2, 155:195.

[51]Minister to Bégon, July 20, 1701. AM, B2, 155:105-110; minister to Iberville, July 20, 1701. AM, B2, 155:108; Margry, *Découvertes*, IV, 487.

[52]Jay Higginbotham, *Old Mobile: Fort Louis de la Louisiane, 1702-1711* (Mobile, 1977), p. 81.

[53]Mémoire, 1702. AC, C 13a, 1:99, 363.

[54]Mémoire, 1703. AC, C 13a, 1:93.

[55]See the full treatment of Iberville's financial dealings in Giraud, *Histoire de la Louisiane*, I, 104-116.

[56]Memoire de d'Iberville, [June 30, 1702]. Margry, *Découvertes*, IV, 603.

[57]Mémoire, 1702. AC, C 13c, 2:47vo. He did obtain 21 girls who with a conductress were sent on the *Pélican* in 1704. Liste des filles et des deux familles qui doivent passer à la Louisiane, October 3, 1704. AC, B, 25:9vo-10vo.

[58]Mémoire, 1701. Paris, Cartes et plans, Vol. 672, no. 4.

[59]Mémoire, 1699. AC, C 13a, 1:163-164.

[60]Giraud, *Histoire de la Louisiane*, I, 99-100.

Chapter V

[1]Basil Williams, "The Foreign Policy of England Under Walpole," *English Historical Review*, XV (1900), 262.

[2] *Ibid.*, pp. 479-480; Arthur McCandless Wilson, *French Foreign Policy during the Administration of Cardinal Fleury, 1726-1743,* (Cambridge, 1936), p. 13.

[3] Quoted in Wilson, *French Foreign Policy,* p. 42.

[4] *Ibid.*, pp. 45-46.

[5] James Rees Jones, *Country and Court: England, 1658-1714* (Cambridge, Mass., 1978), p. 289.

[6] Baxter, *William III,* p. 381.

[7] Geoffrey J. Walker, *Spanish Politics and Imperial Trade, 1700-1789* (Bloomington, Ind., 1979), pp. 19-20. See Jean Meyer and John Bromley, "La Second Guerre de Cent Ans, 1689-1815," in François Berrida, et al., eds., *De Guillaume le Conquerant au Marché Commun* (Paris, 1979), pp. 157-160, for an excellent analysis of the role played by naval rivalry. For the trade rivalry, see Henry Kamen, *The War of the Succession in Spain, 1700-15* (Bloomington, Ind., 1969), pp. 140-166.

[8] "Asiento" simply refers to any contract between the Spanish government and individuals or groups to render a public service. Georges Scelle, "The Slave Trade in the Spanish Colonies of America: The Assiento," *American Journal of International Law,* IV (1910), 614.

[9] *Ibid.*, 640-641.

[10] Charles André Julien, *Les Français en Amérique,* p. 9; Walker, *Spanish Politics,* p. 20.

[11] Scelle, "The Slave Trade," 647; Herbert S. Klein, *The Middle Passage: Comparative Studies in the the Atlantic Slave Trade* (Princeton, N. J., 1978), p. 234.

[12] Louis XIV to Count Tallard, April 17, 1698, in Paul Grimlot, ed., *Letters of William III and Louis XIV and Their Ministers Illustrative of the Domestic and Foreign Politics of England from the Peace of Ryswick to the Accession of Philip V of Spain, 1697 to 1700,* 2 vols. (London, 1848), I, 391.

[13] Scelle, "The Slave Trade," 642-643.

[14] *Ibid.*, 643; Walker, *Spanish Politics,* 20; Kamen, *The War of Succession,* pp. 144, 147, 149.

[15] E. R. Adair, "Anglo-French Rivalry in the Fur Trade during the 18th Century," *Culture,* VIII (1947), 448; Bernadine Pietraszeck, "Anglo-French Trade Conflicts in North America, 1702-1713," *Mid-America,* XXXV, New Series, XXIV (1942), 144-174.

[16] Innis, *The Fur Trade,* pp. 119ff.

[17] Quoted in Yves F. Zoltvany, ed., *The French Tradition in America* (Columbia, S. C., 1969), pp. 129-130.

[18]Jean-François Brière, "Pêche et politique à Terre-Neuve au XVIIIe siècle: La France veritable gagnante du traité d'Utrecht," *Canadian Historical Review*, LXIV (1983), 168-187.

[19]Priestley, *France Overseas*, p. 156.

[20]Julien, *Les Français en Amérique*, p. 7.

[21]*Ibid.*, p. 8.

[22]*Ibid.*

[23]Priestley, *France Overseas*, p. 157.

[24]Wilson, *French Foreign Policy*, p. 8; Williams, "The Foreign Policy of England," 263.

[25]Wilson, *French Foreign Policy*, p. 9.

[26]*Ibid.*, p. 7.

[27]Williams, "The Foreign Policy of England," 262-263; Meyer and Bromley, "La Second Guerre de Cent Ans," 158.

[28]Wilson, *French Foreign Policy*, p. 17. Philip V had never forgiven the regent for entertaining the idea of ascending the Spanish throne himself during the War of the Spanish Succession. His dislike of the regent was a major factor in the estrangement between France and Spain. Meyer, *Le Régent*, p. 99.

[29]Yves F. Zoltvany, *Philippe de Rigaud de Vaudreuil, Governor of New France, 1703-1725* (Toronto, 1974), p.149.

[30]Quoted in Jean Meyer, *La Vie quotidienne en France au temps de la Régence* (Paris, 1979), p. 65.

[31]Paul Vacher, *Robert Walpole et la politique de Fleury (1731-1742)* (Paris, 1924), pp. 289-302.

[32]Zoltvany, *Vaudreuil*, pp. 150ff, related the Canadian governor's struggle against the official policy and the undeclared war he waged against the British ally. See, for example, also Meyer, *Le Régent*, p. 130.

[33]Jean Meyer, *La France moderne de 1515 à 1799*, Vol. III of Jean Favier, ed., *de France* (Paris, 1985), p. 387.

[34]Giraud, *Histoire de la Louisiane*, II, 104-116.

[35]August 5, 1683, Margry, *Découvertes*, II, 310.

[36]Memoir [1684]. AC, C 13c, 3:64.

[37]Iberville to Pontchartrain, September 7, 1700. Margry, *Découvertes*, IV, 372.

[38]"Gravier's Voyage, 1700," in Thwaites, *Jesuit Relations*, LXV, 173.

[39]To de Muy, June 30, 1707. AC, B, 29:278-278vo,.

[40]To M. de la Ranette, October 17, 1708. AC, B, 31:299.

[41]To d'Artaguiette, May 10, 1710. AC, B, 32:42. (Library of Congress copy.)

[42]Building a powerful army was always the priority. During Colbert's entire ministry, the naval expenditure averaged eight percent of the total budget. On the other hand, the expenditures for the army, including fortifications, amounted to forty-seven percent in 1683. Meyer, *Colbert*, p. 272.

[43]Giraud, *Histoire de la Louisiane*, I, 130-131.

[44]October 31, 1708. AC, B, 30:53. (Library of Congress copy.)

[45]To Rémonville, July 13, 1710. AC, B, 32:136vo. (Library of Congress copy.)

[46]To Rémonville, August 10, 1710. AC, B, 32:195vo.

[47]Glyndwr Williams, *The Expansion of Europe in the Eighteenth Century: Overseas Rivalry, Discovery and Exploitation* (New York, 1966), p. 52.

[48]Zoltvany, *Vaudreuil*, pp. 130-131; William J. Eccles, *France in America* (New York, 1973), pp.178-180.

[49]Marcel Giraud, "Un Aspect de la rivalité franco-espagnole au début du XVIIIe siècle (1713-1717)," *Revue Historique*, CCXVII (1957), 256.

[50]Letters patent, October 12, 1712. AC, A, 22:1-8vo.

[51]Giraud, *Histoire de la Louisiane*, I, 232.

[52]To the minister, August 17, 1712. AC, C 13a, 2:688.

[53]To the minister, June 29, 1712. AC, C 13a, 2:676.

[54]Duclos to the minister, October 29, 1713. AC, C 13a, 3:311.

[55]Riola to Surgères, March 23, 1700. AC, C 13a, 1:243-246.

[56]To Arriola, June 3, 1702. AC, C 13a, 1:358.

[57]Iberville au Ministre de la Marine, July 2, 1701. Margry, *Découvertes,* IV, 476.

[58]"Mémoire du sieur d'Iberville sur Pensacola," [1700]. Margry, *Découvertes,* IV, 550-552.

[59]AM, B 4, 21:532.

[60]Memoir, [July 5, 1701. AC, C 13a, 1:413-444.

[61]Le Ministre de la Marine à le duc d'Harcourt, 1700; Margry, *Découvertes,* IV, 572.

[62]"M. de Ricouart au Ministre de la Marine," August 23, 1700, Margry, *Découvertes,* IV, 386-391.

[63]Jack D. L. Holmes, "Dauphin Island in the Franco-Spanish War, 1719-22," in John F. McDermott, ed., *Frenchmen and French Ways in the Mississippi Valley* (Urbana, Ill., 1969), p. 108; D'Artaguiette to Pontchartrain, February 12, 1710. AC, C 13a, 2:531-538.

[64]Nancy M. Surrey, *The Commerce of Louisiana during the French Regime, 1699-1763* (New York, 1916), pp. 422-430. On the shortage of specie in the colony, see pp. 107, 111, 121.

[65]Giraud, "Un Aspect," 257.

[66]*Ibid.*

[67]December 17, 1712. AC, B, 34:444vo-445.

[68]To Crozat, October 1713. AC, C 13a, 3:357-358.

[69]Memoir, October 9, 1713. AC, C 13a, 3:227.

[70]Duclos to Pontchartrain, October 29, 1713. AC, C 13a, 3:313-314.

[71]Cadillac to Pontchartrain, April 10, 1714. AC, C 13a, 3:474.

[72]Ruby Johnson Swartzlow, "The Early History of Lead Mining in Missouri," *Missouri Historical Review*, XXVIII (1934), 191.

[73]Cadillac to Council, June 22, 1716. AC, C 13a, 4:607.

[74]Giraud, "Un Aspect," 263.

[75]Memoir from the king to Cadillac, December 27, 1715. AC, C 13a, 3:684.

[76]Memoir, October 1717. AC, C 13a, 5:143-145.

[77]Holmes, "Dauphin Island," 109.

[78]Julien, *Les Français en Amérique*, p. 20.

[79]Jones, *Country and Court*, p. 289.

[80]Though the Compagnie failed completely because of the exorbitant taxes levied on slaves and of English smuggling. Julien, *Les Français en Amérique*, p. 9.

[81]Utrecht settled the problems in principle only. Since France and England never agreed as to the area ceded, and since the French fishermen obtained the right to exploit the Newfoundland "French Shore" and managed to gain a virtual monopoly. See Brière, "Pêche et Politique," 187.

[82]Quoted in Basil Williams, *The Whig Supremacy, 1714-1760* (Oxford, 1942), p. 300.

[83]*Ibid.*, pp. 300-301.

[84]Priestley, *France Overseas*, p. 155; Duclos, August 31, 1715. AC, D2c, 51:6-8.

[85]Verner W. Crane, "The Southern Frontier in Queen Anne's War," *American Historical Review*, XXIV (1919), 379.

[86]*Ibid.*, p. 383.

[87]Dawson A. Phelps, "The Chickasaw, the English, and the French, 1699-1744," *Tennessee Historical Quarterly*, XVI (1957), 117.

[88]Jay Higginbotham, "Henri de Tonti's Mission to the Chickasaw, 1702," *Louisiana History*, XIX (1978), 285-296.

[89]Iberville to minister, March 26, 1702. AC, F1., 10:288.

[90]Bienville to minister, October 12, 1708. AC, C 13a, 2:180.

[91]October 10, 1706. AC, C 13b, 1:10vo-11.

[92]Bienville to minister, October 27, 1711. AC, C 13a, 2:2570.

[93]Bienville to minister, September 1, 1715. AC, C 13a, 3:786-787.

[94]Memoir of the Council of Marine, February 11, 1721. AC, C 13a, 4:80.

[95]Duclos to minister, June 7, 1716. AC, C 13a, 4:674-675.

[96]Miniutes of Council Meeting, Biloxi, February 8, 17-21, 1721. AC, C 13a, 6:146-146vo.

[97]Giraud, *Histoire de la Louisiane,* II, 173.

[98]Eccles, *Canada under Louis XIV,* p. 245.

[99]Quoted in Salone, *La Colonisation de la Nouvelle-France*, p. 307.

[100]La Chesnaye to Pontchartrain, 1702. AC, C 13a, 1:29.

[101]Vaudreuil and Begon to Pontchartrain, quoted in Frégault, *Le XVIIIe Siècle canadien,* p. 280.

[102]Iberville to Pontchartrain, 1703. AC, C 13a, 1:383.

[103]Guy Frégault, *Pierre Le Moyne d'Iberville* (Montreal, 1968), p. 253.

[104]On the Illinois controversy, see Glenn R. Conrad, "Administration of the Illinois Country: The French Debate" (unpublished paper).

[105]Giraud, *Histoire de la Louisiane,* II, 64.

[106]Memoir [January 11,] 1717. AC, C 13a, 5:231vo.

[107]Memoir to the Council, February 11, 1716. AC, C 13a, 4:55-56.

[108]*Ibid.*, 56-58.

[109]Giraud, *Histoire de la Louisiane,* III, 4.

[110]Letters patent, August 26, 1718. AC, A, 22:69-71vo.

[111]Arrêt, June 20, 1718,. AC, A 22: 65-69; On the early activities of the company, see Marcel Giraud, "La Compagnie d'Occident (1717-1718),"*Revue Historique*, CCXXVI (1961), 23-56.

[112]Giraud, *Histoire de la Louisiane,* III, 63-65. The long-range returns of the Company of the Indies have been obscured by Law's sensational bankruptcy. See Gilles Y. Bertin, "Les Aspects comptables et financiers du commerce colonial de la Compagnie des Indes entre 1719 et 1730," *Revue d'Histoire Economique et Sociale*, XL (1962), 481-482, for an assessment of its strength.

[113]*Ibid.*, p. 19.

[114]The most complete account of the Cellamare conspiracy is in Pierre-Edouard Lémontey, *Histoire de la Régence et de la minorité de Louis XV, jusqu'au ministère du Cardinal de Fleury,* 2 vols. (Paris, 1832). The most recent is in Jean Meyer, *Le Régent,* pp. 188-219.

[115]For the amazing career of the gardener's son turned cardinal and minister, see Simon Harcourt-Smith, *Cardinal of Spain: The Life and Strange Career of Alberoni* (New York, 1944).

[116]Wilson, *French Foreign Policy*, p. 13.

[117]Bienville to the Council, October 20, 1719. AC, C 13a, 5:274-281.

[118]See, for example, "Dissertation particulière sur la Louisiane," *Nouveau Mercure* (1717), pp. 83, 92; "Lettre," *ibid.*, (May 1719), pp. 185-186. On the long-range effect of this propaganda blitz, see Pierre H. Boulle, "Some Eighteenth-Century French Views on Louisiana," in John F. McDermott, ed., *Frenchmen and French Ways in the Mississippi Valley* (Urbana, Ill., 1969), pp. 15-27. For the reluctance of Louis XIV and Pontchartrain to turn for forced immigration, see Marcel Giraud, "Tendances humanitaires à la fin du règne de Louis XIV," *Revue Historique*, CCIC (1953), 226-227.

[119]See Sheila T. Sturdivant, "Rich Man, Poor Man, Beggar Man, Thief: Frenchmen Exiled to Louisiana, 1716-1721" (MA thesis, University of Southwestern Louisiana, 1971).

[120]Glenn R. Conrad, trans. and ed., *Immigration and War: Louisiana, 1718-1721, from the Memoir of Charles Legac* (Lafayette, La., 1970), p. 1.

[121]See passenger lists in Glenn R. Conrad, *First Families of Louisiana,* 2 vols. (Baton Rouge, La., 1970).

[122]Giraud, *Histoire de la Louisiane,* III, 387.

[123]*Ibid.*, p. 390.

[124]Verner W. Crane, *The Southern Frontier, 1670-1732* (Ann Arbor, 1956), pp. 225-234.

[125]Giraud, *Histoire de la Louisiane,* III, 390.

Chapter VI

[1]See Mousnier, "Note sur les rapports," *Revue Historique,* 339-350; Roland Mousnier, *Les Institutions de la France sous la monarchie absolue* (Paris, 1980), II, 489-490; Bordes, "Les Intendants de Louis XIV," 45-62. On the prestige of early governors, see Robert R. Harding, *Anatomy of a Power Elite. The Provincial Governors of Early Modern France* (New Haven, 1978).

[2]Mousnier, "Note sur les rapports," p. 350.

[3]See Eccles, *Frontenac.*

[4]Moreover, few if any of the Louisiana *ordonnateurs* had the training of the metropolitan *intendant.* See Vivian R. Gruber, *The Royal Provincial Intendants: A Governing Elite in Eighteenth-Century France* (Ithaca, 1968), for the training given the *intendants.* O'Neill, *Church and State,* p. 95.

[5]See, for example, "Instructions to Cadillac," December 18, 1712. AC, B, 34:434-439; and "Instructions to Duclos," same date. AC, B, 34:440vo-449.

[6]See Carl A. Brasseaux, *Denis-Nicolas Foucault and the New Orleans Rebellion of 1768* (Ruston, La., 1987).

[7]O'Neill, *Church and State,* p. 259-260.

[8]On Louis and the Protestants, see John B. Wolf, *Louis XIV* (New York, 1968).

[9]In fact, Protestants were present in New France throughout the French regime. See Jaenen, "The Persistence of the Protestant Presence in New France, 1541-1760," 29-40. See also, Marc-André Bédard, "La Présence protestante en Nouvelle France," *Revue d'Histoire de l'Amérique Française,* XXXI (1977), 325-349; and Claude de Bonnault, "Les Protestants au Canada avant 1760," *Bulletin des Recherches Historiques*, LXII (1956), 5-33.

[10]See Cahen, "Les Juifs à la Martinique," 93-122; "Les Juifs dans les colonies françaises," IV (1881), 127-165, 236-248; V (1882), 68-92, 258-272.

[11]O'Neill, *Church and State,* p. 282.

[12]*Ibid.*, p. 259.

[13]See Louis Armand de Lom d'Arce, baron de Lahontan, *Dialogues curieux entre l'auteur et un sauvage de bons sens qui a voyagé*, ed. by Gilbert Chinard (Baltimore, 1931), p. 81, for the opinion that the Indians possess "le caractère du plus honnête homme du monde."

[14]*Joutel's Journal*, p. 80.

[15]Giraud, *Histoire de la Louisiane*, I, 143; II, 342.

[16]Pierre Hamer, *Raphaël de Luxembourg: Une contribution luxembourgeoise à la colonisation de la Louisiane* (Luxembourg, 1966), p. 84.

[17]See Roland Mousnier, *Fureurs paysannes: les Paysans dans les révoltes du XVIIIe siècle (France, Russie, Chine)* (Paris, 1967), pp. 12-17, for an excellent discussion of the difference among caste, class, and order.

[18]Louis XIV's opinion is supported by Harris' study *The Seigneurial System in Early Canada* which examines the geographical evidence and finds no impact of the seigneurial system on the patterns of social and economic activity. He concludes that the system was "largely irrelevant to the geography of early Canada" and to "the way of life which emerged there" (p. 8).

[19]Dechêne, "L'Evolution du régime seigneurial," 145.

[20]See Diamond, "An Experiment in 'Feudalism,' " 3-45, for the failure of feudalism in New France.

[21]Pontchartrain to Cadillac, August 3, 1712. AC, B 24:123. (Library of Congress copy.)

[22]John R. Carpenter, *Histoire de la littérature française sur la Louisiane de 1673 jusqu'à 1766* (Paris, 1966), pp. 16-17.

[23]As Cornelius Jaenen points out, the French have always prided themselves on their excellent relations with the Indians, and on knowing how to gain and keep their affections. "Pelleteries et peaux rouges: Perceptions françaises de la Nouvelle-France et de ses peuples indigènes, aux XVIe, XVIIe et XVIIIe siècles," *Recherches Amérindiennes au Québec*, XIII (1983), 107.

[24]See Eccles, *Frontenac*, pp. 54-55; Colbert to Frontenac, May 17, 1674, in Margry, *Découvertes*, I, 249; "Mémoire de La Salle," *ibid.*, p. 335.

[25]See the lengthy debate "la traite de l'eau-de-vie" October 10, 1678, in Margry, *Découvertes*, vol. I. Cadillac insisted that he, as other well intentioned officials, "felt obliged to tolerate the trade for the good of the state." B. N., Mss. Clairambault 882:146. He and other supporters of the brandy trade, "sought only the glory of God and the King"! *Ibid.*, 882:138vo.

[26]January 5, 1740. AC, C 13a, 25:208. On the flagging religious faith, and the priests' loss of moral

authority, see Marcel Giraud, "Crise de conscience et d'autorité à la fin du règne de Louis XIV," *Annales. ESC*, VII (1952), 297-301.

[27]Cornelius J. Jaenen, "Conceptual Frameworks for French Views of America and Amerindians," *French Colonial Studies*, no. 2 (1978), 3.

[28]*Ibid.*, 9.

[29]Brasseaux, *Comparative View*, p. 52.

[30]"Letter of du Poisson," Thwaites, *Jesuit Relations*, LXVII, 240.

[31]"Relation de la découverte . . . faite en 1673," Margry, *Découvertes*, I, 268.

[32]Brasseaux, *Comparative View*, p. 50.

[33]O'Neill, ed., *Charlevoix's Louisiana*, p. 146.

[34]"Le Petit to Avangour," *Jesuit Relations*, LXVIII, 134.

[35]"Récit d'un ami de l'abbé de Gallinée," Margry, *Découvertes*, I, 351-352.

[36]"Details sur le voyage de Louis Jolliet," *Ibid.*, I, 260; "Cavelier de La Salle de 1679 à 1681," in *ibid.*, I, 488.,

[37]Baron de Lahontan, *Dialogues Curieux*, p. 81.

[38]*Ibid.*, p. 77.

[39]B. N., Mss. Clairambault 1016:164vo, 275. See also, B. N., Mss. fr, N. A., 7485:172vo-173, and the letter by Du Poisson in the *Jesuit Relations*, LXVII, 310-312.

[40]"Gravier's voyage," *Jesuit Relations*, LXV, 150.

[41]B. N., Mss. Clairambault 1016:288-289, 291.

[42]"Le Petit to Avangour," *Jesuit Relations*, LXVIII, 197-199.

[43]Margry, *Découvertes*, I, 410.

[44]June 15, 1740. AC, C 13a, 25:105.

[45]To the minister, January 10, 1731. AC, B, 1:117.

[46]October 26, 1713. AC, C 13a, 3:7.

[47]"Cavelier de La Salle, de 1670 à 1681," in Margry, *Découvertes,* I, 534.

[48]B. N., Mss. Clairambault 1016:62-64.

[49]"Cavelier de La Salle, de 1679 à 1681," Margry, *Découvertes,* I, 534.

[50]"Recit," *Ibid.,* p. 351.

[51]Eccles, *Frontenac,* pp. 279-280.

[52]Beauchamps to the minister, March 12, 1740. AC, C 13a, 25:243vo, 246vo; May 21, 1740, AC, C 13a, 25:253vo.

[53]Memoir of the Council of Marine, February 11, 1716, AC, C 13a, 4:80.

[54]"Le Petit to d'Avangour," *Jesuit Relations,* LXVIII, 196.

[55]Margry, *Découvertes,* I, 347-348.

[56]"Gravier's voyage," *Jesuit Relations,* LXV, 150.

[57]"Letter by Poisson," *ibid.,* LXVII, 309. See also O'Neill, ed., *Charlevoix's Louisiana,* p. 216.

[58]Carpenter, *Histoire de littérature française,* pp. 77-78.

[59]Letter, September 1679-September 29, 1680. Margry, *Découvertes,* II, 32-33.

[60][1725]. AC, C 13a, 12:260.

[61]*Ibid.,* 259vo.

[62]O'Neill, ed., *Charlevoix's Louisiana,* p. 81-82.

[63]AC, C 13a, 7:174.

[64]Bienville to Pontchartrain, July 28, 1706. AC, C 13a, 1:537.

[65]Duclos to Pontchartrain, December 2, 1715. AC, C 13a, 3:822-823.

[66]D'Artaguiette to Pontchartrain, September 8, 1712. AC, C 13a, 2:799.

[67]Royal Memoir to L'Epinay and Hubert, October 28, 1716. AC, B, 38:334.

[68]To minister, July 25, 1732. AC, C 13a, 14:69.

[69]See Daniel H. Usner, Jr., "From African Captivity to American Slavery: The Introduction of Black Laborers to Colonial Louisiana," *Louisiana History*, XX (1979), 25-48. *Engagés*, or indentured servants, were sent to Louisiana by the Company of the West, but the institution was not much more successful than in the Indies. Léon Vignols, "Les Antilles françaises sous l'Ancien Régime. Aspects économiques et sociaux. L'Institution des engagés (1626-1774)," *Revue d'Histoire Economique et Sociale*, XVI (1928), 12-45; Léon Vignols, "Une Question mal posée: Le travail manuel des blancs et des esclaves aux Antilles (XVIIe-XVIIIe siècles)," *Revue Historique*, CLXXV (1935), 308-315.

[70]Deschamps, *Histoire de la question coloniale*, pp. 153-154. James Thomas McGowan, "Creation of a Slave Society: Louisiana Plantations in the Eighteenth Century" (Ph. D. dissertation, University of Rochester, 1976), p. 50.

[71]Michel Foucault, *Folie et déraison: Histoire de la folie à l'époque classique* (Paris, 1961), p. 63.

[72]Stanley Elkins, *Slavery: A Problem in American Institutional and Intellectual Life* (Chicago, 1976), p. 64.

[73]Théophile Malvezin, *Histoire du commerce de Bordeaux depuis les origines jusqu'à nos jours*, 3 vols. (Bordeaux, 1892), III, 205-206.

[74]See Charles Verlinden, "Note sur l'esclavage à Montpellier au bas Moyen Age (XIIIe-XVe siècles)," *Etudes d'histoire dédiées à la mémoire de Henri Pirenne par ses anciens élèves* (Bruxelles, 1937), pp. 451-469; Charles Verlinden, "Problème de la continuité en histoire coloniale," *Revistas de Indias*, XI (1951), 224-226.

[75]Andrew Trout, *Jean-Baptiste Colbert* (Boston, 1978), p. 156. In 1680, there were over 2,000 slaves in the Mediterranean galleys and some 10,000 men were enslaved in a forty year period. Marc Vigié, *Les Galériens du Roi, 1661-1715* (Paris, 1985), p. 68. Moreover, as Vigié points out, the galley rowers were never liberated at the term of their sentence, except through the king's exceptional "grace" so that in fact, they were held in "a curious personal slavery." *Ibid.*, p. 266.

[76]Robert-Joseph Pothier, *Oeuvres*, Vol. IX: *Traité des personnes et des choses . . .* , ed. by M. Bugnet (Paris, 1846), p. 16.

[77]Marcel Trudel, *L'Esclavage au Canada français: Histoire et conditions de l'esclavage* (Quebec, 1960), pp. 84-85.

[78]Albert Duchêne, *Histoire des finances coloniale de la France* (Paris, 1938), p. 50; Christian Schefer, *La France moderne et le problème colonial* (Paris, 1907), pp. 47-48.

[79]Frank Tannenbaum, *Slave and Citizen: The Negro in the Americas*(New York, 1947), pp. 64-65.

[80]*Ibid.*, p. 63.

[81]Blet, *Histoire de la colonisation française,* I, 161.

[82]Pothier, *Oeuvres,* IX, 47.

[83]*Ibid.*

[84]The indifference to the suffering of the lower classes is reflected in the callousness with which Frenchmen condemned to the galleys were kept enslaved as much as thirty years longer than their original sentence. Georges Pagès, "Note sur le recrutement et la libération des galériens sous Louis XIV au début du ministère de Colbert," *Revue d'Histoire Moderne et Contemporaine,* XI (1908-1909), 35-53.

[85]Pothier, *Oeuvres,* IX, 51, 52.

[86]*Ibid.*, Vol. VII: *Traité de la puissance du mari sur la personne et les biens de la femme,* p. 1.

[87]Black Code, Article XLIX, in *Publications of the Louisiana Historical Society*, IV (1908), 88.

[88]AC, C 13a, 35:46. Some earlier laws made the husband liable for the wife's misconduct if he failed to chastise her, as was his duty.

[89]Eugene Genovese, *Roll, Jordan, Roll: The World the Slaves Made* (New York, 1974), pp. 73-74.

[90]Black Code, Article LIII, in *Publications*, p. 89.

[91]Pothier, *Oeuvres,* IX, 52.

[92]Black Code, Articles XXXVIII, in *Publications*, p. 85.

[93]McGowan, "Creation of a Slave Society," p. 49.

[94]See Shelby McCoy, "Negroes and Mulattoes in Eighteenth-Century France," *Journal of Negro History,* XXX (1945), 276-292.

[95]Martineau and May, *Trois Siècles d'histoire antillaise*, pp. 55-56.

[96]Quoted in Leroy-Beaulieu, *De la colonisation,* p. 169.

[97]Quoted in Gabriel Debien, "Gens de couleurs libres et colons de Saint-Domingue devant la Constituante (1789-mars1790)," *Revue d'Histoire de l'Amérique Française,* IV (1950), 214.

[98]Hardy, *Histoire sociale de la colonisation française,* p. 25.

[99]Joe Gray Taylor, *Negro Slavery In Louisiana* (Baton Rouge, La., 1963), p. 19.

[100]Deschamps, *Histoire de la question coloniale,* p. 319.

[101]Black Code, Article XXI, in *Publications,* p. 81.

[102]Black Code, Articles XXVII, XXVIII, XXIX, XXX. in *ibid.*, p. 83; Isambert, Tallandier et al., *Recueil général des anciennes lois françaises* . . . , 29 vols. (Paris, 1821-1823), XX, 614-615.

[103]Henry Peter Brougham, Baron Brougham and Vaux, *An Inquiry into the Colonial Policy of the European Powers*, 2 vols. (1803; reprint ed., New York, 1970), II, 439. In France, domestic theft was punished by death. Isambert et al., *Recueil général,* XXI, 260.

[104]AC, C 13a, 35:45vo-46.

[105]Carl A. Brasseaux, "The Administration of Slave Regulations in French Louisiana, 1724-1766," *Louisiana History,* XXI (1980), 142. Similar conclusions were reached about the Code in the West Indies by Richard and John Brace, "Abstract of Code Noir—Intentions and Practice, 1685-1794," in *Proceedings of the Second Meeting of the Western Society for French History, November 21-23, 1974* (1975), 42.

[106]Memoir on the Mississippi, July 20, 1701, in Margry, *Découvertes,* IV, 484; Memoir by d'Iberville on the Establishment of the Mississippi, 1701. Paris, Cartes et Documents, Vol. 672, No. 4; Memoir on Louisiana by Mandeville, April 27, 1709. AC, C 13a, 2:475.

[107]Dartaguiette to Pontchartrain, June 20, 1710. AC, C 13a, 2:544.

[108]Memoir on Louisiana by Mandeville, April 29, 1709. AC, C 13a, 2:475.

[109]Jean Buvat, *Journal de la Régence (1715-1723),* ed. by Emile Campardon, 2 vols. (Paris, 1865), I, 422, 438, 441, 465; II, 40; Dorothy McKay Quynn, "Recruiting in Old Orleans for New Orleans,"

American Historical Review, XLVI (1941), 832-835; Commandant A. Herlaut, "Les Enlèvements d'enfants à Paris en 1720 et en 1750," *Revue Historique*, CXXXIX (1922), 43-51, 202-223.

[110]Giraud, *Histoire de la Louisiane*, III, 267.

[111]*Ibid.*, III, 237-238, 235.

[112]See Higginbotham, *Old Mobile*, pp. 132-142, 161-187, for a careful and detailed account of the recruitment, voyage, and subsequent fate of the *Pélican* girls.

[113]Charles R. Maduell, Jr., comp., *The Census Tables for the French Colony of Louisiana from 1699 through 1732* (Baltimore, 1972), pp. 1-10; Cadillac to Pontchartrain, October 26, 1713. AC, C 13a, 3:50-51.

[114]Cadillac to Minister, October 26, 1713. AC, C 13a, 3:50-51; Duclos to Minister, July 15, 1713. AC, C 13a, 3:138-139.

[115]Brevet to Sister Gertrude as matron, June 12, 1720. AC, B, 42bis:375; Brevet of Sisters Louise and Bergère as *conductrices*, June 12, 1720. AC, B, 42bis: 376. Though called "sisters" they were not nuns, but lay officers of the Hôpital Général of Paris. Henry Desgranges Légier, *Hospitaliers d'autrefois: Hôpital général de Paris, 1656-1790* (Paris, 1952).

[116] The number of respectable girls brought as *épouseuses* has been greatly inflated, every old family claims descent from a casket girl. Popular imagination seems to have worked in the same way in Canada. The *filles du roi*, king's maids, sent from 1663 to 1673, numbered only 961 according to Gustave Lanctot (*Filles de joie ou filles du roi: Etude sur l'émigration féminine en Nouvelle France* [Montreal, 1952], p. 113) and 774 according to Silvio Dumas (*Les Filles du Roi en Nouvelle France* [Quebec, 1972]), p. 43).

[117]Dumont de Montigny, *History of Louisiana, translated from the Historical Memoirs of M. Dumont*, in Benjamin French, *Historical Memoirs of Louisiana* (New York, 1853), V,15-16.

[118]Giraud, *Histoire de la Louisiane*, IV, 81.

[119]Chassin to (?), July 1, 1722. AC, C 13a, 6:297-297vo.,

[120]Cadillac to Council, January 2, 1716. AC, C 13a, 4:530-531.

[121]Périer and La Chaise to the Company, November 2, 1727. AC, C 13a, 10:108vo.

[122]Father Raphaël to Abbé Raguet, May 15, 1725. AC, C 13a, 8:402-402vo.

[123]Devin to Pauger, August 29, 1724. AC, C 13a, 8:204.

[124] *Ibid.*

[125] On the maintenance of aristocratic values and *préseances* in Canada, see Denys Delâge, "Canada and New York, 1608-1750" (MA thesis, University of Montreal, 1968), p. 175; "L'Affaire du Prie-Dieu, à Montréal, en 1694," pp. 71-110.

[126] Maduell, *Census Tables*, pp. 17-27, 39-47.

[127] *Ibid.*, pp. 51-76.

[128] *Ibid.*, pp. 114-122, 124-141.

Bibliography

PRIMARY SOURCES

Manuscripts

Paris, France. Archives Nationales, Archives des Colonies, Série A, Actes du Pouvoir Souverain.

__________. Archives Nationales, Archives des Colonies, Série B, Correspondance envoyée, Ordres du Roi.

__________. Archives Nationales, Archivres des Colonies, Série C, Sous-série 11, Canada, Correspondance générale.

__________. Archives Nationales, Archives des Colonies, Série C, Sous-série 13a, Louisiane, Correspondance générale.

__________. Archives Nationales, Archives des Colonies, Série C, Sous-série 13c, Louisiane, Correspondance générale, supplément.

__________. Archives Nationales, Archives des Colonies, Série F, Sous-série 3, Collection Moreau de Saint-Méry.

__________. Archives Nationales, Archives de la Marine, Série B, Correspondance.

__________. Archives Natrionales, Archives du Ministère des Affaires Etrangères, Mémoires et Documents, Amérique.

__________. Archives Nationales, Archives Dépôt des Cartes et Plans de la Marine.

__________. Bibliothèque Nationale, Fonds Français, Nouvelles Acquisitions, Fonds Clairambault, Volume 1016.

__________. Bibliothèque Nationale, Fonds Français, Nouvelles Acquisitions, Volumes 7497 (Bernou's correspondence); 7485 (Renaudot's correspondence), 9290, 9292, 9294, 9334 (Margry's papers).

Calendars and Bibliographies

Beers, Henry Putney. *The French in North America: A Bibliographical Guide to French Archives, Reproductions, and Research Missions.* Baton Rouge: Louisiana State University, 1957.

Bonnassieux, Pierre. *Conseil de Commerce et Bureau du Commerce, 1700-1791. Inventaire analytique des procès-verbaux.* Introduction and table by Eugène Lelong. Paris: Imprimerie Nationale, 1900.

Cox, E. G. *A Reference Guide to the Literature of Travel.* 3 vols. Seatle: University of Washington Press, 1939-1949.

Lanctot, Gustave. *L'Oeuvre de la France en Amérique du Nord. Bibliographie séléctive et critique.* Montreal: Fides, 1951.

Menier, Marie-Antoinette, Taillemite, Etienne, and Forges, Gilberte de. *Correspondance à l'arrivée en provenance de la Louisiane.* Tome I (articles C 13a 1 à 37). Paris: Imprimerie Nationale, 1976.

Messier, Jean-Jacques. *Bibliographie relative à la Nouvelle France.* Montreal: Les Editions Univers, 1979.

Rowland, Dunbar. *General Correspondence of Louisiana, 1678-1763.* New Orleans: Polyanthos, 1976.

Surrey, Nancy M. Miller. *Calendar of Manuscripts in Paris Archives and Libraries Relating to the History of the Mississippi Valley to 1803.* 2 vols. Washington: Carnegie Institution of Washington, 1926-1928.

Wroth, Lawrence C., and Annan, Gertrude L. *Acts of French Royal Administration Concerning Canada, Guiana, the West Indies and Louisiana, Prior to 1791.* New York: The New York Public Library, 1930.

Printed Sources

Barbier, Edmond-Jean-François. *Chronique de la Régence et du règne de Louis XV (1718-1763) ou Journal de Barbier.* 8 vols. Paris: Charpentier, 1957-1966.

Bartram-Hill, Henry, trans. *The Political Testament of Cardinal Richelieu: The Significant Chapters and Supporting Selections.* Madison: University of Wisconsin Press, 1961.

Beer, William, ed. "Le Code noir," *Publications of the Louisiana Historical Society,* IV (1908), 75-90.

Bossu, Jean Bernard. *Nouveaux Voyages aux Indes Occidentales . . .* Paris: Le Jay, 1768.

__________. *Nouveaux Voyages en Louisiane: 1751-1768.* Ed. Philippe Jacquin. Paris: Aubier Montagne, 1980.

__________. *Travels Through That Part of North America Formerly Called Louisiana.* Translated from the French by John Forster. 2 vols. London: Printed for T. Davies, 1771.

Brasseaux, Carl A., trans. and ed. *A Comparative View of French Louisiana, 1699 and 1762: The Journals of Pierre Le Moyne d'Iberville and Jean-Jacques-Blaise d'Abbadie.* Lafayette, La.: U.S.L. History Series, 1979.

Buvat, Jean. *Journal de la Régence (1715-1723).* Edited by Emile Campardon. 2 vols. Paris: Plon, 1865.

Campeau, Lucien. *Monumentae Novae Franciae.* Vol. 2: *Etablissement à Québec (1616-1634).* Rome and Québec: Les Presses de l'Université Laval, 1979.

__________. *La première mission d'Acadie (1602-1616).* Vol. 23 of *Monumenta Missionum Societates Jesu.* Quebec: Presses de l'Université Laval, 1967.

Cartier, Jacques. *Voyages en Nouvelle-France.* Texte remis en français moderne par Robert Lahaise et Marie Couturier avec introduction et notes. Ville La Salle: Editions Hurtubise HMH, 1977.

Charlevoix, Pierre François Xavier de, S. J. *History and General Description of New France.* Translated by John Gilmary Shea. Chicago: Loyola University Press, 1962. Reprint of 1870 edition.

Clément, Pierre. *Lettres, instructions et mémoire de Colbert.* 6 vols. in 9 pts. Paris: Imprimerie Impériale, 1861-1873.

Conrad, Glenn R., comp. *First Families of Louisiana.* 2 vols. Baton Rouge: Claitors, 1970.

__________, trans. and ed. *Immigration and War: Louisiana, 1718-1721, from the Memoir of Charles Le Gac.* Lafayette, La.: U. S. L. History Series, 1970.

__________, ed. *The Historical Journal of the Establishment of the French in Louisiana.* Translated by Joan Cain and Virginia Koenig. Lafayette, La.: U. S. L. History Series, 1971.

Cox, Isaac Joslin, ed. *The Journeys of René Robert Cavelier, Sieur de La Salle.* 2 vols. New York: ANS Press, 1973. Reprint of 1922 edition.

Coxe, Daniel. *A Description of the English Province of Carolana, by the Spaniards Called Florida, and by the French La Louisiane.* Gainesville, Fla.: The University Presses of Florida, 1976. Facsimile reproduction of the 1722 edition.

Delanglez, Jean, trans. and ed. *The Journal of Jean Cavelier: The Account of a Survivor of La Salle's Texas Expedition, 1684-1688.* Chicago: Institute of Jesuit History, 1938.

__________, ed. "Louisiana in 1717: Mémoire sur la Louisiane pour estre presenté, avec la carte de ce pais, au Conseil Soverain de Marine par F. Le Maire P. P. Miss. ap," *Revue d'Histoire de l'Amérique Française,* III (1949-1950), 94-100, 256-269, 423-446.

De Ville, Winston. *Louisiana Troops, 1720-1770.* Fort Worth, Texas: American Reference Publishers, 1965.

Dumont de Montigny, Butel. *Mémoires historiques sur la Louisiane,* in Benjamin French, ed. *Historical Collections of Louisiana.* New York: Lamport, Blakeman and Law, 1853.

Du Ru, Paul. *Journal of Paul du Ru (Febuary 1 to May 8, 1700): Missionary Priest to Louisiana.* Translated with introduction and notes from a manuscript in the Newberry Library by Ruth Lapham Butler. Chicago: Caxton Club, 1934.

Garneray, Louis. *Voyages, aventures et combats: Souvenirs de ma vie maritime.* Bruxelles: A. Lebègue, 1851.

Gravier, Gabriel. *Les Voyages de Giovanni Verrazano sur les côtes d'Amérique qvec des marins normands, pour le compte du roi de France en 1524-1528.* Rouen: Imprimerie E. Cagniard, 1898.

Grillon, Pierre, ed. *Les Papiers de Richelieu.* Paris: 6 vols. Editions A. Pedone, 1975.

Hennepin, Louis. *A Description of Louisiana.* Translated by John Gilmary Shea. Ann Arbor: University Microfilms, Inc., 1966. Reprint of 1880 edition.

__________. *A New Discovery of a Vast Country in America.* 2 vols. Chicago: A. C. McClurg and Co., 1903. New York: Klaus Reprint, 1972.

Higginbotham, Jay, trans. and ed. *The Journal of Sauvole: Historical Journal of the Establishment of the French in Louisiana by M. de Sauvole.* Mobile, Ala.: Colonial Books, 1969.

Isambert, François-André, et al. *Recueil général des anciennes lois françaises depuis l'an 420 jusqu'au la révolution de 1789.* 29 vols. Paris, 1821-1833.

Joutel's Journal of La Salle's Last Voyage. Introduction by Darritt B. Rutman. New York: Corinth Books, 1962.

Lahontan, Louis Armand de Lom d'Acre, baron de. *Dialogues curieux entre l'auteur et un sauvage de bon sens qui a voyagé et Mémoires de l'Amérique Septentrionale.* Baltimore: Johns Hopkins Press, 1931.

__________. *Nouveaux Voyages . . .* The Hague: Chez les frères Honoré, 1703.

Le Page du Pratz, Antoine-Simon. *Histoire de la Louisiane contenant la découverte de ce vaste pays; sa description géographique; un voyage dans les terres; l'histoire naturelle; les moeurs, coutumes et religion des naturels, avec leurs origines; deux voyages dans le nord du Nouveau Mexique, dont un jusqu'à la Mer du Sud, ornée de deux cartes et de 40 planches en taille douce.* 3 vols. Paris: De Bure, 1758.

Lescarbot, Marc. *Histoire de la Nouvelle-France suivie des Muses de la Nouvelle France.* Edited by Edwin Tross. 3 vols. Paris: Librairie Tross, 1866.

McWilliams, Richebourg Gaillard, trans. and ed. *Fleur de Lys and Calumet: Being the Penicaut Narrative of French Adventure in Louisiana.* Baton Rouge: Louisiana State University, 1953.

__________, trans. and ed. *Iberville's Gulf Journals.* University, Ala.: University of Alabama Press, 1981.

Maduell, Charles R. *The Census Tables for the French Colony of Louisiana from 1699 through 1732.* Baltimore: Genealogical Publishing Co., 1972.

Malouet, Victor-P. *Collection de mémoires et correspondance officielles sur l'administration des colonies, et notamment sur la Guiane française et hollandaise.* 5 vols. Paris: Baudouin, An X.

Marais, Mathieu. *Journal et mémoires de Mathieu Marais.* 2 vols. Geneva: Slatkine, 1967. Reprint of 1863-1868 edition.

Margry, Pierre. *Découvertes et établissements des Français dans l'ouest et dans le sud de l'Amérique septentrionale (1614-1754). Mémoires et documents originaux.* 6 vols. Paris: Imprimerie D. Jouaust, 1876-1886.

Mousnier, Jehan, ed. *Journal de la traite des noirs: Dam Joulin, Charles le Breton La Vallée, Garneray, Mérimée . . .* Paris: Editions de Paris, 1957.

O'Neill, Charles E., ed. *Charlevoix's Louisiana: Selections from the History and the Journal.* Baton Rouge: Louisiana State University, 1977.

Perrin du Lac, François-Marie *Voyage dans les deux Louisianes.* Paris: Capelle et Renaud, 1805.

Radisson, Pierre Esprit. *Voyages of Peter Esprit Radisson.* Translated by Gideon D. Scull. New York: Burt Franklin, 1967. Reprint of 1885 edition.

Rowland, Dunbar, and Sanders, A. G., eds. *Mississippi Provincial Archives: French Dominion.* 3 vols. Jackson: Mississippi Department of Archives and History, 1927.

Shea, John Gilmary, ed. *Discovery and Exploration of the Mississippi Valley.* Albany, N. Y.: Joseph McDonough, 1903.

__________. *The Expedition of Don Diego Dioniso de Peñalosa, Governor of New Mexico, from Santa Fe to the River Mischipi . . .* New York: J. G. Shea, 1882.

Talon, Jean. "Lettres et Mémoires," *Rapport de l'Archiviste de la Province de Québec pour 1930-1931.* Quebec: Redempti Paradis, 1931.

Thwaites, Reuben Gold. *The Jesuit Relations and Allied Documents: Travels and Explorations of the Jesuit Missionaries in New France, 1610-1791.* 73 vols. New York: Pageant Book Company, 1959. Reprint of the 1896-1901 edition.

Vitoria, Francisco de. *De Indis et de Jure Belli Reflectiones.* Ed. by Ernest Nys. Washington: The Classics of International Law, 1917.

Voorhies, Jacqueline K., comp. *Some Late Eighteenth Century Louisianians: Census Records of the Colony, 1758-1769.* Lafayette, La.: University of Southwestern Louisiana, 1973.

Waldseemüller, Martin. *Cosmographiae Introductu.* Translated by Joseph Fischer and Franz von Wieser. Ann Arbor: University Microfilms, Inc., 1966.

Weddle, Robert S., ed. *La Salle, the Mississippi, and the Gulf. Three Primary Documents.* College Station: Texas A & M University Press, 1987.

William III. *Letters of William III and Louis XIV and Their Ministers Illustrative of the Domestic and Foreign Policy of England from the Peace of Ryswick to the Accession of Philip V of Spain.* London: Longman, Brown, Green and Longmans, 1848.

Wood, George A. "Céleron de Blainville and French Expansion in the Ohio Valley," *Mississippi Valley Historical Review,* IX (1923), 302-319.

Wroth, Lawrence C. *The Voyages of Giovanni de Verrazzano, 1524-1528.* New Haven: Yale University Press, 1970.

Zoltvany, Yves F., ed. *The French Tradition in America.* Columbia, S. C.: University of South Carolina Press, 1969.

SECONDARY SOURCES

Unpublished Dissertations and Theses

Boucher, Philip Poulin. "France 'Discovers' America: The Image of Tropical America in Sixteenth and Seventeenth Century France and Its Impact on Early French Colonization." Ph. D. dissertation, University of Connecticut, 1974.

Daigle, Jean. "Nos amis les ennemis: Relations commerciales de l'Acadie avec le Massachusetts, 1670-1711." Ph. D. dissertation, University of Maine, 1975.

Delâge, Denys. "Canada and New York: 1608-1750." M. A. thesis, University of Montreal, 1968.

Forêt, Michael J. "Irresolution and Uncertainty: French Colonial Indian Policy in Louisiana, 1699-1763." M. A. thesis, University of Southwestern Louisiana, 1982.

Glenday, Daniel. "French Mercantilism and the Atlantic Colonies (With Specific References to New France), 1494-1672." M.A. thesis, McGill University, 1975.

Kilman, Grady. "Slavery and Forced Labor in Colonial Louisiana, 1699 to 1803." M. A. thesis, University of Southwestern Louisiana, 1972.

Lemieux, Donald. "The Office of 'Commissaire-Ordonnateur' in French Administration." Ph. D. dissertation, Louisiana State University, 1972.

Lima, Richard Arthur. "The Extraordinary Voyage Genre in Eighteenth-Century French Prose Fiction." Ph. D. dissertation, University of California-Berkeley, 1979.

McGowan, James Thomas. "Creation of a Slave Society: Louisiana Plantations in in the Eighteenth Century." Ph. D. Dissertation, University of Rochester, 1977.

Schaeper, Thomas J. "The French Council of Commerce, 1700-1715: An Administrative Study of Mercantilism after Colbert." Ph. D. dissertation, Ohio State University, 1977.

Sturdivant, Sheila T. "Rich Man, Poor Man, Beggar Man, Thief: Frenchmen Exiled to Louisiana, 1717-1721." M. A. thesis, University of Southwestern Louisiana, 1971.

Zaccano, Joseph Peter, Jr. "French Colonial Administration in Canada to 1760." Ph. D. dissertation, University of Pittsburgh, 1961.

Books

Atkinson, Geoffroy. *The Extraordinary Voyage in French Literature before 1700.* New York: Columbia University Press, 1920.

__________. *The Extraordinary Voyage in French Literature from 1700 to 1720.* Paris: E. Campion, 1922.

__________. *Les Nouveaux Horizons de la Renaissance française.* Paris: Oroz, 1935.

__________. *Les Relations de voyages du XVIIIe siècle et l'évolution des idées.* Génève: Slatkine, 1972. Reprint of the Paris edition, 1924.

Babelon, Jean-Pierre. *Henri IV.* Paris: A. Fayard, 1982.

Bamford, Paul Walden. *Forests and French Sea Power, 1660-1789.* Toronto: University of Toronto Press, 1956.

Banbuck, C. A. *Histoire politique, économique et sociale de la Martinique sous l'Ancien Régime (1635-1789).* Paris: Marcel Rivière, 1935.

Baxter, Stephen B. *William III and the Defense of European Liberty, 1650-1702.* New York: Harcourt, Brace and World, Inc., 1966.

Beloff, Max. *The Age of Absolutism, 1660-1815.* New York: Harper and Bros., 1962.

Belting, Natalia Maree. *Kaskaskia Under the French Regime.* Urbana: University of Illinois Press, 1948.

Bérenger, Jean. *Pionniers et colons en Amérique du Nord.* Paris: A. Colin, 1974.

Bergin, Joseph. *Cardinal Richelieu: Power and the Pursuit of Wealth.* New Haven: Yale University Press, 1985.

Biggar, H. P. *The Early Trading Companies of New France.* New York: Argonaut Press, 1965.

Bitton, Davis. *The French Nobility in Crisis: 1560-1640.* Stanford, Calif.: Stanford University Press, 1969.

Blet, Henri. *Histoire de la colonisation française. Naissance et declin d'un empire. Des origines à 1789.* 3 vols. Paris: B. Arthaud, 1946.

Bloch, Marc. *Les Caractères originaux de l'histoire rurale frančsaise.* 2 vols. Paris: A. Colin, 1952-1956.

Bluche, François. *Louis XIV.* Paris: A. Fayard, 1986.

Boiteux, Lucas-Alexandre *Richelieu: "Grand Maître de la navigation et du commerce de France."* Paris: Editions Ozanne, 1955.

Bordonove, Georges. *Les Rois qui ont fait la France: Henri IV, le grand.* Paris: Pygmalion, 1983.

__________. *Les Rois qui ont fait la France: Louis XIII, le juste.* Paris: Pygmalion, 1981.

__________. *Les Rois qui ont fait la France: Louis XIV, Roi Soleil.* Paris: Pygmalion, 1982.

__________. *Les Rois qui ont fait la France: Louis XV, le Bien-Aimé.* Paris: Pygmalion, 1982.

Boyer, Raymond. *Les Crimes et les châtiments au Canada français du XVIIe au XXe siècle.* Quebec: Le Cercle du livre de France, 1966.

Braudel, Fernand. *La Méditerranée et le monde méditerraneen à l'époque de Philippe IV.* Paris: Librairie Armand Colin, 1949.

Bridenbaugh, Carl, and Bridenbaugh, Roberta. *No Peace Beyond the Line: The English in the Caribbean, 1624-1690.* New York: Oxford University Press, 1972.

Brougham, Henry Peter. *An Inquiry into the Colonial Policy of the European Powers.* 2 vols. New York: Augustus M. Kelley, 1970. Reprint of 1803 edition.

Brunschwig, Henri. *La Colonisation française du Pacte colonial à l'Union Française.* Paris: Calmann-Levy, 1949.

Burckhardt, Carl J. *Richelieu: His Rise to Power.* New York: Vintage Books, 1964.

__________. *Richelieu and His Age: Assertion of Power and Cold War.* New York: Harcourt, Brace and World, 1965.

__________. *Richelieu and His Age: Power Politics and the Cardinal's Death.* New York: Harcourt, Brace Jovanovich, 1970.

Caldwell, Norman Ward. *The French in the Mississippi Valley, 1740-1750.* Philadelphia: Porcupine Press, 1974. Reprint of 1941 edition.

Carmona, Michel. *Marie de Médicis.* Paris: A. Fayard, 1981.

__________. *La France de Richelieu.* Paris: A. Fayard, 1984.

__________. *Richelieu: L'ambition et le pouvoir.* Paris: A. Fayard, 1983.

Carpenter, John R. *Histoire de la littérature française sur la Louisiane de 1673 jusqu'à 1766.* Paris: A. C. Nizet, 1966.

Caruso, John Anthony. *The Mississippi Valley Frontier: The Age of French Exploration and Settlement.* New York: Bobbs Merrill, 1966.

Chailley-Bert, Joseph. *Les Compagnies de colonisation sous l'Ancien Régfime.* New York: Burt Franklin, 1968. Reprint of 1898 edition.

Chambers, Henry E. *Mississippi Valley Beginnings.* New York: G. P. Putnam's Sons, 1922.

Chaunu, Pierre, and Gascon, Richard. *Histoire économique et sociale de la France.* Tome I: *de 1450 à 1660.* Paris: Presses Universitaires de France, 1977.

Chesnel, Paul *Histoire de Cavelier de la Salle: Exploration et conquête du Bassin du Mississippi . . .* Paris: J. Maisonneuve, 1901.

Chevallier, Pierre. *Louis XIII, roi cornelien.* Paris: A. Fayard, 1979.

Chinard, Gilbert. *L'Amérique et le rêve exotique dans la littérature française au XVIIe et au XVIIIe siècles.* Geneva: Slatkine, 1970. Reprint of the 1913 edition.

Church, William F. *Richelieu and Reason of State.* Princeton, N. J.: Princeton University Press, 1972.

Clark, John G. *La Rochelle and the Atlantic Economy during the Eighteenth Century.* Baltimore: Johns Hopkins Press, 1981.

__________. *New Orleans, 1718-1812: An Economic History.* Baton Rouge: Louisiana State University, 1970.

Clément, Pierre. *Histoire de Colbert et de son administration.* 2 vols. Geneva: Slatkine, 1980. Reprint of 1874 edition.

__________. *Histoire du système protecteur en France, depuis le ministère de Colbert jusqu'à la révolution de 1848 . . .* New York: Burt Franklin, 1968. Reprint of 1854 edition.

Cloulas, Ivan. *Catherine de Médicis.* Paris: A. Fayard, 1979.

Cole, Charles Woolsey. *Colbert and a Century of French Mercantilism.* 2 vols. Morningside Heights: Columbia University Press, 1939.

__________. *French Mercantilism, 1683-1700.* New York: Columbia University Press, 1933.

Colloque sur les institutions coloniales dans les Amériques au XVIIIe siècle. Ottawa: Pan-American Institute of Geography and History, 1972.

Copleston, Frederick Charles. *A History of Philosophy.* 9 vols. Westminster, Md.: Newman Press, 1946-1975.

Corkran, David H. *The Cherokee Frontier: Conflict and Survival, 1740-1762.* Norman: University of Oklahoma Press, 1962.

Crane, Verner W. *The Southern Frontier, 1670-1732.* Ann Arbor: University of Michigan Press, 1965. Reprint of 1928 edition.

Crété, Liliane. *Coligny.* Paris: A. Fayard, 1985.

Crouse, Nellis M. *French Pioneers in the West Indies, 1624-1664.* New York: Columbia University Press, 1940.

__________. *La Verendrye: Fur Trader and Explorer.* Port Washington, N. Y.: Kennikat Press, 1972. Reprint of 1956 edition.

Davies, Kenneth Gordon *The North Atlantic World in the Seventeenth Century.* Minneapolis: University of Minnesota Press, 1974.

Delanglez, Jean. *The French Jesuits in Lower Louisiana (1700-1763).* Washington, D. C.: The Catholic University of America, 1935.

__________. *Some La Salle Journeys.* Chicago: Institute of Jesuit History, 1938.

Delcourt, André. *La France et les établissements français au Sénégal entre 1713 et 1763.* Dakar: Mémoires de l'IFAN, no. 17, 1952.

Denis, Henri. *Histoire de la pensée économique.* Paris: Presses Universitaires de France, 1966.

Dent, Julian. *Crisis in Finance: Crown, Financiers and Society in Seventeenth-Century France.* New Abbot: David and Charles, 1973.

Deschamps, Hubert. *Les Méthodes et les doctrines coloniales de la France (du XVIe siècle à nos jours).* Paris: Armand Colin, 1953.

Deschamps, Léon. *Histoire de la question coloniale en France.* Paris: E. Plon, Nourrit, 1891.

Desgranges, Henry Légier. *Hospitaliers d'autrefois. Hôpital général de Paris, 1656-1790.* Paris: Hachette, 1952.

Dessert, Daniel. *Argent, pouvoir et société au grand siècle.* Paris: A. Fayard, 1984.

Dickason, Olive Patricia. *The Myth of the Savage and the Beginnings of French Colonialism in the Americas.* Edmonton: University of Alberta Press, 1984.

Donnelly, Joseph P. *Jacques Marquette, S. J., 1637-1675.* Chicago: Loyola University Press, 1968.

Doucet, R. *Les Institutions de la France au XVIe siècle.* 2 vols. Paris: Editions A. et J. Picard et Cie, 1948.

Dubois, Marcel. *Systèmes coloniaux et peuples colonisateurs.* Paris: G. Masson, E. Plon, Nourrit, 1895.

Ducasse, André. *Les Négriers ou le trafic des esclaves.* Paris: Hachette, 1948.

Duchêne, Albert. *Histoire des finances coloniales de la France.* Paris: Payot, 1938.

__________. *La Politique coloniale de la France. Le Ministère des colonies depuis Richelieu.* Paris: Payot, 1928.

Dumas, Silvio. *Les Filles du roi en Nouvelle France.* Cahiers d'Histoire, no. 24. Quebec: La Société Historique du Quebec, 1972.

Dunn, William Edward. *Spanish and French Rivalry in the Gulf Region of the United States, 1678-1702: The Beginnings of Texas and Pensacola.* Austin: University of Texas Bulletin, no. 1705, 1917.

Eccles, William J. *Canada Under Louis XIV: 1663-1701.* Toronto: McClelland and Stewart, 1963.

__________. *Canadian Society Under the French Regime.* Montreal: Harvest House, 1968.

__________. *France in America.* New York: Harper Torchbook, 1972.

__________. *Frontenac: The Courtier Governor.* Toronto: McClelland and Stewart Limited, 1968.

__________. *The Government of New France.* Ottawa: The Canadian Historical Association Booklets, no. 18, 1971.

Elkins, Stanley. *Slavery: A Problem in American Institutional and Intellectual Life.* Chicago: University of Chicago Press, 1959.

Faure, Edgar. *La Banqueroute de Law.* Paris: Gallimard, 1977.

Fieldhouse, David Kenneth. *The Colonial Empires: A Comparative Survey from the Eighteenth Century.* New York: Dell Publishing Co., 1971.

Filion, Maurice. *Maurepas, ministre de Louis XV (1715-1749).* Préface de Frédéric Mauro. Montreal: Leméac, 1967.

Folmer, Henry. *Franco-Spanish Rivalry in North America, 1524-1763.* Glendale, Calif.: The Arthur H. Clark Company, 1953.

Foucault, Michel. *Folie et déraison. Histoire de la folie à l'époque classique.* Paris: Plon, 1961.

Fouchard, Jean. *Les Marrons de la liberté.* Paris: Editions de l'Ecole, 1972.

__________. *Les Marrons du syllabaire. Quelques aspects du problème de l'instruction et de l'éducation des esclaves et affranchis de Saint-Domingue.* Port-au-Prince, Haiti: Henri Deschamps, 1953.

Frégault, Guy. *La Civilisation de la Nouvelle-France, 1713-1744.* Montreal: Fides, 1969.

__________. *Le XVIIIe siècle canadien: Etudes.* Montreal: Editions HMH, 1968.

__________. *Le Grand Marquis: Pierre de Rigaud de Vaudreuil et la Louisiane.* Montreal: Fides, 1952.

__________. *Pierre Le Moyne d'Iberville.* Montreal: Editions Fides, 1968.

Frostin, Charles. *Les Révoltes blanches à Saint-Domingue aux XVIIe et XVIIIe siècles (Haïti avant 1789).* Paris: L'Ecole, 1975.

Galloway, Patricia K., ed. *La Salle and His Legacy: Frenchmen and Indians in the Lower Mississippi Valley.* Jackson, Miss.: University Press of Mississippi, 1982.

Garnault, Emile. *Le Commerce rochelais au XVIIIe siècle.* 3e partie: *Marine et colonie.* La Rochelle: E. Martin, 1891.

Garrison, Janine. *L'Edit de Nantes et sa révocation. Histoire d'une intolérance* . Paris: Editions du Seuil, 1985.

__________. *Henri IV.* Paris: Seuil, 1984.

Genovese, Eugene. *Roll, Jordan, Roll: The World the Slaves Made.* New York: Pantheon Books, 1974.

Giraud, Marcel. *Histoire de la Louisiane française.* Vol. I: *Le règne de Louis XIV (1698-1715).* Paris: Presses Universitaires de France, 1953.

__________. *Histoire de la Louisiane française.* Vol. II: *Années de transition (1715-1717).* Paris: Presses Universitaires de France, 1958.

__________. *Histoire de la Louisiane française.* Vol. III: *L'époque de John Law (1717-1720).* Paris: Presses Universitaires de France, 1966.

Girault, Arthur. *Les Colonies françaises avant et depuis 1815.* 6e édition. Paris: Recueil Sirey, 1943.

__________. *Principes de colonisation et de législation coloniale: la Tunisie et le Maroc.* Paris: Librairie du Recueil Sirey, 1936.

Goubert, Pierre. *Louis XIV et vingt millions de Français.* Paris: A. Fayard, 1966.

Gravier, Gabriel. *Découvertes et établissements de Cavelier de la Salle de Rouen dans l'Amérique du Nord.* Paris: Maisonneuve et Cie, 1870.

Guy, Richard. *Noblesse d'affaires au XVIIIe siècle.* Paris: Armand Colin, 1974.

Hamelin, Jean. *Economie et société en Nouvelle-France.* Quebec: PUL, 1960.

Hamer, Pierre. *Raphaël de Luxembourg; Une Contribution luxembourgeois à la colonisation de la Louisiane.* Luxembourg: Publication de la Section Historique de l'Institut Grand-Ducal, 1966.

Hamilton, Raphael N. *Marquette's Explorations: The Narratives Reexamined.* Madison: The University of Wisconsin Press, 1970.

Hammang, Francis H. *The Marquis de Vaudreuil: New France at the Beginning of the Eighteenth Century.* New York: Bruges, 1938.

Hanotaux, Gabriel. *Histoire du Cardinal de Richelieu.* 6 vols. Paris: Librairie Plon, [1932].

Hardy, Georges. *Histoire sociale de la colonisation française.* Paris: Larose-Paris, 1953.

Harmand, Jules. *Domination et colonisation.* Paris: Ernest Flammarion, 1910.

Harris, Richard Colebrook. *The Seigneurial System in Early Canada: A Geographical Study.* Madison: The University of Wisconsin Press, 1968.

Harsen, Paul. *Crédit public et banque d'état en France du XVIe au XVIIIe siècle.* Paris: Droz, 1933.

Hauser, Henri. *La Pensée et l'action économiques du Cardinal de Richelieu.* Paris: Presses Universitaires de France, 1944.

Heinrich, Pierre. *La Louisiane sous la Compagnie des Indes: 1717-1731.* New York: Burt Franklin, 1970. Reprint of 1908 edition.

Higginbotham, Jay. *Fort Maurepas: The Birth of Louisiana.* Mobile, Ala.: Colonial Books, 1968.

__________. *Old Mobile: Fort Louis de la Louisiane, 1702-1711.* Mobile: Museum of the City of Mobile, 1977.

Innes, Harold A. *The Fur Trade in Canada: An Introduction to Canadian Economic History.* Toronto: University of Toronto Press, 1973.

Jacobs, Wilbur R. *Wilderness Politics and Indian Gifts: The Northern Colonial Frontier, 1648-1763.* Lincoln, Neb.: University of Nebraska Press, 1966.

Jacquart, Jean. *François Ier.* Paris: A. Fayard, 1981.

Jaenen, Cornelius. *Friend and Foe: Aspects of French-Amerindian Cultural Contact in the Sixteenth and Seventeenth Centuries.* New York: Columbia University Press, 1976.

__________. *The Role of the Church in New France.* Toronto: McGraw-Hill, Ryerson, Ltd., 1976.

Jaray, Gabriel-Louis. *L'Empire français d'Amérique (1534-1803).* Paris: Armand Colin, 1938.

Jones, James Rees *Country and Court: England, 1658-1716.* Cambridge, Mass.: Harvard University Press, 1978.

Jouan, René. *Histoire de la marine française.* Paris: Payot, 1932.

Julien, Charles-André. *Les Français en Amérique au XVIIe siècle.* Paris: Centre de Documentation Universitaire et Société d'Edition d'Enseignement Supérieur, 1957.

__________. *Les Français en Amérique de 1713 à 1784.* Paris: Centre de Documentation Universitaire et Société d'Edition d'Enseignement Supérieur, 1957.

__________, and Herval, Beauchesne, Th., eds., *Les Français en Amérique pendant la première partie du XVIe siècle. Textes des voyages de Gonneville, Verrazzano, J. Cartier et Roberval.* Introduction de Charles-André Julien. Paris: Presses Universitaires de France, 1946.

Keller, Albert Galloway. *Colonization: A Study of the Founding of New Societies.* Boston: Ginn and Co., 1908.

Kennedy, John Hopkins *Jesuit and Savage in New France.* Hamden, Conn.,: Archon Books, 1971. Reprint of 1950 edition.

Klein, Herbert S. *The Middle Passage: Comparative Studies in the Atlantic Slave Trade.* Princeton, N. J.: Princeton University Press, 1978.

Knecht, Robert J. *Francis I.* Cambridge: Cambridge University Press, 1982.

Krech, Shepard, III, ed. *The Subartic Fur Trade.* Vancouver: University of British Columbia Press, 1984.

Labrousse, Ernest, et al. *Histoire économique et sociale de la France.* Tome II. *Des derniers temps de l'âge seigneurial aux préludes de l'âge industriel (1600-1789).* Paris: Presses Universitaires de France, 1970.

La Chance, André. *Le Bourreau au Canada sous le régime français.* Quebec: La Société Historique de Québec, 1966.

La Cour-Gayet, Georges *Histoire de la marine.* Paris: L'Illustration, 1934.

__________. *La Marine militaire de la France sous le règne de Louis XV.* Paris: Honoré Champion, 1902.

Lamontagne, Roland. *La Galissonière et le Canada.* Préface de Louis de Broglie. Paris: Presses Universitaires de France, 1962.

__________. *Succès d'intendance de Talon.* Montreal: Leméac, 1964.

Lanctôt, Gustave. *Filles de joie ou filles du roi. Etude sur l'émigration féminine en Nouvelle-France.* Montreal: Editions Chantidier, 1952.

Lebigre, Arlette. *Les Grands Jours d'Auvergne: Désordres et répressions au XVIIe siècle.* Paris: Hachette, 1976.

Leconteux, Bernard. *Law et le commerce colonial.* Paris: Jouve, 1921.

Lemontey, Pierre-Edouard. *Histoire de la Régence et de la minorité de Louis XV jusqu'au ministère du Cardinal Fleury.* 2 vols. Paris: Paulin, 1832.

Leroy-Beaulieu, Paul. *De la colonisation chez les peuples modernes.* Paris: Librairie Guillaumin, 1886.

Levasseur, Emile. *Recherches historiques sur le système de Law.* Paris: Librairie Guillaumin, 1854.

Lodge, Eleanor C. *Sully, Colbert, and Turgot: A Chapter in French Economic History.* London: Metheun, 1931.

Lodge, Richard. *Studies in Eighteenth-Century Diplomacy, 1740-1748.* London: J. Murray, 1930.

Lokke, Carl Ludwig. *France and the Colonial Question: A Study of Contemporary French Opinion, 1763-1851.* New York: Columbia University Press, 1932.

Lough, John. *An Introduction to Eighteenth-Century France.* London: Longman's, Green and Co., 1960.

Luthy, Herbert. *La Banque protestante en France de la Révocation de l'Edit de Nantes à la Révolution.* 2 vols. Paris: SEVPEN, 1959.

McCloy, Shelby T. *Government Assistance in Eighteenth-Century France.* Philadelphia: Porcupine Press, 1977. Reprint of 1946 edition.

McCusker, John J. *Money and Exchange in Europe and America, 1600-1775: A Handbook.* Chapel Hill: University of North Carolina Press for the Institute of Early American History and Culture, Williamsburg, Va., 1978.

McDermott, John Francis, ed. *Frenchmen and French Ways in the Mississippi Valley.* Urbana: University of Illinois Press, 1969.

MacKirdy, Kenneth A., Moir, John S., and Zoltvany, Yves F., ed. *Changing Perspectives in Canadian History.* Notre Dame, Ind.: University of Notre Dame Press, 1967.

Malvezin, Théophile. *Histoire du commerce de Bordeaux depuis les origines jusqu'à nos jours.* 3 vols. Bordeaux: Imprimerie Nouvelle, 1892.

Mandrou, Robert. *La Raison du prince. L'Europe absolutiste, 1649-1775.* Paris: Marabout, 1980.

Marquis, Thomas Guthrie. *The Jesuit Missions: A Chronicle of the Cross in the Wilderness.* Toronto: Glascow, Brook and Company, 1916.

Martin, Gaston. *Capital et travail à Nantes au cours du XVIIIe siècle.* Paris: Marcel Rivière, 1931.

__________. *Histoire de l'esclavage dans les colonies françaises.* Paris: Presses Universitaires de France, 1948.

__________. *Nantes au XVIIIe siècle: L'administration de Gérard Mellier (1709-1720-1729).* Nantes: Librairie Ancienne et Moderne, L. Durance, 1928.

__________. *Nantes au XVIIIe siècle: L'ère des négriers, 1714-1774.* Paris: Presses Universitaires de France, 1931.

__________. *Nantes et la Compagnie des Indes (1664-1769).* Paris: Librairie des Sciences Economiques et Sociales Marcel Rivière, n. d.

__________. *Négriers et bois d'ébène.* Grenoble: B. Arthaud, 1934.

Martin, Germain. *La Grande Industrie sous le règne de Louis XIV (Plus particulièrement de 1660 à 1715).* New York: Burt Franklin, 1971. Reprint of 1899 edition.

Martineau, Alfred, and May, Louis-Philippe. *Trois siècles d'histoire antillaise: Martinique et Guadeloupe de 1635 à nos jours.* Paris: Société de l'Histoire des Colonies française, 1935.

Mauro, Frédéric. *L'Expansion européenne (1600-1870).* Paris: Presses Universitaires de France, 1967.

May, Louis-Philippe. *Histoire économique de la Martinique (1635-1763).* Paris: Marcel Rivière, 1930.

Meyer, Jean. *Colbert.* Paris: Hachette, 1981.

__________. *La France moderne de 1515 à 1789.* Vol. III of Jean Favier, ed., *Histoire de France.* Paris: A. Fayard, 1980.

__________. *Le Régent, 1674-1723.* Paris: Ramsay, 1985.

__________. *La Vie quotidienne en France au temps de la Régence.* Paris: Hachette, 1979.

Mims, Stewart L. *Colbert's West Indian Policy.* New Haven: Yale University Press, 1912.

Mousnier, Roland. *La Vénalité des offices sous Henri IV et Louis XIII.* Paris: n.p., 1945.

__________. *Fureurs paysannes: Les paysans dans les révoltes du XVIIe siècle (France, Russie, Chine).* Paris: Calman Lévy, 1967.

__________, ed. *Un Nouveau Colbert. Actes du colloque organisé pour le tricentenaire de la mort de Colbert.* Paris: Sedes, 1985.

Munro, William Bennett. *The Seigneurs of Old Canada: A Chronicle of New World Feudalism.* Toronto: Glascow, Brook and Company, 1914.

Murat, Ines. *Colbert: Portrait d'un grand argentier.* Paris: Livre de poche, 1984.

Murphy, Edmund R. M. *Henry de Tonty: Fur Trader of the Mississippi.* Baltimore: Johns Hopkins Press, 1941.

Néret, Jean-Alexis. *Capitaine Jacques Cartier.* Ottawa: Cercle du Livre de France, 1949.

Nish, Cameron. *Les Bourgeois-gentilhommes de la Nouvelle France, 1729-1740.* Montreal: Fides, 1968.

Nowell, Charles E. *The Great Discoveries and the First Colonial Empires.* Ithaca, N. Y.: Cornell University Press, 1954.

Nute, Grace Lee. *Caesars of the Wilderness: Médard Chouart, sieur des Groseillers and Pierre Esprit Radisson, 1618-1710.* St. Paul: Minnesota Historical Society Press, 1978. Reprint of 1943 edition.

__________. *The Voyageur.* St. Paul, Minn.: Minnesota Historical Society, 1966. Reprint of 1955 edition.

Ogg, Frederick Austin. *The Opening of the Mississippi: A Struggle for Supremacy in the American Interior.* New York: Cooper Square Publilshers, Inc., 1968.

O'Neill, Charles Edwards. *Church and State in French Colonial Louisiana: Policy and Politics to 1732.* New Haven: Yale University Press, 1966.

Osler, Edmund B. *La Salle.* Don Mills, Ont.: Longmans Canada, 1967.

Ouellet, Fernand. *Histoire économique et sociale du Québec, 1760-1850. Structures et conjonctures.* Montreal: Fides, 1966.

Packard, Laurence Bradford. *The Commercial Revolution, 1400-1766: Mercantilism-Colbert-Adam Smith.* New York: Holt, 1927.

Palm, Franklin Charles. *The Economic Policies of Richelieu.* Urbana, Ill.: University of Illinois Studies in the Social Sciences, IX, no. 4, 1920.

Pares, Richard. *War and Trade in the West Indies, 1739-1763.* London: Frank Cass and Co., 1963.

Parkman, Francis. *Count Frontenac and New France under Louis XIV.* Boston: Little, Brown and Company, 1922.

__________. *The Jesuits in North America in the Seventeenth Century.* Boston: Little, Brown and Company, 1892.

__________. *La Salle and the Discovery of the Great West.* Boston: Little, Brown and Company, 1902.

Parry, John H. *The Establishment of the European Hegemony, 1415-1715: Trade and Exploration in the Age of the Renaissance.* New York: Harper Torchbooks, 1966.

Pauliat, Louis. *Louis XIV et la Compagnie des Indes Orientales de 1664.* Paris: Calmann-Lévy, 1886.

__________. *La Politique coloniale sous l'Ancien Régime.* Paris: Calmann-Lévy, 1887.

Perkins, James Breck. *France Under Louis XIV.* 2 vols. New York: Houghton Mifflin, 1897.

__________. *France Under Mazarin, with a Review of the Administration of Richelieu.* 2 vols. New York: G. P. Putnam's Sons, 1886.

__________. *Richelieu and the Growth of French Power.* New York: G. P. Putnam and Sons, 1926.

Pluchon, Pierre. *Nègres et juifs au XVIIIe siècle. Le Racisme au siècle des lumières.* Paris: Tallandier, 1984.

Porchnev, Boris. *Les Soulèvements populaires en France de 1623 à 1648.* Paris: S.E.V.P.E.N., 1963.

Pothier, Robert-Joseph. *Oeuvres.* 10 vols. Paris: Cosse et N. Relamotte, 1845-1848.

Priestley, Herbert Ingram. *France Overseas Through the Old Regime: A Study in European Expansion.* New York: D. Appleton-Century, 1939.

Rameau de Saint-Père, Edme. *Une Colonie féodale en Amérique: L'Acadie (1604-1881).* Paris: E. Plon, Nourrit et Cie, 1889.

Rawlyk, George A. *Nova Scotia's Massachusetts: A Study of Massachusetts-Nova Scotia Relations, 1630 to 1784.* Montreal: McGill-Queen's University Press, 1973.

Roncière, Charles de la. *Nègres et négriers.* Paris: Editions des Portiques, 1933.

Rothkrug, Lionel. *Opposition to Louis XIV: The Political and Social Origins of the French Enlightenment.* Princeton, N. J.: Princeton University Press, 1965.

Sagnac, Philippe, and Saint-Leger, Alexandre de. *Louis XIV (1676-1715).* Peuples et civilisations. Paris: Presses Universitaires de France, 1949.

Saintoyant, Jules-François *La Colonisation européenne du XVe au XIXe siècle.* Tome I: *La Formation des empires coloniaux (XVe-XVIIe siècles).* Paris: La Renaissance du Livre, 1947.

__________. *La Colonisation française sous l'Ancien Régime (du XVe siècle à 1789).* 2 vols. Paris: La Renaissance du Livre, 1929.

Salone, Emile. *La Colonisation de la Nouvelle France. Etude sur les origines de la nation canadienne française.* Paris: E. Guilmoto, n. d.

Schefer, Christian. *La France moderne et le problème colonial.* Vol. I. Paris: Félix Alclan, 1907.

Schmoller, Gustav. *The Mercantile System and Its Historical Significance.* New York: Peter Smith, 1931.

Schoelcher, Victor. *Esclavage et colonisation.* Paris: Presses Universitaires de France, 1948.

Seward, Desmond. *The Bourbon Kings of France.* New York: Barnes and Noble, 1976.

Smith, Donald. *Le "Sauvage" pendant la periode héroique de la Nouvelle France (1534-1663) d'après les historiens canadiens-français des XIXe et XXe siècles.* Ville La Salle: Hurtubise HMH, 1974.

Spears, John R. *A History of the Mississippi Valley from Its Discovery to the End of Foreign Domination.* New York: A. S. Clark, 1903.

Steele, Ian Kenneth *Politics of Colonial Policy: The Board of Trade in Colonial Administration, 1696-1720.* Oxford: Clarendon Press, 1968.

Surrey, Nancy M. *The Commerce of Louisiana during the French Regime, 1699-1763.* New York: Longman, Green and Co., 1916.

Tannebaum, Frank. *Slave and Citizen: The Negro in the Americas.* New York: A. A. Knopf, 1947.

Tapié, Victor-Lucien. *La France de Louis XIII et de Richelieu.* Paris: Flammarion, 1980.

Taylor, Joe Gray. *Negro Slavery in Louisiana.* Baton Rouge: Louisiana Historical Association, 1963.

Terrasse, Charles. *François Ier. Le Roi et le règne.* Paris: Editions Bernard Grapet, 1943.

Tersen, Emile. *Histoire de la colonisation française.* Paris: Presses Universitaires de France, 1950.

Tramond, Joannès. *Manuel d'histoire maritime de la France des origines à 1815.* Paris: Sociéte d'Editions Géographiques, Maritimes et Coloniales, 1927.

__________. *Manuel d'histoire maritime de la France.* Paris: Augustin Challamel, 1916.

Treasure, G. R. R. *Cardinal Richelieu and the Development of Absolutism.* New York: St. Martin's Press, 1972.

Trout, Andrew. *Jean-Baptiste Colbert.* Boston: Twayne, 1978.

Trudel, Marcel. *The Beginnings of New France, 1524-1663.* Translated by Patricia Claxton. Toronto: McClelland and Stewart Ltd., 1973.

__________. *Les Débuts du regime seigneurial au Canada.* Montreal: Fides, 1974.

__________. *L'Esclavage au Canada français: Histoire et conditions de l'esclavage.* Quebec: Presses Universitaires Laval, 1960.

__________. *Histoire de la Nouvelle France.* Vol. I: *Les vaines tentatives, 1524-1603.* Montreal: Fides, 1963.

__________. *Histoire de la Nouvelle France.* Vol. II. *Le comptoir, 1604-1627.* Montreal: Fides, 1966.

__________. *Initiation à la Nouvelle-France. Histoire et institution.* Montreal: Holt, Rinehart and Winston, 1968.

__________. *Le Régime seigneurial.* Ottawa: Les Brochures de la Société Historique du Canada, no. 6, 1971.

Vaucher, Paul. *Robert Walpole et la politique de Fleury (1731-1742).* Paris: Librairie Plon, 1924.

Vigié, Marc. *Les Galériens du roi, 1661-1715.* Paris: A. Fayard, 1985.

Vignols, Léon. *Les Antilles françaises sous l'Ancien Régime.* Paris: M. Rivière, 1928.

Villiers du Terrage, Marc de. *Les Dernières Années de la Louisiane française.* Paris: E. Guilmoto, 1904.

Walker, Geoffrey J. *Spanish Politics and Imperial Trade, 1700-1789.* Bloomington: Indiana University Press, 1979.

Weber, Henry. *La Compagnie française des Indes (1604-1875).* Paris: A. Rousseau, 1904.

Weddle, Robert S. *Wilderness Manhunt: The Spanish Search for La Salle.* Austin: University of Texas Press, 1973.

Wedgewood, C. V. *Richelieu and the French Monarchy.* New York: Collier Books, 1962.

Williams, Basil. *The Whig Supremacy, 1714-1760.* Oxford: Clardneon Press, 1942.

Williams, Glyndur. *Expansion of Europe in the Eighteenth Century: Overseas Rivalry, Discovery and Exploration.* New York: Walker and Co., 1966.

Wilson, Arthur McCandless. *French Foreign Policy during the Administration of Cardinal Fleury, 1726-1743.* Cambridge, Mass.: Harvard University Press, 1936.

Winsor, Justin. *Cartier to Frontenac: Georgraphical Discovery in the Interior of North America in Its Historical Relations, 1534-1700.* New York: Cooper Square Publishers, Inc., 1970.

__________. *The Mississippi Basin . . . : The Struggle in America Between England and France, 1697-1763, with Full Cartographical Illustration from Contemporary Sources.* New York: Houghton, Mifflin and Company, 1895.

Wolf, John B. *Louis XIV.* New York: W. W. Norton and Company, 1968.

Woods, Patricia Dillon. *French-Indian Relations on the Southern Frontier, 1699-1762.* Ann Arbor: University Microfilms, Inc., 1980.

Yacono, Xavier. *Histoire de la colonisation française.* Paris: Presses Universitaires de France, 1969.

Zarb, Mireille. *Les Privilèges de la ville de Marseilles du Xe siècle à la Révolution.* Paris: A. et J. Picard, 1961.

Zoltvany, Yves F. *Phillippe de Vaudreuil, Governor of New France, 1703-1725.* Toronto: McClelland and Stewart, Ltd., 1974.

Articles

Adair, E. R. "Anglo-French Rivalry in the Fur Trade during the Eighteenth Century," *Culture,* VIII (1947), 435-455.

__________. "France and the Beginning of New France," *Canadian Historical Review,* XXV (1944), 246-278.

__________. "The French-Canadian Seigneurie," *Canadian Historical Review,* XXXV (1954), 187-207.

"L'Affaire du prie-dieu, à Montreal, en 1694," *Rapport des Archives de la Province de Quebec,* (1923-1924), 71-110.

Aiton, Arthur S. "The Asiento Treaty as Reflected in the Papers of Lord Shelburne," *Hispanic American Historical Review,* VIII (1928), 167-177.

Allain, Mathé. "French Emigration Policies: Louisiana, 1699-1715," *Proceedings of the Fourth Meeting of the French Colonial Historical Society, April 6-8, 1978*. Washington, D. C.: University Press of America, 1979, 39-46.

__________. "L'Immigration française en Louisiane, 1718-1721," *Revue d'Histoire de l'Amérique Française,* XXVIII (1975), 555-564.

__________. "Manon Lescaut et ses consoeurs: Women in the Early French Period, 1700-1731," *Proceedings of the Fifth Meeting of the French Colonial Historical Society, March 29-April 1, 1979.* Washington, D. C.: University Press of America, 1980, 18-26.

Baker, Vaughan B. "Les Louisianaises: A Reconnaissance," *Proceedings of the Fifth Meeting of the French Colonial Historical Society, March 29-April 1, 1979*. Washington, D. C.: University Press of America, 1980, 6-15.

Bamford, Paul. "Entrepreneurship in Seventeenth- and Eighteenth-Century France: Some General Conditions and a Case Study," *Explorations in Entrepreneurial History,* IX (1957), 204-213.

Bataillon, Marcel. "L'Amiral et les 'nouveaux horizons' français," *Actes du Colloque l'Amiral de Coligny et son temps (Paris, 24-29 octobre 1972).* Paris: Société de l'Histoire du Protestantisme Français, 1974, 41-52.

Beauchesne, Genviève. "Les Sources de l'histoire du port de Lorient et des trois Grandes Compagnies des Indes," *Revue d'Histoire des Colonies,* XLII (1955), 96-109.

Bédard, Marc-André. "La Présence protestante en Nouvelle-France," *Revue d'Histoire de l'Amérique Française,* XXXI (1978), 325-349.

Behrens, Betty. "Nobles, Privileges and Taxes in France at the End of the Ancien Régime," *Economic History Review,* Second Series 2, XV (1962-1963), 451-475.

Belting, Natalia Maree. "The French Villages of the Illinois Country," *Canadian Historical Review,* XXIV, (1943), 14-23.

Bertin, Gilles Y. "Les Aspects comptables et financiers du commerce colonial de la Compagnie des Indes entre 1719 et 1730," *Revue d'Histoire Economique et Sociale,* XL (1962), 449-483.

Besson, Maurice. "La Police des noirs sous Louis XVI en France," *Revue d'Histoire des Colonies Françaises,* XVI (1928), 433-446.

Bilodeau, Rosario. "Liberté économique et politique des Canadiens sous le régime français," *Revue d'Histoire de l'Amérique Française,* X (1956), 49-68.

Bois, Guy. "Against the Neo-Malthusian Orthodoxy," *Past and Present,* no. 79 (1978), 60-69.

Boissonnade, Pierre. "Colbert et la souscription aux actions de la Compagnie des Indes spécialement en Poitou (1664-1668)," *Bulletin de la Société des Antiquaires de l'Ouest,* I (1907-1909), 423-451.

Bolton, Herbert E. "The Location of La Salle's Colony on the Gulf of Mexico," *Mississippi Valley Historical Review,* II (1915), 165-182.

Bondois, Paul-Emile. "Les Centres sucriers français au XVIIIe siècle," *Revue d'Histoire Economique et Sociale,* XVI (1929), 27-76.

__________. "Colbert et la question du sucre: La Rivalité franco-hollandaise," *Revue d'Histoire Economique et Sociale,* XI (1923), 12-61.

Bonnault, Claude de. "Les Protestants au Canada avant 1760," *Bulletin des Recherches Historiques,* LXIII (1956), 5-33.

Bordes, Maurice. "Les Intendants de Louis XV," *Revue Historique,* CCXXIII (1960), 45-62.

Boucher, Philip P. "A Colonial Company at the Time of the Fronde: The Compagnie de la Terre ferme de l'Amérique ou France equinoxiale," *Terrae Incognitae,* XI (1979), 43-58.

__________. "The Caribbean and the Caribs in the Thought of Seventeenth-Century French Colonial Propagandists: The Missionaries," *Proceedings of the Fourth Meeting of the French Colonial Historical Society, April 6-8, 1978.* Washington, D. C.: University Press of America, 1979, 17-32.

__________. "Comment se forme un ministre colonial. L'Initiation de Colbert, 1651-1664," *Revue d'Histoire de l'Amérique Française,* XXXVII (1983), 431-452.

__________. "French Images of America and the Evolution of Colonial Theories, 1650-1700," *Proceedings of the Sixth Annual Meeting of the Western Society for French History, November 9-11, 1978* (1978), 220-228.

__________. "The Search for France's Imperial Past," *French Colonial Historical Studies,* II (1978), 75-96.

Boulle, Pierre H. "Some Eighteenth-Century French Views on Louisiana," in John Francis McDermott, ed., *Frenchmen and French Ways in the Mississippi Valley.* Urbana: University of Illinois Press, 1969, 15-27.

__________. "Slave Trade, Commercial Organization, and Industrial Growth in Eighteenth-Century Nantes," *Revue Française d'Histoire d'Outre-Mer,* LIX (1972), 70-112.

__________. "French Mercantilism, Commercial Companies and Colonial Profitability," in Leonard Blussé and Femme Gastrer, eds., *Companies and Trade: Essays on Overseas Trading Companies during the Ancien Regime.* Leiden: Leiden University Press, 1981.

__________. "The Colonialism of the Ancien Regime," *Proceedings of the Third Meeting of the French Colonial Historical Society, May 5-7, 1977.* Athens, Ga.: French Colonial Historical Society, 1978, 1-2.

Boutruche, Robert. "Existe-t-il une continuité dans la politique coloniale de la France?," *Revue Historique,* CLXXII (1933), 257-278.

Brace, Richard and Jean. "Abstract of Code Noir—Intentions and Practices, 1685-1794," *Proceedings of the Second Meeting of the Western Society for French History,* November 21-23, 1974 (1975), 41-42.

Brasseaux, Carl A. "The Administration of Slave Regulations in French Louisiana, 1724-1766," *Louisiana History,* XXI (1980), 139-158.

__________. "The Image of Louisiana and the Failure of Voluntary French Emigration, 1683-1731," *Proceedings of the Fourth Meeting of the French Colonial Historical Society, April 6-8, 1978.* Washington, D. C.: University Press of America, 1979, 47-56.

Brault, Lucien. "Relation du voyage de l'intendant Jacques de Meulles fait en Acadie entre le 11 octobre 1685 et le 6 juillet 1686," *Revue d'Histoire de l'Amérique Française,* II (1948-1949), 432-439.

Brière, Jean-François. "Pêche et politique à Terre-Neuve au XVIIIe siècle: La France véritable gagnante du traité d'Utrecht?," *Canadian Historical Review,* LXIV (1983), 168-187.

Cahen, Albert. "Les Juifs à la Martinique au XVIIe siècle," *Revue des Etudes Juives,* II (1879), 93-122.

__________. "Les Juifs dans les colonies françaises aux XVIIe et XVIIIe siècles," *Revue des Etudes Juives,* IV (1881), 127-165, 235-248; V (1882), 68-92, 258-272.

Careless, J. M. S. "Frontierism, Metropolitanism and Canadian History," *Canadian Historical Review,* XXXV (1954), 1-21.

Church, William L. "The Decline of the French Jurists as Political Theorists, 1660-1789," *French Historical Studies,* V (1967-1968), 1-40.

Confer, Vincent. "French Colonial Ideas Before 1789," *French Historical Studies,* III (1964), 338-359.

Conrad, Glenn R. "L'Emigration alsacienne en Louisiane, 1753-1759," *Revue d'Histoire de l'Amérique Française,* XXVIII (1974-1975), 565-577.

__________. "Emigration Forcée: A French Attempt to Populate Louisiana, 1716-1720," *Proceedings of the Fourth Meeting of the French Colonial Historical Society, April 6-8, 1978.* Washington, D. C.: University Press of America, 1979, 57-66.

Cooper, J. P. "In Search of Agrarian Capitalism," *Past and Present,* no. 80 (1978), 20-65.

Courville, Serge. "Espace, territoire et culture en Nouvelle-France: Une vision geographique," *Revue d'Histoire de l'Amérique Française,* XXXVII (1983), 417-429.

Crane, Verner W. "Projects for Colonization in the South, 1684-1732," *Mississippi Valley Historical Review,* XII (1926), 23-35.

__________. "The Southern Frontier in Queen Anne's War," *American Historical Review,* XXIV (1918-1919), 379-395.

Croot, Patricia, and Parker, David. "Agrarian Class Structure and Economic Development," *Past and Present,* no. 78 (1978), 37-47.

Crowley, Terence A. "The Forgotten Soldiers of New France; The Louisbourg Example," *Proceedings of the Third Meeting of the French Colonial Historical Society, May 5-7, 1977.* Athens, Ga.: French Colonial Historical Society, 1978, 52-69.

Cruzat, Héloïse H., trans. "Trial and Sentence of Biron, Runaway Negro Slave, Before the Superior Council of Louisiana, 1728," *Louisiana Historical Quarterly,* VIII (1925), 23-27.

Daigle, Jean. "L'Acadie, 1604-1763. Synthèse historique," in Jean Daigle, ed., *Les Acadiens des Maritimes: Etudes thématiques.* Moncton: Centre d'Etudes Acadiennes, 1980, 17-48.

Dart, Henry Plauché. "A Great Louisiana Plantation of the French Colonial Period, 1737-38," *Louisiana Historical Quarterly,* VIII (1925), 589-593.

__________. "Documents Concerning Sale of Chaouachas Plantation in Louisiana, 1737-38," *Louisiana Historical Quarterly,* VIII (1925), 594-646.

__________. "The First Cargo of African Slaves for Louisiana, 1718," *Louisiana Historical Quarterly,* XIV (1931), 163-177.

__________. "First Law Regulating Land Grants in French Colonial Louisiana," *Louisiana Historical Quarterly,* XIV (1931), 346-348.

__________. "The Slave Depot of the Company of the Indies at New Orleans," *Louisiana Historical Quarterly,* IX (1926), 2876-287.

Debien, Gabriel. "La Christianisation des esclaves des Antilles françaises aux XVIIe et XVIIIe siècles," *Revue d'Histoire de l'Amérique Française,* XX (1966-1967), 525-555; XXI (1967-1968), 99-111.

__________. "Engagés pour le Canada au XVIIe siècle," *Revue d'Histoire de l'Amérique Française,* VI (1952), 177-233.

__________. "Gens de couleur libres et colons de Saint-Domingue devant la Constituant (1789-mars 1790)," *Revue d'Histoire de l'Amérique Française,* V (1950), 211-232, 398-426.

__________. "La Nourriture des esclaves sur les plantations des Antilles françaises aux XVIIe et XVIIIe siècles," *Caribbean Studies,* IV, no. 2 (1964-1965), 3-27.

__________, and Houdaille, J. "Les Origines africaines des esclaves des Antilles françaises," *Caribbean Studies,* X, no. 2 (1970), 5-29.

__________, Gaucher, M., and Delafosse, M. "Les Engages pour le Canada au XVIIIe siècle," *Revue d'Histoire de l'Amérique Française,* XIII (1959-1960), 247-261, 402-421, 550-561; IXIV (1960-1961), 246-258, 430-440, 583-602.

Dechêne, Louise. "L'Evolution du régime seigneurial au Canada: Le Cas de Montréal aux XVIIe et XVIIIe siècles," *Recherches Sociographiques,* XII (1971), 143-183.

Delafosse, Jean. "La Rochelle et le Canada au XVIIe siècle," *Revue d'Histoire de l'Amérique Française,* IV (1950-1951), 469-511.

Delafosse, Maral. "La Rochelle et les Iles au XVIIe siècle," *Revue d'Histoire des Colonies,* XXXVI (1949), 238-281.

Delanglez, Jean. "The Natchez Massacre and Governor Périer," *Louisiana Historical Quarterly,* XVII (1934), 631-641.

Delcourt, André. "Fait social et histoire coloniale," *Revue d'Histoire Economique et Sociale,* XLVIII (1950), 252-263.

Deloche, Maximin. "Un Missionnaire français au XVIIIe siècle: Contribution à l'histoire de l'établissement des Français en Louisiane," *Bulletin du Comité des Travaux Historiques et Scientifiques. Section de Géographie,* XLV (1930), 39-60.

__________. "Le Testament politique du cardinal de Richelieu," *Revue Historique,* CLXV (1930), 43-76.

Deschamps, Léon. "Un Colonisateur du temps de Richelieu: Isaac de Razilly," *Revue de Géographie,* (1886), 273-284.

Dessert, Daniel. "L'Affaire Fouquet," *L'Histoire,* no. 32 (Mars, 1981), 39-47.

__________, and Journet, Jean-Louis. "Le Lobby Colbert: Un Royaume ou une affaire de famille," *Annales ESC,* XXX (1975), 1303-1336.

Diamond, Sigmund. "Le Canada français au XVIIIe siècle: Une Société préfabriquée," *Annales ESC,* XVI (1961), 317-354.

__________. "An Experiment in 'Feudalism': French Canada in the Seventeenth Century," *William and Mary Quarterly,* 3rd series, XVIII (1961), 3-34.

Dravasa, Etienne. "Vivre noblement: Recherches sur la dérogeance de la noblesse du XIVe au XVI siècle," *Revue Juridique et Economique du Sud-Ouest,* Série Juridique, XVI (1965), 135-193.

Dubief, Henri. "Gaspard de Coligny et Walter Raleigh: Un Grand Dessein et un échec," *Bulletin de la Société d'Histoire du Protestantisme Français,* CXXVIII (1982), 493-504.

Dunbar-Nelson, Alice. "People of Color in Louisiana," *Journal of Negro History,* I (1916), 361-376.

Dunkley, Kenneth M. "Trading Companies and Privilege in Richelieu's France: The Hundred Associates of Morbihan," *Proceetings of the Third Meeding of the French Colonial Historical Society, Mary 5-7, 1978.* Athens, Ga.: The French Colonial Historical Society, 1978, 3-15.

Dunn, William E. "Spanish Reactions Against the French Advance Toward New Mexico," *Mississippi Valley Historical Review,* II (1915-1916), 348-362.

Eccles, William J. "A Belated Review of Harold Adams Innes, *The Fur Trade in Canada,*" *Canadian Historical Review,* LX (1979), 419-441.

__________. "French Aims and Means in Colonial North America," in Mathé Allain and Genn R. Conrad, eds., *France and North America: Over Three Hundred Years of Dialogue.* Lafayette, La.: University of Southwestern Louisiana, 1973, 57-70.

__________. "The Fur Trade and Eighteenth-Century Imperialism," *William and Mary Quarterly,* 3rd series, XL (1983), 341-362.

__________. "The History of New France According to Francis Parkman," *William and Mary Quarterly,* 3rd series, XVIII (1961), 163-175.

__________. "A Response to Hugh M. Grant on Innes," *Canadian Historical Review,* LXII (1981), 323-329.

__________. "The Social, Economic and Political Significance of the Military Establishment in New France," *Canadian Historical Review,* LII (1971), 1-22.

Everett, Donald E. "Free Persons of Color in Colonial Louisiana," *Louisiana History,* VII (1966), 21-50.

Falardeau, Jean-Charles. "La Paroisse canadienne-française au XVIIe siècle," *Cahiers de l'Ecole des Sciences Sociales, Politiques et Economiques de Laval,* no. 7 (n. d.), 20-38.

Filion, Maurice. "La Crise de la marine française, d'après la mémoire de Maurepas de 1745 sur la marine et le commerce," *Revue d'Histoire de l'Amérique Française,* XXI (1967-1968), 230-242.

Foner, Laura. "The Free People of Color in Louisiana and St. Domingue: A Comparative Portrait of Two Three-Caste Slave Societies," *Journal of Social History,* III (1969-1970), 406-430.

F['orbonnais], [François-Victor] V[eron] D[luverger] de. "Colonie," *Encyclopédie, ou dictionnaire raisonné des sciences, des artes et des métiers.* Edited by Denis Diderot and Jean Le Ronde d'Alembert. Paris and Neufchastel, 1751-1765. VIII, 519-523..

__________. "Compagnie de commerce," *Encyclopédie, ou dictionnaire raisonné des sciences, des artes et des métiers.* Edited by Denis Diderot and Jean Le Ronde d'Alembert. Paris and Neufchastel, 1751-1765. VIII, 739-740.

Frégault, Guy. "Essai sur les finances canadiennes," *Revue d'Histoire de l'Amérique Française,* XII (1959), 307-322, 459-484; XIII (1959-1960), 30-44, 157-182..

__________. "Le Régime seigneurial et l'expansion de la colonisation dans le bassin du Saint-Laurent au XVIIIe siècle," *Canadian Historical Association Report,* (1944), 61-73.

Frostin, Charles. "Les Pontchartrain et la pénétration commerciale française en Amérique espagnole (1690-1715)," *Revue Historique,* CCXLV (1971), 307-336.

Gadoury, Lorraine, Landry, Yves, and Charbonneau, Hubert. "Demographie differentielle en Nouvelle France: Villes et campagnes," *Revue d'Histoire de l'Amérique Française,* XXXVIII (1984-1985), 357-378.

Galloway, Patricia. "Louisiana Post Letters: The Missing Evidence for Indian Diplomacy," *Louisiana History,* XXII (1981), 31-44.

Gérard, Albert. "La Réorganisation de la Compagnie des Indes (1719-1723)," *Revue d'Histoire Moderne et Contemporaine,* XI (1908), 5-34, 177-197.

Girin, Léon. "Le Gentilhomme français et la colonisation du Canada," *Mémoires de la Société Royale du Canada,* (1896), 65-94.

Giraud, Marcel. "Un Aspect de la rivalité franco-espagnole au début du XVIIIe siècle (1713-1717)," *Revue Historique,* CCXVII (1957), 250-269.

__________. "La Compagnie d'Occident (1717-1718)," *Revue Historique,* CCXXVI (1961), 23-56.

__________. "Crise de Conscience et d'autorité à la fin du règne de Louis XIV," *Annales ESC,* VII (1952), 172-190, 293, 302.

__________. "L'Exacte description de la Louisiane d'Etienne Véniard de Bourgmont," *Revue Historique,* CCVII (1957), 29-41.

__________. "La France et la Louisiane au début du XVIIIe siècle," *Revue Historique,* CCIV (1950), 185-208.

__________. "Marins et ouvriers des ports devant la crise de la fin du règne de Louis XIV," *Hommage à Lucien Febvre: Eventail de l'histoire vivante,* 3 vols. Paris, 1953, II, 343-352..

__________. "Tendances humanitaires à la fin du règne de Louis XIV," *Revue Historique,* CCIX (1953), 217-237.

Godwin, J. A. "The Social Origins and Privileged Status of the French Eighteenth-Century Nobility," *Bulletin of the John Rylands Library,* XLVII (1965), 400-401.

Goubert, Pierre. "The French Peasantry of the Eighteenth Century," *Past and Present,* no. 10 (1956), 55-77.

Grant, Hugh M. "One Step Forward, Two Steps Back: Innes, Eccles, and the Canadian Fur Trade," *Canadian Historical Review,* LXII (1981), 304-322.

Grant, William L. "Canada versus Guadeloupe: An Episode of the Seven Years' War," *American Historical Review,* XVII (1911-1912), 735-743.

Grassby, R. B. "Social Status and Commercial Enterprise Under Louis XIV," *Economic History Review,* Second Series, XIII (1960), 19-38.

Groulx, Lionel. "Colonisation au Canada sous Talon," *Revue d'Histoire de l'Amérique Française,* IV (1950-1951), 61-73.

__________. "Note sur la chapellerie au Canada sous le régime français," *Revue d'Histoire de l'Amérique Française,* III (1949-1950), 383-401.

Harsen, Paul. "La Création de la Compagnie d'Occident (1717). Contribution à l'histoire du système de Law," *Revue d'Histoire Economique et Sociale,* LIV (1956), 7-41.

Hauser, Henri. "Les Caractères généraux de l'histoire économique de la France du milieu du XVIe siècle à la fin du XVIIIe," *Revue Historique,* CLXXIII (1934), 312-328.

Hecht, Jacqueline. "Un Problème de population active au XVIIIe siècle en France: La Querelle de la noblesse commerçante," *Population,* XIX (1964), 267-290.

Herlaut, A. Commandant. "Les Enlèvements d'enfants à Paris en 1720 et en 1750," *Revue Historique,* CXXXIX (1922), 43-61, 202-223.

Higginbotham, Jay. "Henri de Tonti's Mission to the Chickasaw, 1702," *Louisiana History,* XIX (1978), 285-296.

______. "Who Was Sauvole?," *Louisiana Studies,* VII (1968), 144-149.

Hill, Henry Bertram. "French Constitutionalism: Old Regime and Revolutionary," *Journal of Modern History,* XXI (1949), 222-227.

Hilton, R. H. "A Crisis of Feudalism," *Past and Present,* LXXX (1978), 3-19.

Hobsbawm, E. J. "The Crisis of the Seventeenth Century," in Trevor H. Aston, ed., *Crisis in Europe, 1560-1660.* New York: Basic Books, 1965, 5-58.

Holmes, Jack D. L. "Dauphin Island in the Franco-Spanish War, 1719-1722," in John F. McDermott, ed., *Frenchmen and French Ways in the Mississippi Valley.* Urbana: University of Illinois Press, 1969, 103-125.

Jacquemin, Jeanine. "La Colonisation protestante en Floride et la politique européenne au XVIe siècle," *Bulletin de la Société de l'Histoire du Protestantisme Français* (1955), 181-208.

Jaenen, Cornelius J. "Le Colbertisme," *Revue d'Histoire de l'Amérique Française,* XVIII (1964-1965), 64-84, 252-266.

__________. "Conceptual Frameworks for French Views of America and Amerindians," *French Colonial Historical Studies,* II (1978), 1-22.

__________. "Images of New France in the History of Lescarbot," *Proceedings of the Sixth Annual Meeting of the Western Society for French History, November 9-11, 1978* (1979), 209-219.

__________. "Pelleterie et peaux rouges: Perceptions françaises de la Nouvelle-France et de ses peuples indigènes aux XVIe, XVIIe et XVIIIe siècles," *Recherches Amerindiennes au Québec,* XIII (1983), 107-114.

__________. "The Persistence of Protestant Presence in New France, 1541-1760," *Proceedings of the Second Meeting of the Western Society for French History, Nov. 21-23, 1974* (1975), 29-40.

Jaray, Gabriel Louis. "Les Principes de la politique américaine de la France sous Henri IV, Richelieu et Colbert," *Revue de Synthèse,* XIII (1937), 97-113.

Kilman, Grady. "Slavery and Agriculture in Louisiana, 1699-1731," *Attakapas Gazette,* VI (1971), 39-50.

Labrousse, Ernest. "Le 'Tragique' XVIIe Siècle," in Fernand Braudel and Ernest Labrousse, eds., *Histoire économique et sociale de la France,* 2 vols. Paris: Presses Universitaires de France, 1977, II, 329-365.

Lamontagne, Roland. "Les Dépenses du roi au Canada à l'époque de Jean Talon (1665-1672)," *Revue d'Histoire de l'Amérique Française,* XIII (1959-1960), 335-343.

__________. "L'Influence de Colbert sur l'oeuvre de Jean Talon," *Revue d'Histoire de l'Amérique Française,* VI (1952-1953), 42-61.

Lanctot, Gustave. "Un Parlement colonial au temps de Louis XIV (1647-1663)," *Revue d'Histoire des Colonies,* XLII (1955), 277-290.

Lart, Charles E. "The Noblesse of Canada," *Canadian Historical Review,* III (1922), 222-232.

Lebrun, François. "Le Colbertisme a-t-il existé?," *L'Histoire,* no. 60 (Oct., 1983), 52-54.

Lemieux, Donald J. "The Mississippi Valley, New France and French Colonial Policy," *Southern Studies,* XVII (1978), 39-56.

Lonn, Ella. "The French Council of Commerce in Relation to American Trade," *Mississippi Valley Historical Review,* VI (1919-1920), 192-219.

Lunn, Jean E. "The Illegal Fur Trade Out of New France, 1713-1760," *Canadian Historical Association Report,* (1939), 61-76.

McCloy, S. T. "Negroes and Mulattoes in Eighteenth-Century France," *Journal of Negro History,* XXX (1945), 276-292.

MacDonald, L. R. "France and New France: The Internal Contradiction," *Canadian Historical Review,* LII, no. 2 (1971), 121-143.

McWilliams, Richebourg Gaillard. "Iberville at the Birdfoot Subdelta: Final Discovery of the Mississippi River," in John Francis McDermott, ed., *Frenchmen and French Ways in the Mississippi Valley.* Urbana: University of Illinois Press, 1969, 127-140.

Martin, Gaston. "Nantes et la Compagnie des Indes (1664-1769)," *Revue d'Histoire Economique et Sociale,* XV (1927), 231-253.

__________. "Le Système de Law et la prosperité du port de Nantes," *Revue d'Histoire Economique et Sociale,* XII (1924), 461-477.

Mathieu, Jacques. "La Balance commerciale. Nouvelle France-Antilles au XVIIIe siècle," *Revue d'Histoire de l'Amérique Française,* XXV (1971-1972), 465-497.

__________. "La Vie à Quebec au milieu du XVIIe siècle. Etudes des sources," *Revue d'Histoire de l'Amérique Française,* XXIII (1969-1970), 404-424.

Mauro, Frédéric. "Concepts économiques et économie coloniale à l'époque du capitalisme commercial (1500-1800)," in *Deuxième Conférence Internationale d'Histoire Economique, Aix-en-Provence, 1962.* Paris: Mouton et Cie, 1965, 713-723.

May, Louis-Philippe. "La France, Puissance des Antilles," *Revue d'Histoire Economique et Sociale,* XVIII (1930), 451-481.

__________. "Nicolas Fouquet et la politique coloniale de Louis XIV," *Revue d'Histoire des Colonies,* XXXIII (1940-1946), 70-83.

Miceli, Mary Veronica. "The Christianization of French Colonial Louisiana: A General View of Church and State in the Context of Eighteenth-Century French Colonization and a Theory of Mission," *Southern Studies,* XXI (1982), 384-397.

Micelle, Jerry A. "From Law Court to Local Government: Metamorphosis of the Superior Council of French Louisiana," *Louisiana History,* IX (1968), 85-107.

Miller, E. T. "The Connection of Peñalosa with the La Salle Expedition," *Quarterly of the Texas State Historical Association,* V (1901-1902), 97-112.

Moogk, Peter N. "Rank in New France: Reconstructing a Society from Notarial Documents," *Histoire Sociale/Social History,* XV (1975), 34-53.

__________. "Charles de Monseignat," *Dictionnaire biographique du Canada.* Toronto and Quebec: Les Presses de l'Université Laval, 1969. II, 504-507.

Mousnier, Roland. "Conclusion," *XVIIe siècle,* no. 122l (1979), 73-77.

__________. "L'Evolution des institutions monarchiques en France et ses relations avec l'état social," *XVIIe Siècle,* Nos. 58-59 (1963), 57-72.

__________. "La Fonction publique en France du début du seizième siècle à la fin du dix-huitième siècle," *Revue Historique,* CCLXI (1979), 321-335.

__________. "Note sur les rapports entre les gouverneurs de provinces et les intendants dans la première moitié du XVIIe siècle," *Revue Historique,* CCXXVIII (1962), 339-350.

__________. "Le Testament Politique de Richelieu," *Revue Historique,* CCI (1949), 55-71.

Mullin, Gerald W. "Rethinking American Negro Slavery from the Vantage Point of the Colonial Era," *Louisiana Studies,* XII (1973), 398-422.

Musset, G., ed. "Le Voyage en Louisiane de Franquet de Chaville, 1720-1724," *Journal de la Société des Américanistes de Paris,* IV (1902), 98-143.

Noël, Karl "La Condition matérielle des esclaves à l'Ile de France, période française (1715-1810)," *Revue d'Histoire des Colonies françaises,* XLI (1954), 303-313.

O'Neill, Charles E. "The Death of Bienville," *Louisiana History,* VIII (1967), 363-369.

Ouellet, Fernand. "La Formation d'une société dans la vallée du Saint-Laurent: D'une société sans classe à une société de classes," *Canadian Historical Review,* LXII (1981), 407-450.

__________. "Liberé ou exploité: Le Paysan québécois d'avant 1850," *Histoire Sociale/Social History,* XIII (1980), 339-368.

Pagès, Georges. "Le Conseil du Roi et la vénalité des offices pendant les premières années du ministère de Richelieu," *Revue Historique,* CLXXXII (1938), 245-282.

__________. "Note sur le recrutement et la libération des galériens sous Louis XIV au début du ministère de Colbert," *Revue d'Histoire Moderne et Contemporaine,* XI (1903-1909), 35-53.

Palm, Franklin C. "Mercantilism as a Factor in Richelieu's Policy of National Interests," *Political Science Quarterly,* XXXIX (1924), 650-664.

Pelletier, Monique. "Des Globes pour le Roi-Soleil: Les Origines des 'globes de Marly'," *Revue de la Bibliothèque Nationale,* I (1981), 80-86.

Petitjean-Roget, Jacques. "Les Protestants à la Martinique sous l'ancien régime," *Revue d'Histoire des Colonies,* XLIII (1955), 220-265.

__________. "Les Juifs à la Martinique, sous l'ancien régime," *Revue d'Histoire des Colonies,* XLIII (1956), 138-158.

Phelps, Dawson A. "The Chickasaw, the English, and the French, 1699-1744," *Tennessee Historical Quarterly,* XVI (1957), 117-133.

Pietraszeck, Bernadine. "Anglo-French Trade Conflicts in North America, 1702-1713," *Mid-America,* New Series, XXXV (1953), 144-174.

Pigeonneaux, Henri. "La Politique coloniale de Colbert," *Annales de Sciences Politiques,* I (1886), 487-509.

Pluchon, Pierre. "Un Négociant juif et deux esclaves nègres à Paris: Aspect du racisme au siècle des lumières," *Recherches Haïtiennes,* No. 1 (1979), 5-77.

Postan, M. M., and Hatcher, John. "Population and Class Relations in Feudal Society," *Past and Present,* LXXVIII (1978), 24-37.

Quynn, Dorothy McKay. "Recruiting in Old Orleans for New Orleans," *American Historical Review,* XLVI (1940-1941), 832-836.

Rankin, David C. "The Tannebaum Thesis Reconsidered: Slavery and Race Relations in Antebellum Louisiana," *Southern Studies,* XVIII (1979), 5-31.

Ranum, Orest. "Richelieu and the Great Nobility: Some Aspects of Early Modern Political Motives," *French Historical Studies,* III (1963), 184-204.

Reid, Allana G. "General Trade Between Quebec and France during the French Regime," *Canadian Historical Review,* XXXIV (1953), 18-32.

__________. "Intercolonial Trade during the French Regime," *Canadian Historical Review,* XXXII (1951), 236-251.

__________. "Representative Assemblies in New France," *Canadian Historical Review,* XXVII (1946), 19-26.

Renault, François P. "Etude sur le pacte de famille et la politique coloniale française, 1760-1792," *Revue d'Histoire des Colonies Françaises,* IX (1921), 1-52; X (1922), 213-264.

Rennard, J. "Arrivée des femmes aux Antilles," *Revue d'Histoire des Colonies,* XXVIII (1935), 135-148.

Richard, Guy. "Un Aspect particulier de la politique économique et sociale de la monarchie au XVIIe siècle," *XVIIe Siècle,* no. 49 (1960), 11-41.

Rothensteiner, John E. "Earliest History of Mine La Motte," *Missouri Historical Review,* XX (1926), 199-213.

__________. "Le Four banal dans la Nouvelle France," *Le Bulletin des Recherches Historiques,* XXX (1924), 257-260.

Roy, Pierre-Georges. "Le Moulin banal dans la Nouvelle France," *Le Bulletin des Recherches Historiques,* XLIX (1943), 3-9.

__________. "Les Seigneuries de la Nouvelle France," *Bulletin des Recherches Historiques,* LIV (1948), 301-316.

Roy, Régis. "La Noblesse au Canada avant 1760," *Bulletin des Recherches Historiques,* L (1944), 16-19.

Rule, John C. "Jean-Frédéric Phélypeaux, comte de Pontchartrain et Maurepas: Reflections on His Life and His Papers," *Louisiana History,* VI (1965), 365-377.

__________. "Jérôme Phélypeaux, comte de Pontchartrain and the Establishment of Louisiana, 1696-1715," in John F. McDermott, ed., *Frenchmen and French Ways in the Mississippi Valley*. Urbana: University of Illinois Press, 1969, 179-197.

__________. "King and Minister: Louis XIV and Colbert de Torcy," in Ragnhild M. Hatton and J. S. Bromley, eds., *William III and Louis XIV: Essays, 1680-1720, by and for Mark A. Thompson.* Toronto: University of Toronto Press, 1968, 213-236.

__________. "Louis XIV, Roi-Bureaucrate," in John C. Rule, ed., *Louis XIV and the Craft of Kingship.* Columbus: Ohio State University Press, 1969, 3-101.

__________. "The Old Régime in America: A Review of Recent Interpretations of France in America," *William and Mary Quarterly,* 3rd series (1962), 575-581.

Saintoyant, Jules-François "Des Politiques religieuses et indigènes des diverses colonisations européennes avant le XIXe siècle," *Revue d'Histoire des Colonies Françaises,* XXIII (1935), 285-304.

Salmon, J. H. M. "Venality of Office and Popular Sedition in 17th Century France: A Review of a Controversy" *Past and Present,* no. 37 (1967), 21-43.

Sanfaçon, Roland. "La Construction du premier chemin Québec-Montréal et le problème des corvées (1706-1737)," *Revue d"histoire de l'Amérique Française,* XII (1958-59), 3-29.

Scelle, Georges. "The Slave Trade in the Spanish Colonies of America: The Asiento," *American Journal of International Law,* IV (1910), 612-662.

Schapper, Bernard. "A Propos de la doctrine et de la politique coloniales de Richelieu," *Revue d'Histoire des Colonies,* XLI (1954), 314-328.

Schaeper, Thomas J. "Colonial Trade Policies Late in the Reign of Louis XIV," *Revue Française d'Histoire d'outre-Mer,* LXVII (1980), 203-215.

Sée, Henri. "Les Armateurs de Saint-Malo au XVIIIe siècle," *Revue d'Histoire Economique et Sociale,* XVII (1929), 29-35.

__________. "Les Economistes et la question coloniale au XVIIIe siècle," *Revue d'Histoire des Colonies Françaises,* XXVII (1929), 381-392.

__________. "Esquisse de l'histoire du commerce français à Cadix et dans l'Amérique espagnole au XVIIe siècle," *Revue d'Histoire Moderne,* XIII (1928), 13-31.

__________. "Le Grand Commerce maritime et le système colonial dans leur relations avec l'évolution du capitalisme (XVIe-XIXe siècles)," *Revue de Synthèse Historique,* XXXIX (1925), 15-35.

__________. "Que faut-il penser de l'oeuvre économique de Colbert?," *Revue Historique,* CLII (1926), 181-194.

Soboul, Albert Marius. "The French Rural Community in the Eighteenth and Nineteenth Centuries," *Past and Present,* no. 10 (1956), 78-95.

Swartzlow, Ruby Johnson. "Early History of Lead Mining in Missouri," *Missouri Historical Review,* XXVIII (1933-1934), 184-194, 287-295; XXIX (1934-1935), 27-34, 109-114, 195-205.

Szarka, Andrew S. "Louis XIV and Brazil: The French Probe into Maranhao, 1697-1700," *Proceedings of the Second Meeting of the French Colonial*

Historical Society. Athens, Ga.: French Colonial Historical Society, 1977, 133-147.

Taillemite, Etienne. "Colbert, legislateur de la Marine royale," *La Nouvelle Revue Maritime,* No. 380 (1983), 44-70.

Tarrade, Jean. "L'Administration coloniale en France à la fin de l'Ancien Régime: Projets de réforme," *Revue Historique,* CCXXIX (1963), 103-122.

Taylor, George V. "Noncapitalist Wealth and the Origins of the French Revolution," *American Historical Review,* LXXII (1966-1967), 469-496.

Teall, Elizabeth S. "The Seigneur of Renaissance France: Advocate or Oppressor?," *Journal of Modern History,* XXXVII (1965), 131-150.

Thomas, H. M. "The Relations of Governor and Intendant in the Old Regime," *Canadian Historical Review,* XVI (1935), 27-40.

Trigger, Bruce G. "The French Presence in Huronia: The Structure of Franco-Huron Relations in the First Half of the Seventeenth Century," *Canadian Historical Review,* XLIX (1968), 107-141.

Trudel, Marcel. "Les Débuts d'une société: Montreal, 1642-1663. Etude de certains comportements sociaux," *Revue d'Histoire de l'Amérique Française,* XXIII (1969-1970), 185-207.

__________. "Enfin les fleurs de lis, 1524," *Revue d'Histoire de l'Amérique Française,* XV (1961-1962), 411-508.

__________. "Louis XIV et son projet de deportation, 1689," *Revue d'Histoire de l'Amérique Française,* IV (1950-1951), 157-171.

__________. "Les Obligations du censitaire à l'époque des Cent-Associés," *Revue d'Histoire de l'Amérique Française,* XXVII (1973-1974), 3-41.

Turgeon, Charles. "Les Idées économiques de Sully," *Revue d'Histoire Economique et Sociale,* X (1922), 249-269.

Usner, Daniel H., Jr. "From African Captivity to American Slavery: The Introduction of Black Laborers to Colonial Louisiana," *Louisiana History,* XX (1979), 25-48.

Vachon, André. "L'Eau-de-vie dans la société indienne," *Canadian Historical Association Report*, (1960), 22-32.

_________. "Etat des recherches sur le régime français (1632-1760)," in Fernand Dumont and Yves Martin, eds., *Situation de la recherche sur le Canada français.* Québec: Les Presses de l'Université Laval, 1962, 11-26.

Varille, Mathieu. "La Politique coloniale de Law," *Revue du Lyonnais,* Série 5, I (1921), 55-74.

Verlinden, Charles. "Etude sur l'esclavage à Montpellier au Moyen Age (XIIIe-XVe siècles)," *Etudes d'Histoire dédiées à la mémoire de Henri Pirenne par ses anciens élèves.* Bruxelles: Nouvelle Société d'Editions, 1937, 451-469.

_________. "Les Origines coloniales de la civilisation atlantique: Antécédents et types de structure," *Cahiers d'Histoire Mondiale,* I, No. 2 (1953), 378-398.

_________. "Le Problème de la continuité en histoire coloniale," *Revista des Indias,* XX (1951), 219-236.

_________. "Sentido de la historia colonial americana," *Estudios Americanos,* (1952), 551-564.

Vignols, Léon. "Les Antilles françaises sous l'Ancien Régime: L'Institution des engagés," *Revue d'Histoire Economique et Sociale,* XVI (1928), 12-45.

_________. "Les Antilles françaises sous l'Ancien Régime: Un Produit social de la guerre: filibuste et boucane (XVIe et XVII siècles)," *Revue d'Histoire Economique et Sociale,* XVI (1928), 137-181.

_________. "Les Esclaves coloniaux en France au XVIIe et XVIIIe siècles et leur retour aux Antilles," *Annales de Bretagne et des Pays de l'Ouest,* (1927), 211-221.

_________. "L'Importation en France au XVIIIe siècle, du boeuf salé d'Irlande: Ses Emplois—Les Tentatives pour s'en passer," *Revue Historique,* CLIX (1928), 79-95.

_________. "La Mise en valeur du Canada à l'époque française," *Revue d'Histoire Economique et Sociale,* XVI (1928), 720-795.

__________. "Une Question mal posée: Le Travail manuel des blancs et des esclaves aux Antilles (XVIIe-XVIIIe siècles)," *Revue Historique,* CLXXV (1935), 308-315.

Wallot, Jean-Pierre. "Le Régime seigneurial et son abolition au Canada," *Canadian Historical Review,* L (1969), 367-393.

Ware, Marion. "An Adventurous Voyage to French Colonial Louisiana: The Narrative of Mother Tranchepain, 1727," *Louisiana History,* I (1960), 212-229.

Webster, Jonathan Howes. "Colbertism and Colonial Commerce: The Case of Bordeaux's Trade to the French West Indies," *Proceedings of the Third Meeting of the French Colonial Historical Society.* Athens, Ga.: French Colonial Historical Society, 1978, 16-38.

__________. "The Concern sof Bordeaux's Merchants and the Formation of Royal Commercial Policy for the West Indies," *Proceedings of the Second Meeting of the Western Society for French History, November 21-23, 1974* (1975), 12-20.

Wedel, Mildred Mott. "The Bénard de la Harpe Historiography on French Colonial Louisiana," *Louisiana Studies,* XIII (1974), 9-67.

Williams, Basil. "The Foreign Policy of England under Walpole," *English Historical Review,* LXV (1900), 251-276, 479-494; XVI (1901), 67-83, 308-327, 439-451.

Woods, Patricia D. "The French and the Natchez Indians in Louisiana, 1700-1731," *Louisiana History,* XIX (1978), 413-435.

Zitomerski, J. "Urbanization in French Colonial Louisiana (1706-1766)," in *Annales de Demographie Historique, 1974.* Paris: Mouton, 1974, 263-277.

Zoltvany, Yves F. "Esquisse de la Coutume de Paris," *Revue d'Histoire de l'Amérique Française,* XXV (1971), 365-384.

__________. "The Frontier Policy of Philippe Rigaud de Vaudreuil, 1713-1725," *Canadian Historical Review,* XLVIII (1967), 227-250

__________. "New France and the West, 1701-1713," *Canadian Historical Review,* XLVI (1965), 301-322.

Zysberg, André. "L'Irresistible ascension de Jean-Baptiste Colbert," *L'Histoire,* No. 60 (Oct., 1983), 34-42.

Index